LEGEND OF A ROCK STAR

LEGEND OF A ROCK STAR

a memoir

BY DEE DEE RAMONE

THUNDER'S MOUTH PRESS
New York

LEGEND OF A ROCK STAR: A Memoir

© 2002 by Dee Dee Ramone

Published by
Thunder's Mouth Press
An Imprint of Avalon Publishing Group Incorporated
161 William St., 16th Floor
New York, NY 10038

"Johnny Ramone Stays Tough" by Colin Devenish from Rollingstone.com, June 24, 2002 © 2002 Rollingstone.com. All rights reserved. Reprinted by permission.

"Musician Dee Dee Ramone Found Dead" by Jeff Wilson with a contribution from AP writer Larry McShane. Reprinted with permission of The Associated Press.

From "New York Honors Dee Dee" by Christian Hoard from Rollingstone.com, July 3, 2002 © 2002 Rollingstone.com. All rights reserved. Reprinted with permission by Christian Hoard.

"Dee Dee Ramone 1952-2002" by John Holmstrom first appeared on punkmagazine.com. All Rights Reserved. Reprinted with permission by John Holmstrom.

From "The 50 Greatest Rock Bands of All Time," first published by *Spin* magazine. February 2002 © 2002 *Spin* magazine. All rights reserved. Reprinted with permission of *Spin* magazine and the authors.

Library of Congress Cataloging-in-Publication Data

Ramone, Dee Dee
     Legend of a rock star: a memoir / by Dee Dee Ramone.
     p.cm.
     ISBN 1-56025-389-4 (trade paper)
1. Ramone, Dee Dee. 2. Punk rock musicians -- United States -- Biography. I. Title

ML419.R32 A3 2002
782.42166'092 -- dc21
2002028500

Designed by Paul "Scratchy" Paddock

Distributed by Publishers Group West

Dee Dee would like to thank Barbara, Joey, Tommy, Johnny, Marky, CJ, Paul and Mark Kostabi, Christian Hoard, Stefan Adika, Arturo Vega, Johnny Thunders, Stiv Bators, Sid Vicious, Chris Spedding, Tina Weymouth, Chris Fantz, Eddie Vedder, Daniel Ray, Trigger, Ira Herzog, Erik Kahn, Dan O'Connor, Monte Melnick, anyone Dee Dee insulted in this book, anyone Dee Dee didn't insult in this book, but should have, all those who attended the Continental Divide memorial service.

For Barbara

CONTENTS

Foreword

WHEN I FIRST MET DEE DEE at the Chelsea Hotel, he reminded me of another author who became my friend, Gregory Corso. The term "marching to your own drummer" doesn't even scratch the surface. Both of these guys defined cool, and had a cultural impact that few of us are lucky to even get near. Neither of them hung out at Elaine's, or mingled with Tina Brown.

They were real New Yorkers, the kind you remember. Once, I was telling Corso of my admiration and gratitude for how he and Kerouac, Burroughs, Ginsberg, and others had impacted on the bland culture of the fifties, and Gregory's response was "Hey, get out of the bongo days." Always unexpected, like a jazz solo, always on the money. These two guys, in a different era, could have done one-man shows like Leguizamo. All you had to do was get them going, and a rainbow of spontaneous, original, and unpretentious wisdom and poetry would arise and it was usually funny as hell. And yes, Dee Dee was a poet. He was the poet of the Ramones, the guy who lived the life and walked the walk. He was a poet after he left the Ramones and lived his life making music, painting, writing, and talking the words in the everyday language of a poet.

I remember driving around near Venice Beach with Dee Dee and his wife Barbara. Dee Dee had just finished talking about the death of his father, and how he had gone to the grave to talk to his father "privately," to put things right. A dutiful son, Dee Dee was always trying to make things better, if sometimes a bit late on the execution. The description was childlike and from a place that was entirely pure, and there was much of that pureness in Dee Dee. And like many people blessed and burdened with the talent of purity, Dee Dee found many ways throughout his life to cast away this inherent quality.

LEGEND OF A ROCK STAR

His death may have been the ultimate middle finger to the oppression of his pure side, to the challenges of middle age, to the expectations that come from being famous. The last time I saw Dee Dee was at Roseland, where he did one of his last gigs as a favor to me. He was playing with his band as well as Marky and C.J. Ramone, and Paul Kostabi. It was classic Ramones—full throttle, adreneline fueled, burning down the house. There was a big sign that Arturo Vega made that read, "Happy Birthday Joey." Dee Dee wanted to honor Joey in public, since Joey's birthday was a few days away. Print articles had been covering the conflict between the various Ramones as Joey's posthumous birthday closed in. Dee Dee wanted to clear the air, make sure fans knew he really loved Joey, no matter how bad things may have gotten from time to time. When Jerry from the Misfits first raised the sign on the old stage at Roseland, the packed house responded with a volcanic wave of cheers. I raised the sign a few seconds later, and again, the crowd screamed in unison. An hour earlier, Dee Dee, C.J., and Marky played a spontaneous acoustic set of Ramones hits, down in the dressing room. It was a magical moment, unchoreographed, pared down, and straightforward. No bullshit, just the music. "Lobotomy," "Sheena Is a Punk Rocker," "Chinese Rock," the small group listened quietly as Dee Dee sang, C.J. played guitar, and Marky used his boot soles as percussion.

A week earlier, Dee Dee and I were hanging out at the Knitting Factory in L.A. for a literary reading. We were listening to Harry Dean Stanton, but Dee Dee had been upset with me for twisting his arm a few weeks back, the night before he accepted his Rock and Roll Hall of Fame award. That night I asked him to do the Roseland gig, an event for booksellers, publishers, agents, and book types. We would have Dee Dee come with his band, and share the stage with Tom Tom Club—his old pals Tina Weymouth and Chris Frantz from Talking Heads. As it turned out, the addition of Marky and C.J. created a mini Ramones reunion, but that night at the Knitting Factory Dee Dee was still angry that I had talked him into yet another gig. I had also made Dee Dee attend two book signings that weekend, one at Borders and the other at the L.A. Bookfair for *Lobotomy* and *Chelsea Horror Hotel*, his two books. Dee Dee had called me after the second signing and told me he really just wanted to be a painter and a writer, and do his art in peace and quiet. He was pissed off that I had taken advantage of his good will, the night before his Rock and Roll Hall of Fame award, and had gotten him to agree to another gig. He had been doing gigs most of his adult life and at this point all they brought were heartache and bad hotels. He was struggling to find a center in his life that would be appropriate for a fifty-year-old aging rock star, and life on the road was not, in his mind, going to be part of his next act. After Dee Dee finished screaming at me, he grew quiet and as Dee Dee would, after an explosion, he became apologetic. I told him we would meet at the Knitting Factory and discuss the whole thing, and if he didn't want to do the Roseland gig, I'd understand.

As Harry Dean Stanton continued his reading, Dee Dee and I were huddled at the bar, and I listened to Dee Dee talk about the early days of the Ramones with affectionate remembrances of Johnny Thunders, Sid Vicious, Stiv Bators, people now departed. It had been an electric time for Dee Dee, and there were certain moments when he would draw that time back from his memory, and it was like a big movie screen with all his friends as stars, young and unstoppable. He forgave me for the Roseland gig, and agreed to come. Maybe it would be good to be on stage at Roseland, with all its history, and ghosts of the past. I was grateful, and put my arm around Dee Dee to thank him. He was enjoying his generosity, and had that childlike Dee Dee look, even behind his sunglasses in that dark room.

All of a sudden Dee Dee jumped up and said it was time to go. We hugged and he left. Fifteen seconds later he came back and presented me with a dragon ring, which I wear now. He said it was a present for me, and then he rushed out of the room, spontaneous, unpredictable, guileless, just like that.

The day I heard Dee Dee was dead, it didn't seem possible, and yet it was, if you read this book, always just beneath the surface. I have a painting that Dee Dee gave me near my bed. It's a portrait of Sid Vicious with the words: "You can't trust no fuck'en body." It stands as the alter ego to the dragon ring I sport on my right index finger.

Neil Ortenberg
Avalon Publishing Group

CHAPTER ONE

I'AM TRYING TO SETTLE DOW
D ENJOY MY LAST MORNING
R A WHILE IN LOS ANGELES AND
ENTALY ADJUST TO WHAT I'AM
BOUT TO HAVE TO FACE, WHICH
MERCILESS TOUR OF EUROPE T
RT OF SUPPORT MY NEW C.D, O
W OF OLD RAMONES SONGS THA
RE RECORDED WITHOUT ME AN
AD SINGING THE SONGS MYSELF
STEAD OF JOEY, THE FORMER
WGER FOR THE RAMONES.
I WANTED TO DO THIS ALBUM
O HEAR MY SELF SING AND PLA
HESE RAMONES SONGS ON MY
WN AS A GOOF, I NEVER THOUG
O MAKE ANOTHER CAREER OU

CHAPTER ONE

YO   EWERFU
NAGER TO GUIDE YOU THRE
E PIT FALLS OF THIS BUSSINE
DONT HAVE, AND THE
OF A STRONG RECHOR
TOUR

I'M TRYING TO SETTLE DOWN now and enjoy my last morning home for a while in Los Angeles and mentally adjust to what I'm about to have to face, which is a merciless tour of Europe to sort of support my new CD, out now, of old Ramones songs that I rerecorded without them, singing the songs myself instead of Joey, the former singer for the Ramones.

I wanted to do this album to hear myself sing and play these Ramones songs on my own as a goof. I never thought to make another career out of it.

You need a powerful manager to guide you through the pitfalls of this business, which I don't have, and the support of a strong record label to tour. Now I'm caught in this weird situation. My labels for the CD in Japan and Europe are pretty good. There's a future there if I want. I feel like I better tour Europe like I did Japan to keep the labels happy for the next time. If I don't, there won't be a next time.

If I play ball I can keep getting press from the publicist these labels have hired and use it to sell my other projects and to get publicity for the paintings that I'm doing with Paul Kostabi and Barbara Zampini, which is my real focus now.

Now I'm stuck with a band and all the bills that come along with this kind of foolishness and all the financial responsibilities are coming out of my own pocket.

I'm also aggravated and worrying how I'm going to get through a twenty-seven-shows-in-thirty-days tour. It just seems impossible.

The drives every day are ten to twenty hours long. Sometimes they will be overnight after we've played a show and the band, the driver of the van that we will be riding in with all the equipment, and I will be tired, stoned, drunk, and careless, and we will more than likely get into a serious accident along the highway somewhere. So this is heightening my predictions of doom and gloom.

Also the fact that we won't have a road crew either to carry the amps and set up the drums, or anyone to tune the guitars or change strings while we're on stage, or that we don't have anyone to do the sound is disturbing me.

And I don't like it that I only have a three-piece band now, and that I had to switch back to the bass from the guitar, and it worries me because I haven't played the bass in eleven years since I quit the Ramones and threw all my basses away.

A lot of things are upsetting me. Rob, the promotor at Paper Clip, calling me every day to badger me about this nightmare tour has worn out my resistance to doing it.

My flight today has a stopover in France, which I hate. Then I get on a connecting flight to Amsterdam. After that we're driving in a van straight to Rot-terdam. There we catch the ferry across the Eng-lish Channel to Britain, where there's a hoof-and-mouth crisis. Hope-fully we will have work permits.

We're expected to drive right away from the ferry landing in England to the first show, which is in Scotland, in Glasgow, at King Tut's

3

LEGEND OF A ROCK STAR

Wa Wa Hut. When we get to the club we'll be expected to set up the equipment and do a show without going to a hotel or getting any rest from the flight or the drive or ferry ride. After the show at King Tut's Wa Wa Hut we'll have to break down the equipment, pack it back into the van, then drive overnight straight to London. If the police don't pull us over, or whatever else wrong that could happen doesn't happen, then our expected arrival time in London is at seven in the morning.

I would bet my miserable life on it that we won't be able to check into our hotel till twelve o'clock and will probably be on the street till then. This happens a lot because pubs don't open till eleven-thirty in London.

My interviews start at the hotel at twelve o'clock and last till show time. How am I going to be able to sneak over to Earl's Court to cop some dope? I worry some more.

What am I going to do, I wondered later as I'm trying to dial England and I can't. I couldn't bear the humiliation of asking my wife how to do it so I called the long distance operator, which you can do in America by dialing zero.

"Hello," I said, "this is Dee Dee Ramone, give me Eagle Rock Records in London, England." I knew that my call was being monitored so I was trying to be extra polite.

In about a half a second that creepy, so-full-of-it, whoever-she-is receptionist that works at Eagle Rock answered the phone. I'm used to this one already and not very impressed, but rather than be safe than sorry I started the attack first.

"This is Dee Dee Ramone!" My voice stabbed through the telephone line. "Get me Faye now! And don't give me any bullshit," I sinisterly added.

Not too many people can stand up to me in a fight and this New Age snob or whatever she is backed off pretty easily. I miss the good old seventies, I thought to myself, reminiscing about when the women who worked at record companies were babes and wore short miniskirts, had nice asses and big tits, and would score dope for you when you got to town, or at least take the band to a Chinese restaurant to get them drunk before the show.

After a brief pause Faye answered the phone. I was so lost, momentarily, in so many escape fantasies that I forgot why I was calling.

"Faye, hello, it's me, Dee Dee, Ramone."

"Yes," Faye answered. "Oh, hello Dee Dee, what do you want?" she said, out-maneuvering me right away.

"Well . . . we're not coming," I said, expecting trouble.

"Don't be ridiculous," she countered me. "Get the hell over here with your band, do you understand? I mean it! You have a slight advantage because of the fuss being made over the twenty-fifth anniversary of punk. It's been so long since then that you're one of the last few punks left alive to ask about what it was like. Let's make the most of this, Dee Dee. You never know, you might sell some copies of your new CD and make back some of the goddamn money that you owe us.

"It will be a rugged tour, I'll give you that, but that's how it goes," she said, and then added a "See you at the gig in London," and hung up.

I always keep the bedroom door closed and the sliding door between the bedroom and the hallway shut, so that Barbara doesn't hear me in the living room in the morning on the telephone. As my line was going dead I was overwhelmed by the jarring noise of the sliding door being thrown violently open and a shockingly just-as-jarring voice shouting at me.

This person shouting at me is my wife Barbara and she's very hung over from the seven gin and tonics which she drank while watching TV last night.

"Dee Dee, you fucking bastard, it's six o'clock in the morning. How could you be so damn inconsiderate?" she started up, sticking one leg out from behind the half-open sliding door and kicking over my cup of coffee that was sitting on the floor on the morning paper, sending the contents all over the rug.

"The lady downstairs is angry, she says that you're walking around too hard on the floor."

"No! No! I'm not," I responded back to this belittling attack from my spouse, turning purple with rage and yelling now at the top of my lungs, unable to contain myself anymore.

"Yes! Yes! You! Dooooo!!!" Barbara yelled back at me, also making a miserable face. "And," she continued yelling, "you slam things around. And you let the water run. You miserable motherfucker. You have to get up early so you wake up everyone else too, don't you! Don't you, motherfucker!"

"No! No I fucking don't," I protested then. Losing my head for a minute, in a fit of rage, I pounded the receiver of the telephone on the

LEGEND OF A ROCK STAR

table violently up and down, smashing it to pieces and cutting my hand by accident in the process. My blood was dripping on the carpet now. In the hallway between the bedroom and the living room there are two closets, next to where Barbara is now standing. The most logical thing for her to do now to make a statement would be to throw my clothes that are in the closet right next to her into the swimming pool in our apartment building's courtyard, so this is exactly what she does. She grabs my things off the shelf in the closet and barges past me, opened the door, and throws my stuff over the railing downstairs into the pool one story below us.

"Get out! Get the fuck out and don't ever come back," she yelled, slamming the door off its hinges as I was running out the door laughing. I had my bass guitar, and my bag for the tour was already packed anyway. The only bad thing was that I didn't have any pot. Fucking hell, I thought to myself. Then I went downstairs to join my possessions by the pool. My landlord keeps a staff with a hook on one end of it, for cleaning the pool, by the fence near the stairs that go to the laundry room. I fetched this staff and then fished my clothes out of the swimming pool. Then, I hung everything out to dry in the clear morning sun over some lounge chairs by the barbecue area of the court-yard, since it's the most private place and hidden from view from my neighbors' apartments. Nobody realized that I wanted to be alone to lick my wounds though, and I had to see everybody in the building and explain everything to them.

Later on someone in a van came to pick me up to take me and Chase, who will be playing drums, and also Chris the Creep, who will be playing the guitar for me, to the Los Angeles airport. There doesn't seem to be a lot I can do now about not going on this tour, I realize sadly.

This is shit, everybody happily complained from the steel floor of the van where we are sitting and cant get comfortable. Limo's went out a long time ago due to the bitter complaints of aging old fart and has-been journalists like Tony Parsons. He criticized the jet-set lifestyles of rock stars in the seventies.

WELL... THAT'S IT! I HAD IT. YOU'RE NOT GETTING ANYTHING ELSE FROM ME TODAY... MAYBE I'LL FEEL BETTER IN TWO WEEKS, WHO KNOWS, MAYBE NOT. I THINK I'M GONNA GO TO HONG KONG AND DO SOME MODELING! I HEAR THEY PARTY ALOT OVER THERE, EVERYBODY DRINKS ALOT AND GOES OUT ALL NIGHT LONG, JUST WHAT I NEED!
WHEN WE WERE IN JAPAN WE PARTIED NIGHT AND DAY, WE EVEN THREW THE T.V. OUT THE WINDOW AND DIDN'T PAY THE BILL. BECAUSE WE'RE ROCK STARS.

THANK YOU VERY MUCH!
BARBARA ZAMPN

LEGEND OF A ROCK STAR

At least Tony isn't a hypocrite. We saw him waiting for a bus in the pouring rain after our show at The Garage in London. We made him even wetter when we splashed the old geezer with water from a puddle as we sped by in our rented transport on the way back to the party at the Columbia Hotel. It was quite a laugh to see the anger on this creep's wrinkly old face—what's a-matter, that's punk, ain't it?

Anyway. Back to today. At the French airlines counter the prepaid economy tickets were actually waiting there for us, ending my worries that they wouldn't be there. Chris showed up with a Sid Vicious makeover. He had done this overnight due to peer pressure all around, and he also brought with him the first Sex Pistols album on CD, but it was scratched.

This is wonderful, I thought when I first saw him like this, but then I noticed he was also chewing bubble gum in a Sid Vicious style. This means constantly pulling it out of his mouth and stretching it and all that kind of stuff and the sneering to go along with it, which is important to the style. He wouldn't stop doing this till finally I couldn't take it anymore and pleaded with him to stop.

"Chris, my nerves are shot. How about giving me a break. Okay?" I asked him.

"What do you mean, a break, Dee Dee, huh, how about giving me one? What the hell am I doing now? Huh?"

"It's the gum chewing, Chris," I answered him back. "Your jaw is going a million miles a minute. It's like you're a twitching spastic or something. Just try to calm down. And get rid of the gum. All right?"

"I quit smoking! That's why I am chewing gum. God! Damn! It! I'm doing this for the band! So I'll be good on the tour and a lot of reasons that aren't making me too happy right now! So I'll tell you what! I'm! Not! Going! Noooow!! Do! You! Understand me?"

I respond, "Nooooo!!! No way! No way, no fucking way!"

He yelled, flailing his arms excitedly in the air and making an incensed face. Then he spit the huge wad of gum that he'd been chowing down on into his hand and then threw it violently down the corridor of the airline terminal.

"Ouch!," I heard an elderly female voice complaining. Turning around to look, I noticed an old lady wiping goo from her face and clutching her heart. Then I heard someone else yell out in concern, "Somebody get a doctor!"

"Let's get out of here right now, guys! Come on, let's go, before the police come and try to arrest us. Now listen up you two," I explained as we were moving along. "I don't like smart alecks. I hate gum chewing. It makes me dislike young people. I hate back talk. And I hate punk rock nose-picking and consistant itching.

"So now that you guys know this, let's try to all be a little nicer to each other. Come on. We've got a plane to catch."

So sullenly, without talking anymore, we go through the gate check, boarded the plane, and find our seats, which are right next to each other. Then we buckled our seat belts and wait to take off.

Now Chris seemed to have picked up high-speed nervous foot-tapping from Chase, who, unknowing of how much he was wrecking my sanity, was enthusiastically chewing a wad of about five or six sticks of gum.

Chris has replaced his gum chewing with a heavy frown. There's nothing I can do about it except try and ignore it. Later on, a stewardess noticed how jumpy we were and offered us twelve Mandrex for 300 dollars. We greatly appreciated the offer and gladly accepted it, and flew the rest of the way stoned.

LEGEND OF A ROCK STAR

At CBGB's 1976.

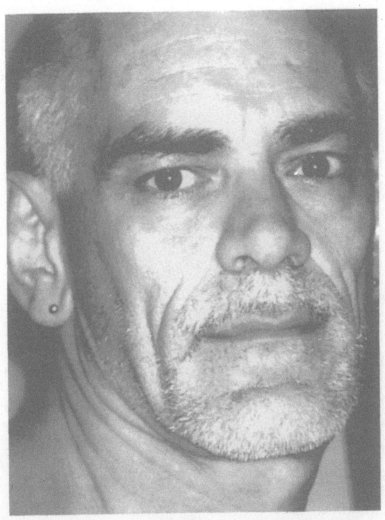

DEE DEE RAMONE
SEPTEMBER 18, 1951 - JUNE 5, 2002

CHAPTER TWO

UR CONNECTING FLIGHT LEF
S ANGELES TWENTY MINUTES
ATE WHICH ISNT TO BAD BY
DAYS STANDARDS BUT IT SCREW
S UP. WHEN WE LANDED AT
HARLES DE GAUL AIRPORT IN PA'
UR CONNECTING FLIGHT HAD
LREADY DEPARTED. WHEN WE
ACHED A DESERTED AREA TH
AS SUPPOSED TO BE WHERE WE
OULD OF BEEN LEAVING AMSTE
ROM, WE STARTED TO WORRY A
T ANGRY.
THERE WASNT ANY ONE TO ASK
FLIGHT INFORMATION ON H

CHAPTER TWO

ERE VILE. THEY SUCKED SI
HREW ONE PASS PORT CHECK
CAREFULLY WADED THREW
E NEATLY ARRANGED

OUR CONNECTING FLIGHT LEFT Los Angeles
twenty minutes late, which isn't too bad by today's standards, but it
screwed us up. When we landed at Charles De Gaulle Airport in Paris
our connecting flight had already departed. When we reached a
deserted area that was supposed to be where we would have been
leaving for Amsterdam from, we started to worry and get angry.

There wasn't anyone to ask for flight information on how to get to
Amsterdam, either. The French customs officials were vile. I carefully
wade through the neatly arranged, roped-off area where you wait your
turn to go through the passport check. Though it is completely normal
by any standards, I wouldn't think then to cut the line or cross over a
rope divider to get to another line, especially since I'm entering into a
hostile foreign country and I don't want to bring any attention to myself.

There were two couples in front of me and I was politely minding my
own business when the French official serving a booth two lines down
from the one that I was waiting in started angrily, glaring at me. He was
very frustrated. Something about me had provoked him. Then he
started pointing his finger at me threateningly, and when that didn't
work he started pounding on the glass walls of his booth with his keys.
Then he started yelling at me in French. I couldn't understand what he
was saying but I think he was yelling for me to get my ass over there.
This meant nothing to me, except "You've got to be kidding."

His eyes were bugging out of his head now and this action was esca-
lating as quickly as a street fight. I easily turned the tables on him with

a few snobbish facial gestures in the direction of the official checking passports in the booth that was serving the line I was waiting in, suggesting that I would be a good guy, especially since I just wanted to leave France as fast as possible and ignore this crazy motherfucker instead of reporting this incident to the State Department.

I then snob-marched myself, Chris, and Chase into France. Then we tried everywhere we could to get information on how we could catch another flight to Amsterdam. Everywhere we went in the terminal we were followed by police, security guards, and undercover agents trying to catch us doing something against the law.

Finally we found the French airlines information booth, but as soon as it was my turn in line the clerk slammed the window shut and hung up a "Closed for lunch" sign and gave me the finger.

Undaunted, I spotted a money-change place and went over to it. *I know what I'm going to have to do,* I realized, and changed what few dollars I had saved for fun into French francs, which was easy. Then I herded Chris and Chase back inside the terminal to a general departure area. In no time at all I was able to find a French airline worker that would take a bribe and procure three fares on a small 450 horsepower Potez 25 French biplane. This is an old fashioned airplane from the 1930s. It has two sets of wings and a single motor up front with only one propeller. It used to be used for delivering the mail but now this one is being used to smuggle marijuana between Holland and France.

The pilot was from France though, and he was a very large man. *He's too big and fat to be flying a light aircraft,* I worried when I saw him. Paulo, the crooked French airlines employee, introduced me to him right away after sneaking me, Chase, and Chris to a secret runway partially hidden far afield in a remote section of the airport. After we got to talking he didn't seem to be too bad of a guy, so I exchanged the money with him and then gave Paulo his commission on the deal.

I couldn't expect him to be doing this and not have a few defects, though. That wouldn't be normal. But I was a little worried. This guy did smell like booze, but he wasn't wasted, but he did keep grinding his teeth into his jaw like speed freaks do, which is probably why he was somewhat alert. But of course he had no hash or marijuana or speed for us, so the flight to Amsterdam was rather grim. We landed a few hours later not far from Schiphol, the main Dutch airport, in the pouring rain,

LEGEND OF A ROCK STAR

on a dirt road that had turned to mud. Then we had to walk over four kilometers till we found the French airlines terminal and tried to claim our luggage.

"Forget it," the clerk told us sarcastically when we couldn't produce any receipts for our baggage or any identification either. Besides our suitcases, we lost our guitars and the bass, and some other things we need to play a show with. When trying to get the bags didn't work out, we went to look for our tour manager. We didn't know who he was or where he would be waiting for us.

FINALY FOUND HIM AFTER
RCHING ARROUND AND LOOSIN
A OTHER WHEN WE WOULD SP
OR WHEN THE PERSON WAITING
SPOT FOR THE OTHERS WOULD
VE HIS POSITION AND GET LOST.
FINALY WE FOUND HIM. HIS NAME
MINNA. HE LOOKED LIKE AN
LCOHOLIC WHO WAS STILL SLEEP-
ON A PARK BENCH ANY WAY AND
HING HAD GOTTEN BETTER. AND NEV
ULD. HE LOOKED LIKE HE NEEDED A
ATION. LIKE HE NEEDED THE SUN
BEACH AND THE OCEAN AIR BUT HE
GET THERE.
SURE DIDNT LOOK LIKE HE
A THIRTY THREE

CHAPTER THREE

DROP
DIDNT HAD A DECENT MEAL
NCE HE'D LEFT HIS PARENTS HOUS
IFTEEN YEARS AGO. NOW HE
AS MOSTLY LIVING ON THE
REETS OF ROTTERDAM AND
METIMES WORKED AS A
RIVER TO SUPPLEMENT HIS

WE FINALLY FOUND HIM, after much searching, losing each other when we would split up, or when the person waiting in one spot for the others would leave his position and get lost. His name was Minna. He looked like a reformed alcoholic who was still sleeping on a park bench anyway and nothing had gotten better. And never would. He looked like he needed a vacation. Like he needed the sun and beach and the ocean air but he'd never get there.

He sure didn't look like he could do a thirty-three-in-thirty-five-days tour without dropping dead. Like he hadn't had a decent meal since he'd left his parents' house fifteen years ago. Now he was mostly living on the streets of Rotterdam and sometimes worked as a driver to supplement his low-level street dealing and the aid for the totally disabled persons he gets from the state, for Dutch people who don't want to work.

When everybody was feeling a common affinity we exchanged greetings and tried to break the ice. I started first by asking him if he had any money. "No," he answered, "I'm skint." His shifty eyes were following my hands' every movement as we were speaking. And his own hands would move automatically towards his waistband, where he probably had a folding knife stashed, and he would step back a half a step any time my hands accidentally grazed my own pockets.

At least he gave me a direct answer, I thought, summing up the situation so we could start trying to lock objectives:

"How about we drive now straight away to Scotland nonstop. It's the only way we can make the gig, I'm sure we can borrow the support band's gear, so don't worry."

"Well, I am worried, Minna," I answered him. "Rob must be sick in the head. Why didn't he just fly us direct to Glasgow? What kind of routing is this? It's shit."

I then looked towards Chris for some encouragement but didn't get any. He looked very despondent from losing his suitcase and his guitar. He was in an "I'm in no mood" mood that he would remain in for the rest of the tour, till finally Chase and I had to run away from him for dear life on the last day of the tour, when we were back at Schiphol airport in Amsterdam, and Chris threw another one of his loud and violent temper tantrums and the police started coming.

It was a lot warmer in L.A. than it is here. We've literally been on the street in front of the airport now for five hours since our late arrival, trying to get organized. We are all shivering in the cold and wet weather. This is even making sitting in the van for twenty-four hours and driving straight through to Glasgow look good. But Minna will probably want to keep the heat off so he won't fall asleep at the wheel. So it looks like were going to have to do something. Chris is only wearing a little T-shirt and his bronchitis is really acting up now.

As we piled into the van he started having a violent coughing fit.

"Are you all right Chris," I asked him. "We're going to drive to Scotland. Is that okay?"

"No, I am not well, Dee Dee," he could barely answer. "I am very sick now, I think I am getting pneumonia. I might have to go back to Los Angeles and check into a hospital."

There was nothing we could really do for him now except hope he wouldn't die. We had to drive to Rotterdam then, and take the ferry to England, and then drive furiously to Scotland. The drive was even more miserable because we had to suffer through listening to Chris' hacking, coughing, and sneezing the whole way there.

We took turns driving and made very good time, but alas.

WE ARRIVED IN GLA...
ONE HAD GIVEN US THE ...
...ESS AND WE COULDN'T FIND ...
...WHERE WE WERE SUPPOSED
...AYING THAT EVENING. FINAL...
...OUR OCLOCK IN THE MORNING ...
...ED WITH MINNA AND DECIDED 7...
...UP AND WITH OUT CHECKING IN...
...TEL TO GET SOME SLEEP, INSTE...
...DESPAIRINGLY DROVE TOWARDS ...
...OW. "TO BAD GUY'S I SAID." ...
...YBODY SOLD ED BACK ...

CHAPTER FOUR

...AST NIGHT WE STAYED AT THE...

CHAPTER FOUR

...WHICH IS RIGHT NEXT TO HYD...
...T. THIS IS A REAL FUN PLAC...
...E IN AUGUST WHEN ITS SUMMI...
...WHEN WE GOT THERE IT WA...
...O WINDY AND RAINING. I...
...O FEEL MYSELF CATCHING...
...D AND CHRIS LOOKED VER...

WHEN WE ARRIVED IN GLASGOW, someone had given us the wrong address and we couldn't find the club where we were supposed to be playing that evening. Finally at four o'clock in the morning we agreed with Minna and decided to give up, and without checking into a hotel to get some sleep, we despairingly drove towards London.

"Too bad guys," I said.

"Yeah," everybody soloed back.

Last night we stayed at the Columbia Hotel in Lancaster Gate, which is right next to Hyde Park. This is a real fun place to be in August, when it's summer, but when we got there it was cold, windy, and raining. I could feel myself catching a cold and Chris looked very bad. He was coughing now constantly.

After our mad dash overnight from the King Tut's Wa Wa Hut fiasco it seemed like I just got to the Columbia, barely put my bags in my room, and then I was doing press all day till show time.

I met Faye right away. I'd only talked to her on the phone before this. She was waiting in the hotel lobby wearing a leopard car coat and she had a very nice hairstyle, much to our excitement and relief. We'd just had a record company rep in Japan that didn't seem to realize what she looked like but who insisted on coming on to us.

After my last interview for the day till after the show, one of the other reps from Eagle Rock drove me straight to the venue and I just kind of bounced on to the stage. I was very disoriented by then and barely knew where I was or what I was doing. The stage was as crowded with admirers as was the club we were playing in. It's called The Garage, and is in Islington, a neighborhood in London. It's always a high playing here and it also perverts my old memories as well as my sense of humor because I have a lot of fond recollections about Islington in the old days when I used to come to London with the Ramones.

"If you don't make them get me some dope, I'll go down to Islington . . . on the subway and cop some myself on the street! Do you understand me!?" Ha ha, he he he, that's me, a young Dee Dee Ramone in the seventies threatening Monte Melnick, the Ramones' road manager, and stooge for Joey and Johnny Ramone, but no friend of mine. I never liked Monte and this hardly ever worked out for me. I did even end up having to go to Islington a few times by myself to cop dope.

It was a little rough back then but I got away with going there to score because I was a good customer and looked just as sleezy as the locals. I even ended up making one or two friends at the time, and one of them became my steady drug dealer in London. He was reliable and we had a good relationship for many years and this made going to England a little bit more tolerable for me back then. We lost touch with each other when I finally had to go to Switzerland to get my blood changed to get off of dope.

I won't mention his real name because that's not nice, but he was at The Garage playing bass in the support band. It was wonderful to see him. The only thing about him that had changed was that he had switched his Superfly afro for dread shorty-shorts. We got to snort a few lines of coke together before I went on stage. It was great shit and really hit me hard, giving me a skyrocketing lift, just the energy my body was begging for. Charlie Parker, ex-U.K. Subs front man, was there to visit. He always comes to see me when I play The Garage and I think he must live in the neighborhood.

When I positioned myself in front of my microphone on the stage in front of the London audience, I felt quite elated from the few lines of coke I had snorted and right away I counted "One, two, three, four and went into "Rockaway Beach." It all was good. I took a few cocaine breaks between numbers, faking equipment failures and walking backstage for a second, where I'd hurriedly snort another line and then go back on and continue playing. Mostly I played Ramones songs except for Chris Spedding's "Motorbikin'," and "Do You Love Me," "The Locomotion," and "Mr. Postman."

CHAPTER 5

THE NEXT MORNING WE LEFT LON
NINE OCLOCK SHARP. EVERY O
O A HARD TIME GETTING UP BO
E WERE EAGER TO GET OUT OF
NGLAND. I DONT DRIVE SO I A
ELCOMED THE TWO HOUR RIDE
E FERRY BECAUSE THE VAN
E MOST NATUERIAL PLACE FO
AY TO SLEEP AND I W
ILL THAT I SOON F
EEP SLEEP
WE GOT TO DOVER W
THE FERRY I COULD
UP MY BRAIN
LIKE THEY WE
FUL SEOITIVE

CHAPTER FIVE

THE FERRY IM A DEEP TO
I AM EXHAUSTED FROM DEP
AND BEING OVERWORKED
THERES A BIG HOOF AN
DISEASE SCARE IN EURGPE NOW
THE BORDER CHECK WHEN WE
IN CALAIS WAS PRETTY DE

THE NEXT MORNING we left London at nine o'clock sharp. Everyone had a hard time getting up but we were eager to get out of England. I don't drive so I almost welcomed the two-hour ride to the ferry because the van is the most natural place for a muscian to sleep and I was so tired still that I soon fell into a deep sleep.

When we got to Dover, where you board the ferry, I could hardly wake up. My brain and body felt like they were on a powerful sedative. I rode across the Channel on the ferry in a deep fog. I was exhausted from depression and overwork.

There's a big hoof-and-mouth disease scare in Europe now but the border check when we landed in Calais was pretty decent, despite all the horror going on. I won't be eating meat on this tour except at McDonald's, though. That's because McDonald's comes from America so it's got to be okay.

Because of the Mad Cow disease there's patrols at the ferry's landings dressed head to toe in hooded white slaughter suits. They're armed with wooden mallets, golf clubs, baseball bats, and electric cattle prods. The purpose of these patrols is to look inside all vehicles entering the continent from Britian and inspect them for livestock or family pets. If an animal is discovered it will be bludgeoned to death on the spot. When we were driving out of England we passed by burning pits used to dispose of the carcasses of slaughtered animals. The stench of burning flesh coming from these pits was horrendous and the moans coming from

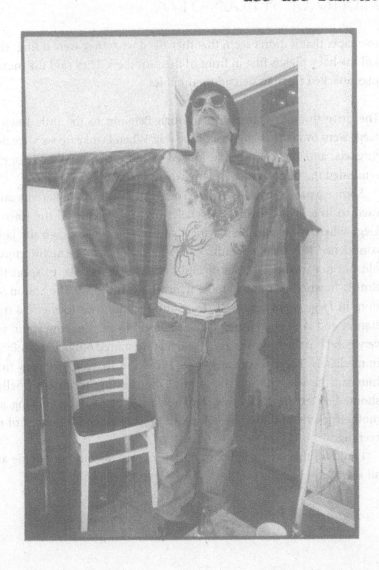

the few animals that were still not dead and slowly roasting alive was quite disturbing. I wonder to myself if this will be England's "Vietnam."

I read in my favorite papers today, the *Sun* and the *Mirror* and the *Star*, that there's going to be an armed resistance in Scotland by the farmers to defend their livestock, and since Scotland is basically a sub-nation of farmers, the whole country will probably rebel against the English. In all fairness to the killers, I also read in one of the articles in

27

the paper that it didn't seem that they liked what they were doing. They kill the baby piglets first in front of their mothers. They said the mother pigs attacked them to defend their babies.

The drive through France and through Belgium to the little town of Liège went by fast. I slept most of the way. When I woke up we were near Brussels, and the countryside looked friendly and familiar to me. It reminded me of parts of Germany where I grew up as a boy.

Soon we passed by Antwerpen. This is also near where Barbara and I used to live, in the town of Mechelen. When we entered the town of Liège where we would be playing that night, it broke down my jaded confidence. It is such a breathtakingly beautiful city. The architecture is old but not medieval. It's a nice place to live if you like to sport that British "town and country" look, which I do. The gig at The Sound Station, in Liége, went very well. The Sound Station was formerly a train station and is now a concert hall. The food in the dressing room was very good but the host was gay. A real fag. He started out being annoying immediately. There wasn't anywhere I could really go to get away from him and he was chasing me around the dressing room till finally I shouted, "Get the fuck away, I'm not a faggot like you fucking are, motherfucker!" and then he left me sheepishly alone for the rest of the evening.

I enjoyed this one, a Belgium outlaw crowd. My kind of people and all is well.

CHAPTER 6

AMSTERDAM WAS
SORT OF IN AND OUT THING. TO
AD BECAUSE I'AM SORT OF INFATUATE
ITH THIS TOWN. I'AM WRITING THIS
THE MORNING AFTER THE GIG AT
HE PARADISO.
I'VE BEEN PLAYING THIS
LUB ALOT ALL MY CAREER
ITH THE RAMONES AND THIS
LUB IS THE PLACE I SAW
HE RAMONES BEFORE THE
ROKE UP
I AM PLAYING IN THE SMALLER
ALL HERE THE ONE UPSTAIRS
HE SHOW LAST NIGHT FELT SPECIA
ND I ENJOYED IT BUT I HAVE
FEE

CHAPTER SIX

REL DOW
HAT THIS IS AS FAR AS I'VE GOTT
N MY OWN SINCE I'VE LEFT THE
RAMONES
I KNOW I COULD NEVER COMPET

AMSTERDAM WAS A SORT OF in-and-out thing. Too bad because I'm sort of infatuated with this town. I'm writing this in the morning after the gig at The Paradiso.

I've played this club a lot, all during my career with the Ramones, and this club is the last place I saw the Ramones play before they broke up.

I am playing in the smaller hall here. The one upstairs. The show last night felt special and I enjoyed it but I have a feeling I've been stupid. That it really is sort of a big letdown. That this is as far as I've gotten on my own since I've left the Ramones is pretty bad.

I know I could never compete with the Ramones and the success that they and I had together. That's normal. But as I'm leaving Amsterdam, now, today, I have a sinking feeling that this will be my last gig here in this city. I've been playing rock and roll music since I was a young man and I'm forty-nine years old now. People keep telling me how great I look, that they can't believe how much energy I have. Women keep complimenting me on how sexy I am, really. But this isn't practical anymore. I've been touring and making records since I left the Ramones, nonstop, as if I never left the business. If ever there's a time to quit it's now.

The band and our driver and I drove out of Amsterdam in silence. It was raining again, as usual. Raining again in my heart, too.

I have an "it's my last meal, walking the plank, you can try to hurt me as much as you want too but can't" aura corralling up my feelings.

I'm starting to miss California, my home. Hollywood has a golden amber ambience of its own, like Amsterdam has hers.

But I can't tell you where my heart is.

CHAPTER 7

THE LAST ONE I SAW HERE WAS
CALLED MY DYING BRIDE
THAT'S THE NAME OF A BAND I HOPE
INWA UTTERED IN HIS STIFF
UPPER LIPPED DUTCH ACCENT.
OH YES IT WAS A HUGE FELLOW
IN A BLACK MOTORCYCLE JACKET
WITH A WHITE SKULL AND CROSS
BONES PAINTED ON THE BACK OF
IT AND A THICK GRAY BEARD
FROM WHERE HE
A RATTY
FROM PEERING OVER
SHOULDER THREW THE
INTO THERE THAT
TWO SEXY UNDERAGE

CHAPTER SEVEN

SEEMED TO BE HAVING A VERY
GOOD TIME
ARE YOU SURE FOR THE
BACKSTAGE AREA
CAUTIOUSLY MEANWHILE
HE NOW WAS TRYIN
TO BLOCK THE BAND FROM
GOING INSIDE THE DRESSING ROOM

"THE LAST ONE I SAW here was called My Dying Bride."

"That's the name of a band, I hope," Minna uttered in his stiff-upper-lipped Dutch accent.

"Oh yes, it was," a huge fellow in a black motorcycle jacket with a white skull and crossbones painted on the back of it and a thick gray beard answered, from where he was sitting on a ratty-looking couch.

I could see from peering over Minna's shoulder through the door frame into there that he was with two sexy, underage groupies in flimsy halter tops and short miniskirts. They seemed to be having a very good time.

"Are you security for the backstage area?" Minna cautiously inquired. He now was trying to block the band from going inside the dressing room by jamming his whole thin frame inside the doorway and giving the dressing room a visual scan, checking things out before deciding to let us go inside now or not.

Before this bloke in the motorcycle jacket and beard could answer back, the whole lot of us pushed our way gleefully past Minna inside the room, without waiting for him to okay the situation. The friendly sounds of laughing young girls and the thick cloud of marijuana leaking out to the hallway where we had been trailing behind Minna were too tempting for us to stand there and let the spoils inside go to waste on just one person.

"Don't worry, everybody," I bellowed, as I burst into the dressing room ahead of everyone else. "It's only my old friend Maxi Dex. Don't worry, he's harmless. He just looks scary because he's a hardened criminal and sells drugs to all the motorcycle gangs in Austria and Germany and Switzerland."

"*Wie geht's mein mawn,*" I enthusiatically greeted him in German, clicking my heels, too, and giving him a salute. "*Sehr gutt danka, und Ich haba diesen madschen mitt gebracht fur dich und zwie grossen packatt en; mean green' fur dich zoom rauchen, mein herr. Wunder barr, das is herlich, nicht var jungs,*" I squealed in delight. "This is my friend Maxi Dex," I said, introducing him all around to everybody.

"He's still selling drugs?" Minna hopefully inquired, pretending that he didn't understand what we had just said in German.

"Yeah," I smirked at him.

He brought us two bags of mean green. Some Top 44 and some Nebula. Real strong smoke. The best. And it seemed like we can take turns having sex with these girls and just pass them around if we liked.

"Why don't we skip the sound check and party till show time?"

"Okay," Minna authorized, "but let's leave later at an appropriate time for dinner. That way we get the most out of everything and no one will have to use their own money today for food or drugs."

"What a good plan," I agreed. "By the way, Minna," I continued, "where the hell are we? I have no idea, I'm losing track of everything. I've been taking too many drugs and my head feels a little cloudy."

"That's all right," Minna answered me back. "There's nothing wrong with you pal, we all feel like that, especially me, but I've got to drive us over these mountains every day. But anyway, we're in Saltzburg, in Austria. I don't know how I got us here, but I did. Tomorrow we go back to Germany, then to Austria again, and then directly to Italy. Don't bring any of that mean green with you, okay? I mean it. The borders are going to be rough from now on. Especially Germany, where almost everything is illegal."

After Minna's sour speech things loosened up and got pretty upscale. Within minutes I had a young babe in a miniskirt sitting on my knee and rubbing her private parts on my leg.

"I want you so bad, Dee Dee," she whispered to me then, kissing my lips. "Do you like to fuck," she said, "do you like me, yes please, and my sister, she likes you too, very much, she gives great head, do you want us both?"

LEGEND OF A ROCK STAR

"Oh yes, very much, yes I do," I answered her. "I love you both. I'm very happy."

How could I not have been? By then I was pretty trashed and her sister had come over to us and was flashing her tits at me. This girl couldn't have been more than a year older than her sister who was squirming on my lap now, begging for sex. They were both most likely fourteen and sixteen years old. What can you do when they want you this bad except go along with it, especially when they have as nice a set of newly developed curves as these two did? Maxi had probably broken them in, anyway.

Everyone else was in similar situations, so by the time we left the dressing room two hours later there were forty-four empty bottles of beer and seven empty wine bottles, which we had consumed between all of us, trashed on the floor.

There were bodily fluids splashed on the walls and couch, but no empty condom wrappers. Everyone in our party is married or in a long-term relationship. But there's no harm in accepting a blow job once in a while and that's not cheating for the guy. After two hours in that small room with everybody smoking mean green furiously, we could hardly see or breath anymore and had to get out of there.

The Rock House has one of the best cooks on the club circuit. We had turkey loaf for dinner. The cook told me later that she was writing a rock and roll cookbook and that she'd like to dedicate the recipe for the turkey loaf to the Ramones. Minna told me later on that even the most jaded and listless phlegmatics were impressed by the courtesies at this venue. Even Dutch rock star Herman Brood and his band the Wild Romance ended up preferring Austria to Germany, and even to Holland, where they were from. The only thing I didn't like were the opening band the Tolle Frosch who were crap. Some of the graffiti on the dressing room wall that I remember were "J. Haider & Beethoven had enemas on this couch," "Mozart and Stalin had anal sex on this couch," and "The annihilator sound check":

"Bubble bath"

"Brick wall"

"Refresh the mailman."

THE DRIVE TODAY TO BIELLA, ITALY
WAS 438 MILES. THINGS ARE BETTER
TOURING EUROPE NOW THAN BEFORE
BECAUSE OF THE OPEN BORDERS.
ONLY IN GERMANY DO YOU
HAVE TO WATCH OUT IF YOUR AN
ALTERNATIVE TYPE OF PERSON OR
EXPECIALY IF YOU HAVE DUTCH
PLATES ON YOUR VEHICLE. THIS
IS BECAUSE IN GERMANY AND
EXPECIALY IN THE GERMAN STATE
BAVARIA THERE ARE SWARMS
OF UNDERCOVER COP'S. THEY
LOVE TO SNEAK UP ON PEOPLE
EXPECIALY AT THE REST STOP
AREAS ALONG THE AUTOBAHN

CHAPTER EIGHT

OF COURSE THE COPS SNUCK
UP BY US IN GERMANY BUT
WE WERE VERY CLEVER AND
THE DRUGS WE HAD
CAREFULLY HIDDEN
SEARCHED US AND
HAD TO LET US GO
CONT REVEAL THIS INFO

THE DRIVE TODAY TO BIELLA, Italy, was 438 miles.

Things are better touring Europe now than before because of the open borders. Only in Germany do you have to watch out, if you're an alternative type of person, or especially if you have Dutch plates on your vehicle. This is because, in Germany and especially in the German state of Bavaria, there are swarms of undercover cops. They love to sneak up on people, especially at the rest stop areas along the autobahn. So please be careful.

Of course, the cops snuck up on us in Germany, but we were very clever and all the drugs we had were carefully hidden. They searched us and then had to let us go. I wouldn't reveal this infomation if I ever planned to go back to Bavaria. Too bad for me, as it's one of the most beautiful places in the world. Since Germany has become like it is lately, with this zero tolerance shit, I've replaced the area mentally with Switzerland, which looks very similar but is more normal and friendly.

The drive to Biella was long because it's a lot of mountain roads, but the scenery makes me remember why I love Europe so much. All was ruined again, though, because Chris had to get another attack of bronchitis and was coughing and wheezing the whole ride to Biella. I was a little angry at him because he stayed at the club to hang out instead of coming back to the hotel after the show in Salzburg. Before we left I asked him, "How are you going to get home?" The rock house was only three blocks to the hotel. But it was pouring cats and dogs. The perfect getting-sick kind of weather. Well, I, hope he's happy now.

The gig at Biella was at a club somewhere out in the countryside. There were a lot of excited dogs running around and barking and having the time of their lives at all the attention they were getting from all these people showing up in what, when they don't have concerts, is probably a very peaceful area that they usually have all to themselves. I allmost didn't want to go inside the club because the neatly plowed fields that outlined the venue and the calm night sky, filled lushly with bright beautiful stars instead of stormy clouds for once, was very soothing. There just was too much tail-wagging and barking from the dogs for this to last, and I had to abruptly exit this illusion of tranquillity. Soon I had absorbed myself in our dressing room backstage, which I was determined to keep completely empty tonight except for band members, and waited for the support band to finish.

The show was really good and the audience worshipped us. Chris had lots of energy, even though he's a little ill. He drinks a lot of whisky, honey, and lemon water, and that makes him feel good. Sometimes I worry about him hurting himself when he falls off the stage or trips and falls over a cable or monitor speaker on his back, but he won't listen and always gives his crowd-pleasing performances anyway. Later, I was very happy to go back to the hotel.

CHAPTER NINE

MILANO ITALY, THE HOTEL
DURANTE, THIS PLACE LITERALLY
STINKS LIKE CAT PISS, THERE
WAS EVEN A STRAY CAT SITTING
IN MY BED IN MY ROOM THAT
PROBABLY LET ITSELF IN THRU
THE WINDOW.

I FEEL LIKE SHOUTING
I HATE YOU!) AT THE PROMOTOR
FROM THE TUNNEL, THE CLUB
WHERE I AM PLAYING TONIGHT
BOOKED THIS HOTEL, NOW ALL I
CAN DO IS CURSE IN MY
ROOM FOR THE FIRST TWO
HOURS I HAVE HAD OFF ON
THIS CREEPY TOUR
THIS THE REWARD I GET
FOR BEING DEE DEE RAMONE, I
SCREAM TO THE HEAVENS, STOMP
MY FEET ON THE FLOOR AS I DO SO
I PRAY TO GOD TO GIVE ME A HEART
ATTACK AND DIE SO I DONT
HAVE TO FACE ANOTHER MISSERABL
DAY OF EXISTENCE, JUST DON'T CALL
ME ROCK STAR, OR —
AND KONAO YES AND ——
SPEN ——

MILANO, ITALY. The Hotel Durante. This place literally stinks like cat piss. There was even a stray cat sitting on my bed in my room that probably let itself in through the window. I feel like shouting "I hate you!" at the promoter from The Tunnel, the club where I'm playing tonight. They booked this hotel. Now all I can do is curse in my room for the first two hours I have had off on this creepy tour.

Is this the reward I get for being Dee Dee Ramone? I complain to the heavens, stomping my foot on the floor as I do so. Just don't call me "rock star," or I might come and kidnap you and force you to spend a night in this chamber of horrors. The furniture in my room is frayed and old and stained with wine, vomit, and tomato sauce. No traveler could be comfortable here. It could only make you feel even more weary to stay in this hotel. Weary of your life. You could only imagine you were a failure and that your life was pathetic and that everything had been for nothing. It would lower any musician's self-esteem to zero and make him feel like he's on the lower end of the social scale to be put here.

I couldn't even laughingly call this joint a section-eight palace. This is no joke. I wouldn't even feel safe walking around the halls or even in my room with the door locked after dark. Milan is known all over the world for being a dangerous city due to its crime and instability. So is all of Italy.

One of the first things I noticed when I entered my room after getting my key from Minna was that theres no bath tub. If there were one, you would have to have a lot of courage to use it. I know, because when I went to visit the toilet down the hall it was filthy. The first thing I saw when I jarred open the bathroom door was an angry centipede fiercely coiling in a corner, giving me a don't-give-me-any-shit attitude on the garbage-covered floor. There were lots of cobwebs on the ceiling with lethal-looking black widow spiders calmly hanging down from them, giving me looks of death.

If that wasn't enough to give me the creepy crawlies, then the bent spoon, resting on the edge of the slop sink, that was burnt underneath and had a dried-up, brown-colored dab of cotton in it that some junkie had used to cook up with did the trick.

It makes me wonder if the only way to get comfortable in this hopeless miserable place would be with a hot shot of dope. I decided to leave and go and piss out of the window in my room.

Our food money comes to only eight dollars a day, and that's only the start of that problem. The other problem is how to communicate in a foreign language in order to get something, let alone pay for it. No one at the reception desk at the Hotel Durante will even look at me, let alone offer me any service. The breakfast that should come with the room won't this time.

We depend on that meal to get by. It's almost always the only decent meal of the day because hotels couldn't stay in business if they fed people like the venues that I've been playing at on this tour have been feeding us.

This is the sacrifice that I have made to play for my fans. Everything doesn't have to be perfect. But the business people are charging my fans a lot of money to see me. Where's it going?

I've worked my way out of flop-house hotels. I've been in enough of them all my life because I was poor and had nowhere else to live. There were plenty of times in my life that I would have been happy to have this room instead of the street, but not now. That was a long time ago and I don't want to relive it because it isn't necessary. This is depressing. If this is all this promoter could do, he shouldn't have booked us here under any circumstances.

These kids coming to The Tunnel tonight are like my babies to me. I mean, yeah, I'd still love to go to the airport right now and get on a plane and go home but in about ten minutes the Italian Ramones fans

LEGEND OF A ROCK STAR

waiting around the van, where I'm trapped now, and can't escape them, wear me out. They love me too much. It could all be for the love of rock and roll but it's also very much for the fans. Even the meanest of the mean types, like myself, would have to throw his meanness away over his shoulder rather than give it to any of these young Ramones fans that are surrounding me outside this club right now.

The show in Milano ended up great. The place was sold out. The

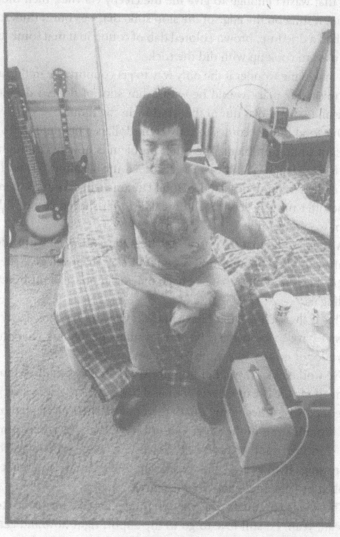

atmosphere was heavy and very punk. It was the closest concert that I've been to or played at since the late seventies.

There was no security to protect me while I was playing. Whatever's gonna happen up there is gonna happen. This is punk rock. So, I hate this, but because it's punk, some of the hardcore punks in the audience are gonna come to disrespect you or start up with you when you're playing, like the spitters in Argentina, who have forced me to admit that there's nothing I can ever do about it, except never play a show there again because they will never stop. Pretty stupid, but, I fight back.

But what can you do if something like what happened to one of my dearest friends happens? I spoke to Jimmy last night. He was home in bed. The night before was his birthday.

Jimmy played guitar in the Vapids, one of the all-time best and most organized punk bands ever. Last night was his birthday and the Vapids were playing a show in Toronto, Canada, where they're from.

While he was playing the set, someone from the support band doused Jimmy and his guitar with lighter fluid and set him on fire. He was very badly burned. This was no joke. He told me last night that his face was so badly burned that he looked like a monster. That his hands were bandaged, that he would never be able to play the guitar again.

"If it was my Mosrite I would have killed them," he told me before we said good-bye.

It sounds like premeditated murder to me, but Jimmy insisted that wasn't the case. It was basically the audience trying to participate with the band while they were playing the show. Huh??? What???

When I'm playing on stage I hold the mike stand down with my foot so I don't get smashed in the teeth with the mike while I'm singing. This happens because of stage divers who, when they hit the stage, hit it with a belly-flop effect. This bounce makes the mike stands spring at you, so you've got to watch out that the mike doesn't hit you in the teeth.

This makes it hard to play neatly and I usually hit loads of bad notes and make lots of mistakes. Sometimes I go blank and can't remember parts of the songs because my mind is elsewhere. The audience likes to get on the stage the most to sing "Blitzkrieg Bop." When one of them makes it up there they want to lock their arms around me and kiss me while I'm trying to sing and play the bass. It's usually a male skin. Then he will make the Nazi salute to the crowd and shout "Hey ho, lets go" into the mike, and then either summersault or swan dive back into the crowd as his boots knock into people's heads. Then another one will take the last one's place immediately.

The front of the stage is always one huge mosh pit. It reminds me of a human meat grinder. The action spreads itself throughout the crowd. A few punks will lock arms together and whirl themselves around the dance floor, spraying beer in the air and smashing and bumping into the other beasts in the pit. I hate getting sprayed with beer, but I always do. It shorts out my bass. Then I have to borrow another one from the support band. This is punk rock.

After the show I was trapped in a crescent hollow, dead center behind the stage. It had a barely adequate curtain that served as a makeshift door. The effect was that the audience could still see me when the show was over. And they wouldn't leave. What a day. What a long day.

Later we had to bum-rush our way out of the building through the crowd and throw ourselves into our van. As I was slamming the door shut I caught the fingers of a young fan who was trying to hand me a paper to sign on the metal door frame and accidentally cut them off.

Minna put the van in gear, stepped on the gas, and plowed indiscriminately through the crowd. As we were speeding away, Minna hit a young Italian football fan who was holding the first Ramones album in his mitts, probably killing him on the spot. I don't know for sure, but the one that got his fingers cut off looked a mess, shouting in pain, and blood spraying from the amputated stumps.

CHAPTER TEN

THE NEXT DAY, FRIDAY THE
WENTY THIRD OF MARCH W
EFT MILANO ITALY AND HE
R SWITZERLAND. WE HA
D SHOWS THERE, ONE IN A
ND ONE IN LUZERN.

CHASE AND I HAVE BE IN
EFORE ON LAST YEARS T
F EUROPE BUT WE JUST S
VERNIGHT AND DIDNT PLAY
IONY THINK YOU COULD P
PUNK SHOW HERE BUT
RONG EVEN THO IT NO
NONEVENTFUL PLAC
THE FIRST DRA
O TODAY WAS BEING STOPP
Y THE CHAPTER TEN DER
PASSPORT CHECK
THE TWO ITALIAN POLICE
EAN BUT THEY WERE FAIR
ARGAINED WITH US FOR
OPY OF MY LATEST C.D.
HEN LET US GO ACROSS
WITZERLAND. AS CHRIS W

THE NEXT DAY, Friday the twenty-third of March, we left Milano, Italy and headed for Switzerland. We have two shows there, one in Aarau and one in Lucerne.

Chase and I have been in Aarau before on last year's tour of Europe but we just stayed overnight and didn't play. I didn't think you could play a punk show here. But I was wrong, even though it's kind of a non-eventful place.

The first drama that happened today was being stopped at the Italian border for a passport check. The two Italian police looked mean but they were fair. They bargained with us for a copy of my latest CD and then let us go across into Switzerland. As Chris was pulling the CD out from his suitcase to give to them, I cringed, seeing how old and horrible I looked on it, especially with my dyed, blue-black Prince Valiant hairstyle and the awful pancake makeup that they made me wear to hide my horrible, beat-up, wrinkled old face.

At the Swiss border we were stopped and pulled over for a check. They opened the door of the van to look around, but before things could get serious we were saved, when the border police at another check point were attempting to pull over a vehicle with Islamic nationals in it that wouldn't stop for them at the booth.

Instead, the driver of the vehicle started trying to run the gauntlet of road traps between no man's land and the Swiss border.

A policeman ran up to this person's car when he was trying to squeeze it through a purposely narrow "L" turn and smashed the fellow's windshield with a large wooden mallet that had a head on it the size of one of those wooden barrels that Saint Bernards wear hanging from their collars for mountain rescues.

After the windscreen of this car was smashed it went out of control. The Islamic national who was driving it was blinded by the spray of glass and couldn't see any more, and couldn't drive safely anymore, so he jumped out of it. He was followed by two other blokes, one of whom hurled a grenade at the border police as he was bailing out of the vehicle. In return the police sprayed them with machine gun fire.

We were all hiding on the floor of the van, shaking to death with fear by then. As the smoke started clearing and in the ensuing chaos due to what had just gone down, we were eventually allowed to cross the border into Switzerland without any further delay. Switzerland is a very nice place. It's a very liberal country. Weed is pretty much not against the law there, although you really can't be sure. I wouldn't bring it across the border or drive in a car with it. You can buy it in stores, though, in a nice section of town, with no hassle. It's high quality and inexpensive.

The club I play at in Lucerne used to be a women's prison. I know this sounds gruesome but whatever it used to be like it's not like that now. My friend Martin runs this place and he's done a lot for music by sacrificing everything he's got for all this. It's a great place to play. Martin has kept a lot of the German and Swiss local scene going for years, as well as bringing acts out of nowhere, like me and Chris and Chase. It has none of the atmosphere of a prison anymore. This is probably because it's a big weed-smoking place. It must have been harvest time when we arrived. This joint is now named The Sedel.

I have no way of relating to this name. No one I asked knows what Sedel means in either Swiss or German.

Last year when I was here on tour, Barbara was playing bass and I was playing guitar. We had a CD out called *Hop Around*. In an article in the local paper they wrote that she was my daughter. They didn't know we were married and that she was my wife. I guess that's how it must look because of our extreme age difference.

Everybody had read this article but Barbara and me. Then all the guys at The Sedel were trying to come on to her. The sound check got quite annoying. They didn't know. They thought Barbara was my daughter. They thought she was single. She's very beautiful and has a lot of money. Everybody seemed to want to join the Ramone family that day. Barbara loves me and sensed that something was irritating me despite her reaction to all the lavish attention she was getting, which put her in rather a jubilant mood. But then to let everybody know that I was her man she started to get very sexy with me, giving me big kisses and lots of loving hugs. Once she even attempted to grab my private

parts. After the show I tried to venture over by The Sedel's bar, which they keep open all night. It's usually a fun place to hang out. This time I felt very uncomfortable. I was getting the look of death from a lot of people.

I found out soon why everybody was being the way they were. I was just plain embarrassed, but I stood up for myself and my wife.

"I'm her husband, not her dad," I proclaimed to the horror of all of Barbara's admirers. "We've been together for five years. Too bad, so sad, but this girl belongs to me! Got it? To me! Okay!" Then I grabbed her ass. This year when I arrived at The Sedel everyone asked me where my wife was. "I . . . didn't bring her," I responded to their inquiries. "And it's partially all you people here's fault."

I'm sour that she's not here with me but I can't take any more chances like that. It makes it too hard to play in a band together. This tour ends April 16. Wilco Johnson is playing at Dingwall's in London on April 25. I desperately want to go. I'm thinking of just staying in Europe and resting after I finish all my dates, and having Barbara fly from Los Angeles to Amsterdam to meet me, and then going to London the next week to see Wilco.

"Punk rock started in Ireland," the angry Swiss psycho sitting next to me in my dressing room after the show at The Sedel announced, in my face.

"Wott," I answered this freak back, reaching over and shutting his tape recorder firmly off.

"How the hell can you explain that? Huh?" I grrrrred, "The fucking Ramones started punk rock music in New York, right?"

Instead of answering me back this weirdo picked up an apple out of the fruit basket and started loudly eating it, smacking his lips and all and looking at me all funny like, and then, undaunted, this lunatic happily continued his spiel.

"My favorite group is the Angelic Upstarts," he told me angrily. I knew that the Upstarts are very anti-American. I usually try to play things down and be nicer, but now there's a need to teach this asshole a lesson and stick up for America and N.Y.C.

I know from experience that this situation won't get any better now anyway so I pull an "out!" and "out!" on him which I learned from a street-hardened member of the Anti-Nowhere League, many years ago in London. I suddenly shot out of my chair with out warning and viciously kicked the leg of the chair that he was sitting in so hard that it knocked him "out!" of it and on his skinny ass to the floor. Then in one continuous motion I picked up the chair that I had been sitting on and to his complete horror and surprise hit him over the head three or four times with it. His eyes rolled back in his skull and he posed no threat to me anymore.

"Way to go, Dee Dee," I heard someone comment over my shoulder. "Oh, I'm not through with him yet," I shot back, incriminating myself but not giving a damn. Grabbing his feet, I then dragged him outside down two flights of steel fire escape type of stairs to the street, banging him up a lot more.

It was raining and cold and I was huffing and puffing, but the demon in me hadn't been satisfied. Since The Sedel is in the Swiss countryside I then dragged this poor, half-dead person and left him bleeding on a cow pile.

...UNCHEN

...WHEN WE WERE A FEW KILOMETE...
...M MUNICH I STARTED GETTING VE...
...RIED. WHERE WAS IT. MUNICH WAS
...TED CORRECTLY ON MY ITINERA...
...SAID MUNICH. THE KULTURSTATION...
...HE KULTURSTATION IS ACTUALY...
...K WHERE THE OLD GERMAN CIRC...
...ONE USED TO WAIT OUT THE WIN...
...WHERE GERMAN DIRECTOR TOD BROU...
...T MANY OF THE SCENES FROM TH...
...IE FREAKS. IT IS SOMEWHERE VE...
...R FROM MUNICH ... TH...
...T SUBURB OF THAT CITY...
...PLACES LIKE THE KULTURSTATION...
...SOME KIND OF FREE ZONES FR...
...POLICE. THE PEOPLE WHO RUN T...
...E DO IT IN A COMMUNAL WAY, TH...
...TO ... ART ...
...SIC CLUB FOR THE YOUNG PEOPLE
...THIS AREA OF BAVARIA
...HE CLUB'S INTERIOR, THE FORT...
...E WALLS SURROUNDING THE PAR...
...T IT SITS IN ... THE OLD CIRCU...
...AILERS THAT LOOK LIKE THEY WERE...

CHAPTER ELEVEN

MÜNCHEN

When we were a few kilometers from Munich I started getting very worried. Where was it? Munich was listed correctly on my itinerary. It said Munich. The Kulturstation.

The Kulturstation is actually a park where the old German circus Krone used to wait out the winter. And where German director Tod Browning shot many of the scenes from the movie *Freaks*. It is somewhere very far from Munich in an out of the way suburb of that city.

Places like the Kulturstation are sort of free zones from the police. The people who run this place do it in a communal way. They got together and made an art and music club for the young people in this area of Bavaria.

The club's interior, the fort-like walls surrounding the park that it sits in, and the old circus trailers that look like they were dumped there, are all heavily covered with graffiti which could match a lot of the graffiti in America for its quality and its dedication.

My band and I, playing music like we do, are of the same sort of tribe. We're very passionate, dedicated, and have a very hard way to go! The people who run the Kulturstation and my band and I are okay. We're like Mad Max people. We have no security for all our hard work and a predictable disastrous ending. All stars burn out.

I try to make the best of it. But the human body does wear out whether you're young or old. It's still about how much abuse you have to take versus how much you have left to give.

When I was in my dressing room, before the show, the promoter brought a journalist from an Internet magazine backstage. This is a super privilege. I was nice but I didn't invite him there or want him there or care to talk to him, but he turned on his recorder and like an idiot and an asshole asked me a shitty question right away. Did you keep writing songs for the Ramones, after you left them, for the money?

Oh, how tired. I didn't even answer him back. I walked out of my own dressing room instead. I was hungry. So I went to the kitchen bar area. This area got a little too over-cozy for me right away. Still, I tried to ignore the developing situation and get something to eat. Chase and Chris were following right behind me. They were also hungry and wanted to get something to eat, and they were bored, and they wanted to sit where there were some people to look at. So I sat down at a table near the bar with them, which all my defensive instincts warned me not to do, but one of Chris' continuous smart-alecky remarks coming my way put me in a fighting mood instead of a running mood.

I was again angered by the food. Carrot soup, vggg. And the main course, ooooh nooo, noodles and hot salad sauce. For dessert you can have my meanness, me and my complaining, my fearless sarcastic anger, etc. But I will still try not to act out and show how I feel. I know better by now.

I also tried to ignore that the empty table next to where we are having dinner is filled up now with unworthy journalists and everyone of them impatient for my time. It was obvious that I was the center of tension, so I got up from my chair, leaving my crap dinner untouched, to go back to the dressing room so as to avoid any trouble. Before I could escape it was announced from the bar that the cup of coffee that I had been waiting and waiting for was finally ready and I could come over to the counter to get it. I politely pushed my way through the crowd of curiosity-seekers, who had gathered by the bar and had been sticking their asses in my face while I had tried to eat my dinner and fetch my coffee. One idiot had to make a comment. He went "How do you like your coffee?" to me. I didn't like the tone of his voice so I took my coffee black and slowly poured it up and down over his arm, which was stretched out on the bar blocking the milk and sugar.

I remember last year on the ferry from England to France I literally had to fart in the face of a man who wouldn't stop. He kept coming over to my table at which I was sitting and trying to have dinner, and pestering me. I ignored him. He wouldn't stop. Then he pretended to be looking at a painting that was hanging behind me on the wall where I was sitting at my table. Finally I got up on my seat, turned around, and let a big fart off in his face.

So this fucking journalist follows me back from the bar area to the dressing room then, and starts up.

"Will you be playing the songs tonight that Joey Ramone made famous with the Ramones?"

Okay. That's his opinion and he's entitled to it. But my reaction to him was, "Can you get the fuck out of here? Yes, leave. No, I will not do your Internet magazine a big favor. Good-bye. I could care less. Then do it with Joey. Get the fuck out."

He left. Later he gave me a sad peace sign from where he was hiding down the hall as I was walking by.

BERLIN WE PLAYED A C...
...ED THE KNACK WHEN W...
...ED TO THE CLUBS ENTR...
...HAD BEEN DRIVING AB...
...HOURS FROM MUNICH...
...D AND SNOWING IW...
...N WE GOT OUT OF THE VAN...
...NOWHERE YOU COULD...
...TING YOUR FEET WET...
...WASN'T FEELING GOOD...
...COMING OFF...
...KING WET WAT...
...D DUNGEON LIKE C...
...ESSING ROOM...
...HING A BAD...
...UM WAITING AFTER...
...THE EQUIPMENT TO...
...O THE VAN WHILE THE...
...RS IN BACK OF THE CLUB...

CHAPTER TWELVE

...N RUN BACK AND FORTH WITH
...R DUTIES...
...IT'S ALL TAKING A TOLL ON
...PHYSICAL AS WELL AS MENTAL
...TA...
...STUFF IN
...THERE'S

IN BERLIN WE PLAYED A CLUB called The Knack. When

we pulled over to the club's entrance we had been driving about ten hours, from Munich. It was cold and snowing in Berlin. When we got out of the van there was nowhere you could step without getting your feet wet.

I wasn't feeling good anymore from coming off the hot stages soaking wet into the cold, damp, dungeon-like German dressing rooms, and was catching a bad cold. And from waiting after the shows for the equipment to be loaded into the van, while the exit doors in back of the club where you load out are left open so that the humper can run back and forth with his duties.

It's all taking a toll on my physical as well as my mental health. The support band put their guitars and stuff in my dressing room. There's so little space in here as it is. There's only room for maybe two people to sit down. I really don't want a bunch of people in here. I don't want any backstage dramas. I am not looking for anything. The drugs or girls. I just want to go home to the hotel and get in bed like I always do. And call my wife.

The show had gone really, really well. It was very satisfying. It had made me very happy. The crowd was really good. I liked playing for them very much. Even Chris was happy. He said we were really tight. So did Chase. Everyone had a good time. But what followed afterwards in the dressing room after the show ruined everything.

Twenty-four hours later I am still enraged. I didn't need this know-

Der Warthog Schläft Heute Abend (The Warthog Sleeps Tonight). Onstage at Joey's birthday bash at the Continental, NYC, May 19, 1997

it-all German creep coming backstage to provoke me. Even though I wasn't feeling good because of my cold I was elated because the show I'd just done in Berlin was the best one I'd ever done either in the Ramones or solo. I knew no solo Ramone could come close to doing what I had just done so my pride was high, and rightfully so.

But I still wasn't in the mood to party or whatever. The hospitality spread at The Knack was cheap and depressing, as was the meal which was the most uninteresting one of the tour. I was peeved by this lack of respect from the German promoter IBD and The Knack. And fed up with my promoter, Paper Clip, in Holland. Chris and Chase were in too good of a mood now to let anything worry them, until something bad actually happened, which we all knew would. But being young, they let their guard down.

Chris had a big smile on his face instead of his usual frown because a sexy fräulein had taken off her T-shirt in front of the band and given it to him after he came off stage after the show, because he had the sniffles.

She took off her dry T-shirt and gave it to him to wear and then stood there in front of all of us completely topless.

And she was smiling. Chris started smiling back at her because he thought it was a German custom and you had to do that. Also, she had very big tits. Then Chase spotted this German girl that was quite beautiful. She was dressed in a Nazi youth outfit. The Nazi armband, the black tie and white business shirt, pigtails, a pleated skirt, thigh-high black seamed stockings, high heels, and an innocent school girl demeanor.

We had already heard all about Berlin, but didn't expect this much. And it was right here, now, for us.

She walked into the dressing room with Chase, making quite a cheerful appearance, walked over to where I was sitting on this decrepit couch, sat down next to me, and gave me a card with a drawing of the Ramones on it. The card read: the Berlin Bastards play dirty with the German Beach Balls and D-J Lickie, up, this, mess, and D-J Stuponic. I couldn't imagine what this was all about, especially as she then tried to grope my cock.

"What do you think you're doing?" I reprimanded her. "Keep your hands to yourself or you'll have to leave, okay?"

She may as well have not heard me, and continued to try to get sexy with me.

"Would you come into the toilet with me, Dee Dee, and let me kneel in front of you, and urinate all over me? Please," she whispered, loud enough for everyone in the cramped dressing room to hear.

"What did you just say?" I asked. I was annoyed. She didn't answer me at first. Instead she got up off the couch where she had been sitting next to me uninvited and knelt down in front of me.

"Dee Dee," she then pleaded again, "please come into the toilet with me. I am at your complete disposal. Please use me. I am nothing but a common turd. I beg you to humiliate me."

"Whatever," I observed, "but you have to get out of my dressing room. Everybody in here heard what you said. Aren't you embarrassed? You could have been a little bit more discreet, if that's what you really wanted," I added nonchalantly.

All the while this was taking place, a line of people were waiting to get inside the small dressing room. They would have already been in there but there wasn't any room, just a constant annoying parade of ill-wishers, angry for the small success they thought I was having.

The girl that wanted me to urinate on her was still there. I guess she was waiting for her boyfriend, who predictably was next in line.

"Hi, I am Herman Gross, with the German Beach Balls," he said, introducing himself to me.

"Welcome Herman," I said, getting up out of my seat on the couch to escape. "Why don't you sit down and make yourself comfortable," I added, as a delay diversion attempt. Herman happily complied and sat down next to this nut-job girl who had been hassling me. I thought they would be happy, but no such luck. I wasn't going to get away that easily. I was trapped and would literally have to fight my way out of the dressing room if I wanted to leave now. Shit, I thought to myself, I better make the best of this.

"Herman," I spoke to him in perfect English, "I hear that the German Beach Balls are a pretty good punk rock band."

"Oh no, *mein gott im himmel*." He winced, squishing his ugly face in pain. "We're not punk, I hate punk, we're rock and roll."

"Then what the fuck are you doing here?" I shouted, losing my temper. "Aren't the Ramones punk? Aren't I the king of punk?"

"Errrr, I don't know, but I think the Ramones are *scheiss*. I hate them."

"What? You hate the Ramones?," I yelled in his face.

"Yes, I hate the Ramones," he scowled back at me defiantly. "And I hate punk. And I hate all Americans."

"But America gave the world rock and roll music," I defended myself.

"So what?" he said, "Germany did it better. Some of the early

German rock and roll songs like that one, 'My Baby, Baby, Balla Balla' . . ."

With that I cut him right off in mid-sentence. Losing all self-control I started yelling at him and his weirdo girlfriend, who was now trying to be nice and on her best behavior, trying to rectify the situation.

"Dee Dee, *mein shact's*. Don't get so worked up. Please, Dee Dee, that's just what Herman wants. That's why he's my boyfriend, he's a bona fide masochist freak. All the members of the German Beach Balls are into water sports. Maybe I could shit in his mouth for you. Would you like that?"

"Oh that's all right, you bunch of creeps," I finally cracked, getting up on the small coffee table and unzipping my fly. I then pulled out my cock and indiscriminately began pissing on everyone concerned.

"Is this what you want? Get out, get out now!"

No one would listen. Especially Herman Gross, who selfishly stuck his face right in the line of my fire, enjoying every minute of my rage. The girl who started this was ecstatic.

"This is all I've ever dreamed about," she squealed, "I would rather Joey Ramone be doing this to me *mein shatz*, but I saw on the MTV news that he has cancer and is in the hospital. So now I have to make do with your pee pee," she went on in a very suspicious sounding accent that was sounding more Swiss than German the more excited she got.

"I love it, I love sick things and fucked up people. Joey, I heard Joey say that they threw you out of the Ramones because you're so fucked up. Dee Dee, would you mind if I pretend you're Joey and close my eyes and then would you piss on me?"

My God, can this freak talk, I thought to myself.

"She's from Berne," someone else told me later. That makes sense, I realized. No real German girl would let a Jewish man (Joey) pee on her, ever. It would be bad form to say the least. Why me, I moaned zipping up my trousers. I had had just about enough of this shit already and was feeling an overwhelming sense of claustrophobic panic. I started pushing my way out of the dressing room, crewka crewka, punching a few cretins as I did so.

I didn't get very far. It's not that easy being me. There's a high price to pay for having been a Ramone. "Oh, Deeeee Deeeeee," a familiar voice called to me as I was running down the hall towards the van. That voice, it stopped me dead in my tracks. It was Allie, the big-promise-maker, loyal-to-Johnny-and-Joey-Ramone-and-completely-against-me German filmmaker who wants to direct a film called "Too Tough to Die," starring the Ramones.

"Hey Allie," I fearlessly smirked at him. "What the fuck are you doing at my show in Berlin? You didn't call me for five months. What about all those promises you made me?"

Allie let all this slide and started acting all innocent and stuff, and putting up a guiltless front. Where did this fool think he learned how to hustle? I grinned to myself, walking over and extending my hand. "Hello, hello Allie." I smiled at him and reassuringly shook hands with him. I could tell Allie was semi-pleased.

"Dee Dee," he started, "We're friends. You're the only one in the Ramones that I have a friendship with."

"We're not friends," I shot back at him. "I like you but not that much. This is business. All right? Can't you see that I'm a very busy and harassed man? Anyway, I have to go right now. But if I ever give you another chance again you've got to talk turkey. That's t-u-r-k-e-y, Allie. Not the loaf okay, understand me. That's turkey, as in the whole bird, the stuffing, gravy, mashed potatoes, and cranberry sauce. And the pumpkin pie.

"Don't fuckin' invite me to Burger King while you fuckers are eating *weiner schnitzel* in Germany."

"Dee Dee, I am not pleased by this, we love you, be the nice bunny. Good chicken, duck, beak, boy, the good Dee Dee that, that, that . . . oh why are you so difficult?"

No way, get out of my life or give me back the value of what you want from me. I'm feeding myself, my enemies aren't going to, so what's in this for me?"

"Dee Dee," Allie interupted, "I am hurt. I really do like you. I hate the Ramones. They're a right bunch of bastards. We need your song "Sheena Is a Surf Punk" for the sound track."

"Well, why doesn't Joey write the song?"

"Come on, Dee Dee. Be professional."

"What do you mean be professional? I already gave you 'Side Walk Surfin'.' I had the song already written. What did they do? What happened? Nothin'. It's too annoying. This is bullshit."

LEGEND OF A ROCK STAR

"But Dee Dee, we can't do the movie without your song. Joey will never have one. If he did, you could be assured I wouldn't be talking to you now in this shitty club."

"Allie, this is what I want. Twenty thousand under the table for aggravation money. Act fast or be last. I'm really outgrowing all this."

The Ramones with Iggy Pop

AST   NIGHT WE PLAYED IN
ENHAGEN DENMARK. THE
    THERE FROM BERLIN WAS HE
FERRY FROM GERMANY TO
NMARK WAS TWO HOURS LAT
LY WHEN YOU GET ON A FER
CAN GET A GOOD MEAL, T
STAURANTS ARE VERY GO
THEM AND YOU CAN ALWA
    THE BRITISH NEWSPAPE
SUN, DAILY MAIL THE W
THE STAR FOR THE HOR
OPES

CHAPTER THIRTEEN

HIM... OFFER, IT WA
ED OF ANY HUMAN COMF
SHOP... NO FOOD NO CAFE
E PEOPLE ON BOARD IT
BAD... SPRE
EMSELVES OVER THE MOSTLY E

LAST NIGHT WE PLAYED in Copenhagen, Denmark. The ride there from Berlin was hell. The ferry from Germany to Denmark was two hours late. Usually when you get on a ferry you can get a good meal. The restaurants are very good on them and I can always buy the British newspapers. the *Sun*, *Daily Mail*, the *Mirror*, and the *Star* for the horoscopes.

This German ferry had nothing to offer. It was naked of any human comforts. No shops, no food, no cafeteria. The people on board weren't too bad, though. The band sprawled themselves over the mostly empty benches and napped till we got to Denmark. We went straight to the club, The Stengade.

Copenhagen is a lovely city. I like it there a lot. The show was really good but very wild. The staff tried very hard at The Stengade. There was good security to protect the stage but the human tidal wave of Ramones fans overwhelmed us and everybody in the audience was able to get up on the stage. All the mike stands were continuously knocked over but we still gave a stunning performance.

There was a poor lost soul that I met at the sound check. He had come to The Stengade to ask me how to get off of drugs. I told him that I remembered him from last year. That he had asked me the same question when I played then.

He looked much worse. It's life threatening to do what these guys do here in Copenhagen. The main problem is vodka. And beer. If you pass out on the street or in some alley in this place the cold will fuck you up.

All the alcoholics in these countries have a frostbitten look on their faces. I felt so, so, sorry for him.

"My book is just a book," I told him. "This is just talk. Promise me you'll go to a hospital?" I asked. I made him say to me he would.

After the show was over they let about twenty-five young girls backstage that wanted to meet me. Of course I was strictly professional and I wouldn't kiss anybody or sign their T-shirts over their newly developing breasts and as usual I went straight back to the hotel as soon as they would let me.

In the morning, before we left for Oslo, the maid entered the room without knocking while I was rocking the bowl. What! Do these creepy old ladies get their jollies doing these things? Taking advantage of the trust the hotel managers give them? She should have been fired, but I have a good heart and didn't tell on her.

Barbara, Dee Dee, and Hiroya.

...E GOT TO THE NORWEGIA...
...ER WE GOT TURNED AWAY
...EY WERE REALY MEAN TO...
...TUALY HATEFUL. THE
...STOMS OFFICIALS WERE
...TERMINED TO LAY SOMETHIN...
...US. WHEN THEY COULDNT
...ND ANY DRUGS OR THE
...RCASS OF A DEAD COW
...E DECIDED TO CHARGE US
...EXORBATANT TAX ON THE
...ITARS AND EQUIPMENT.
...E COULDNT PAY IT. WE
...LSO HAVENT GOTTEN OUR
...Y YET AND THE TOUR IS
...LF OVER. I KEEP NAGGING

CHAPTER FOURTEEN

...NN...BODY
...RE PAY TO NO AVAIL. BUT
...S US ONE TIME MY NAGGING
...GHT OF HELPED INDIRECTLY
...HE DECIDED NOT TO PAY
...E TAX. MAYBE...
...WAS THAT ONE

WHEN WE GOT TO the Norwegian border we got turned away. They were really mean to us. Actually hateful. The customs officials were determined to lay something on us. When they couldn't find any drugs or the carcass of a dead cow they decided to charge us an exorbitant tax on the guitars and equipment. We couldn't pay it. We also haven't gotten our pay yet and the tour is half over. I keep nagging Minna to give everybody their pay, to no avail, but this is one time my nagging might have helped indirectly.

He decided not to pay the tax, maybe because it was that or everybody lose two weeks pay so we could play Oslo.

I didn't want to enter Norway. "Fuck 'em," I complained. "Let's stay in Sweden or go back to Copenhagen."

"No, no, no." Minna put his foot down, sticking up to me, Chris, and Chase.

"I have the keys to this van and we're going to go where I say or I am going to leave you all by the side of the highway. I am sick of the lot of you."

"Well, what do you want to do?" I moaned. "They won't let us into Norway. We've been driving since nine o'clock this morning. The show is in a few more hours. What do you want?"

"We're going to have to drive 400 kilometers out of our way, we'll cross on a border that isn't so watched, and we can make it to the show about five minutes before you guys have to go on stage."

"Fuck this," everybody complained.

It was horrible. The weather couldn't have been worse. Also, it was all small country roads. When the Norwegian border patrol ambushed us an hour later we were deep in the backwoods of Norway.

"I told you so, I told you this would happen. Didn't I, didn't I?"

They surrounded the van. Nothing was good enough for them.

"We know who you are," they complained. "You're Dee Dee Ramone, right?"

"It says Douglas Colvin on this passport, don't it?" I sounded back at 'em.

"Oh, motherfucker," the lady cop remarked rudely back in my face. "Well, do you remember 1980, Oslo University?"

"Yeah," I said, "I played there with the Ramones."

"I was there," she hard-stared through me. "You had to stop the show, remember?"

"Oh yeah. So we were pissed off at the Ramones. Norwegian people hate foreigners. Especially Americans and the American government."

"When the Ramones played Oslo we organized against you. That's why the whole audience stormed the stage that night. To push you off and out of Oslo. You Reagan-loving bastard."

"Do you mean Reagan like in the Exorcist movie or Ronald Reagan like a former American president?"

"Oh, so now you're giving me back talk. Okay, I've had enough. Strip search these bastards," she ordered, to a very gay-looking Norwegian cop with a rubber glove on.

They had us standing on the side of the road now for over half an hour in the cold and snow without coats or jackets. Now they wanted us to take our pants off and have this queer cop stick his finger up our assholes to try and find drugs and to punish us for being Americans.

"Oh, sure, anything you say, dear," I said back.

I guess that's the last words she ever heard because instead of pulling down my pants and bending over I dropped her with a spinning back fist that just about took off her jaw and when she fell from the blow I was on top of her. I grabbed her pistol and emptied it into the other two cops as Minna and the boys stomped the lady cop to death where she lay. It looked like a long day at a slaughterhouse after we got through with them. There was blood and guts all over the snow. We hid the bodies but we couldn't really clean up the scene of our crime and left evidence lying around everywhere that we had done it.

"Who cares?" Minna happily commented when we were safely in the van and on our way to Oslo. "By the time they find out we'll be long gone."

"That was worth it," all agreed.

Later, when we got to the So What Club, we really started getting pissed off. "This is shit," the guys groaned, seeing the one bag of potato chips that was in the closet-sized dressing room. The show was sold out. I was lucky I got to escape the sound check and go to Burger King.

I did tell on Rob from Paper Clip though. Faye called the next day from London. I was in the van. I took the phone call on Minna's mobile phone.

"Hello Faye," I spoke into the receiver.

"How are you dear?" she hopefully inquired.

"This tour sucks!" I started up. "I'll never work with Paper Clip again. I hate them."

"Yes, yes," Faye responded noncommittally. "Well, it's your own fault. You'll just have to grin and bear with it and soon it will be over. Okay, dear?"

"What else Faye?" I asked.

"Make sure you leave for Stockholm at seven in the morning. You've got loads of interviews."

"But Faye, it's already a nine-hour drive!"

"Tuff titty," she scowled and hung up on me.

CHAPTER 15

GOT TO THE NEXT TOWN
IN SWEDEN I WAS IN
MOOD. WE HAD BEEN
FOR A GROUCHY
SEARCH. IT WAS ENUFF
BEING IN EUROPE
REAL
WE OBVIOUSLY SINGLED
BECAUSE HAVE DUTCH PLATE
MEANS DRUGS TO THE CUSTO
CIALS AND NINE TIMES OUT OF
THEY ARE ALLWAYS RIGHT.
WE MIGHT LOOK TIRED AND
THAT, BUT EVEN AS LOW CLA
ERICANS, CHASE, ME AND CHRIS
LOOK AS BAD AS AN ARM
GGLER DOPE DEALERS, OR
NOT
CAUSE OF US THAT WERE SO
SECTED, IT'S BECAUSE OF
DUTCH PASSPORT IT'S
TO ALL KINDS

CHAPTER FIFTEEN

WHEN I GOT TO THE NEXT TOWN, Eskilstuna, in Sweden, I was in a sarcastic mood. We had been stopped again for a grouchy van-and-body search. It was enough to make me hate being in Europe already.

Obviously we are singled out because we have Dutch plates. That means drugs to the custom officials and nine times out of ten they are always right.

We might look tired and all that, but even as low-class Americans, Chase, Chris and I don't look bad enough to be arms smugglers, or dope dealers, or junkies. No, it's not because of us that we're so persecuted. It's because of Minna's Dutch passport. It's getting to be too much already. I am pissed off at having to stand in the snow and I stepped right into a puddle of slush getting out of the van, soaking my sneakers with cold water. How nice.

I told the customs officials off. "I have a right to protest," I said. "What the hell could we be doing illegal coming out of Norway with all the heavy border checks from Denmark, and Sweden, also?" I scoffed at the cop.

They were polite in a bored way. I am grateful that they somehow professionally controlled themselves while I was reacting like I was, which was obviously spoiling for a fight, and let us go, to get rid of us.

"Don't ever fucking ever come back to Norway," they shouted to us as we were pulling away from the checkpoint.

"American motherfuckers!" one yelled, shaking his fist at us.

When we got to the venue in Eskilstuna I had low expectations. As soon as I waded through the slush and inside the hall through the loading entrance I was confronted by Jari-Pekka, a Ramones historian. *Oh no*, I thought, *I don't have the energy for this.*

People like Jari are so dedicated to keeping the spirit of the Ramones alive that it's almost heart wrenching, and soon we were both sitting down in a corner of the club and gossiping like the old friends that we are.

Jari is from Finland and can't speak English or German very well, but we communicated the best we could and it was very friendly. He also gave me an over-fifty page manuscript that he had written and put together on current Ramones activities. But soon it was getting too cold for me at the club, with all the open doors so that the humpers could race back and forth inside and out with equipment. I was also very tired.

Rocco Gustafsson, the promoter, went out of his way to be a nice guy. He drove me personally to the Stads Hotel so I could have a few hours rest and ordered me a dinner from room service delivered to my room, which he paid for out of his own pocket.

After a meal and long hot shower I started feeling like a million dollars. Then I washed my cloths in the sink and hung everything up to

Joey, Barbara, Marky, Dee Dee, and Walter Lure, ex-Heartbreakers.

dry on the heaters. I love it when they have heated towel racks in the bathrooms.

The concert at the Club BLA went really well. I felt that the audience was treating me almost as if I were godlike. There was so much love being exchanged.

The band and the audience were connecting and all was good. A lot of the reason everything was going so well was because the promoters were no-nonsense types. They were pro's and we had a pro situation. The stage was on risers and I was worried, but there were steel fence barricades in front.

People still got hurt. Jari lost a few teeth. I really feel bad about this. I think Chris head-butted him by accident when he jumped on stage to sing "Pinhead" with me.

When Jari was on my side of the stage I knew that he was going to go over and tried to help him, but he fell anyway, knocking a mike stand into a fan's head, splitting it open. People were ducking the blood spraying from his wound and from where I was on stage I could see some of his brains and some blood on my monitor speaker.

There were a lot of beautiful Goth chicks up front, flashing us. These Swedish girls look great with the blue-black dyed blond hair and the magnificent figures that these girls sport.

There were also three Swedish roughnecks up front. I loved these guys. I asked Robert, our guitar tech, to go and please get me three bottles of beer for them, which they drank, thank god, instead of spraying me with them. It was too hot up front though, and there was very little air, and people were passing out and fainting. One girl up front was very, very beautiful and she was determined to get my attention. Swedish girls are big, and mature fast, but this one still looked no older than sixteen to me.

I did meet my wife Barbara when she was sixteen, though. She has smashing good looks and could have anyone she wants. She chose me. I'm very lucky and I know that. I deeply love her and it would kill me if I lost her. But I expect to somehow. Every year I get older and she just gets better looking. It's scary. Then all these other ones chase after me sometimes. It's weird. It doesn't make sense and I don't expect it or think that that's what should happen because I am a rock star or whatever. They always try to get me away from Barbara. I'm always shocked that young sixteen- and seventeen-year-olds with drop-dead gorgeous looks come looking for sex. People are always hitting on Barbara also. When my friend Joan Jett tried to put the make on her I was pissed off.

After the show tonight was finished and we had done three encores someone was fanatically pounding on the dressing room door. "Dee Dee, Dee Dee. Open up. You're gonna like me, come on. Give me a chance." Finally, out of curiosity, Minna opened up the door. He's only human, but sometimes I don't have that luxury. "Oh my god," I gulped, seeing what was walking into my dressing room.

Every guy in the world's wet dream. The goddess of the Golden Triangle. She had dyed her hair blue-black and in her short miniskirt, silver panty hose, black patent leather Doctor Martins, and black chiffon halter top, she was quite well put together. All this gear looks best on young girls who top it off with rock and roll leather accessories and have a nice ass and great tits. This girl was the crème de la crème. I know a lot of you reading this now will be jealous, but believe me, all this is what really happened, except I have to play much of it down for my own personal security.

As soon as she got inside the backstage dressing room she made a bee-line towards the couch where I was sitting and planted her body right next to mine, as close as she possibly could. She barely introduced herself and then let it be known that she had come here to Eskilstuna from her home in Stockholm for one reason. To get me first before her girlfriends could, when I played the Mango Rock Bar in a few days. She tried every sexy trick in the book, but I couldn't let them work.

"Listen, little one," I gently told her. "How old are you?"

"Seventeen," she lied.

"How did you get in?" I questioned her. "You have to be eighteen to get into this club."

"My mother brought me," she answered.

"Where's she now?" I answered her back.

"She's in the car waiting for me. This is Sweden, Dee Dee. I love you. I want to fuck you. Mom agreed that I could bring you home, back to Stockholm with us to spend the night. She's very understanding."

"Well your mother is the one I probably should have been with," I spoke up nervously. "Not that I would want to. I'll admit you're a very hot young lady. I'll probably never get a chance like this ever again and maybe that's a good thing, because I have too much to lose."

She didn't want to leave without me. It was hard to believe that this beauty wanted me so much. Finally she actually started crying softly. "I love you so much, Dee Dee. I can't let you go."

"You have to," I told her, and gave her a peck on the cheek and sent her on her way. I was really relieved to go back to the hotel alone but the bad Dee Dee in me felt a bit insecure that I had thrown her phone number away. If Barbara ever left me I could have called her, I fantasized. Now I'll never meet anyone like her again, I realized.

Oh well, I guess that was the big test that god had to give me.

CHAPTER 16

ODAY ON THE WAY TO TH
T OF VARA WHICH I FOUND
ER IS ACTUALY A SMALL
LAGE IN THE MIDDEL OF NO
RE LAND WE ... ABLE TO
MINNA INTO ... OVER
THE HIGHWA ... NO TO STOP
MCDONALDS FOR LUNCH.
IS WASNT EASY. MINNA CAN BE
EAL PAIN IN THE ASS. HE AVOIDS
FOR ANYTHING BUT GAS
GETS BEHIND THE WHEEL.
MCDONALD ARCH BECKON-
LONG THIS TIME IN THIS
ARTIC OF SAMENESS IT
LIKE A LITE UP CHRISTMAS
EE AMONGHTS A BOUQUET OF
A DESERT OASIS AND
RE'LL BE TREAT

CHAPTER SIXTEEN

GOBBL
THERE WILL
IN A FEW MOR
ROAD

TODAY ON THE WAY TO THE CITY of Vara, which I found out later is actually a small village in the middle of nowhere land, we were able to nag Minna into pulling over off the highway and stopping at McDonald's for lunch.

This wasn't easy. Minna can be a real pain in the ass. He avoids stopping for anything but gas once he gets behind the wheel. But the McDonald's arch beckoned too strongly this time; in this desolate arctic of sameness it stood out like a light-up Christmas tree amongst a bouquet of palms in a desert oasis and there would be treats underneath it for Santa's good children to gobble up.

But there will be a war in a few more hours and everything will be blown up by bombs. There will be no more McDonald's tomorrow, only fire, rubble, and smoke. All of Santa's children will have to starve to death then, and this is our last meal, even Minna knows that.

I would love to go to Denny's in Los Angeles now but I cant. I'm stranded in Sweden. Everybody's half crazy from riding in the van. We can't take a chance on being stuck having to have Swedish mystery meat hot dogs for dinner at the gas station convenience store again. That's no good.

They say that these hot dogs are made from ground-up pig testicles and penises and that the Swedes aren't too worried about the hoof-and-mouth crisis. We're not either and we thought we'd be all right. But we weren't. Just like we had predicted, when we entered McDonald's, which is an American institution, it was very obvious that

Americans weren't wel-
come and that this was a
Swedish McDonald's.
The atmosphere of hos-
tility towards us was very
heavy as we cautiously
entered what should
have been familiar terri-
tory and made our way
politely towards the
counter to wait in line
and order some burgers
and fries, which we could
tell would be a good
idea to order to take out
because everyone in
McDonald's was giving
us angry stares, as if we
were intruding and they
weren't intimidated by
our party one bit.

How could they be, these six-foot-and-over beasts? Almost at once,
an angry Swedish women started pacing back and forth right next to
me, creating unbearable tension. It was obvious that she wanted to cut
the line and that she didn't care what I thought, and that since I was in
her country now I better get out of her way, or else.

"Excuse me, miss," I finally said, turning around to confront her.
"You're being very rude, don't you think?"

"What!" she scoffed right back at me. "Am I supposed to be a typical rude Swedish woman? Is that what you're accusing me of?" She
was staring intently at me now with her big blue eyes and batting her
lashes at me. Giving me a sexy I-want-to-fuck-you look.

"I was only trying to get your attention, cutie," she explained, low-
ering her voice. "We girls get bored up here in the boondocks and we
don't see many men like you, ya know."

"Well, this is what typical American men are like" I said,
responding to her obvious sexual advances and, stepping out of line,

LEGEND OF A ROCK STAR

I offered her my place, which is not what she was expecting, and said to her, "Ladies first."

"You little pussy bitch," she sourly laughed, and then sucker-pushed me out of the line. "So you're stereotyping all Swedish women now, are you!" Then to clarify her point she bumped into me with her tray and raked one of my shins with her boot.

"Not the one I was with last night," I smirked as I backed off and retreated to the van outside empty-handed. "Ouch! That smarts," I cursed to myself, feeling very frustrated.

Later on, during the ride to Vara, Chris and Chase told me that they had let some people they met last night after the show come back to their room at the hotel for a party.

"What happened in there, guys" I asked? "It sounded really noisy. I could tell you were partying. You two look terrible today."

"We're really hung over," Chase said. "We really drank a lot last night, Dee Dee. And we did a couple of grams of speed. I feel very dehydrated and my head's pounding. I'm sick, and look at this," he said, showing me his smarting finger that he'd injured, banging it on the rim of his snare. It looked horrible. It was all swollen and puffy and it looked infected.

I felt bad for Chase. If I had had some painkillers I would have given them to him, but I was out. Chris looked horrible. I could tell that he had contracted pink eye. His left eye was running puss and looked awful and you just knew that everyone was going to catch it, too, because it's so damn contagious. Neither of them was in the best of moods.

I had noticed the empty cases of beer bottles outside their door in the hotel this morning on my way to breakfast. I kept quiet but they didn't make it to breakfast. That's why we stopped at McDonald's. For them.

When we let everybody into the van, Chris started telling the story about last night's shenanigans, and how they got out of control.

"Yeah," Chase added, "one guy started ranking on me for playing a Kiss CD. It's my room, my party, my boom box, and Kiss is my all-time favorite rock and roll group, besides Cheap Trick. Finally I yelled at him to get the fuck out of my room. That the party was over."

With Jayne County

"Wow! That's great, Chase" I said.

Chris then finished this sordid tale. "I really scared the shit out of them," he started. "They said everything they could think of to put America down, till finally I couldn't take it anymore and I started taking the empty beer bottles and throwing them against the wall, splattering glass everywhere. It was crazy. Then I also shouted at them to fuck off. That they were a bunch of spoiled assholes. When they left we still had all the speed, so we finished it off ourselves and we were up all night smoking one cigarette after another."

Yeah, yeah, I thought drifting off in a sea of troubles, worries, woes, and aches and pains of my own.

CHAPTER (17)

THIS MORNING I WOKE UP IN
AL. ACTUALY ITS BEEN
ED TO A HOTEL, ITS NAME
VERTORP SLOTT. EVEN THE
HOTEL THIS PLACE HAS
INTACT AND IT STILL LOOKS
A CASTEL. IT HAS THE WINDOW
EPY STAIRCASES
PLACE, CANDLE CHANDELIER
A STUFFED MOOSE HEAD, LOT'
TEM ACTUALY AND A STUFFED
LYING UNDER AN ANTIQUE
SO PIANO AND THERE'S ALSO
UFFED BEAR IN THE MAIN H
THAT TO THE DININ
A

CHAPTER SEVENTEEN

EW WHERE THERE'S
DING AVENUE THE FOOD
T CAME HERE FOR TH
K FEAST. IT WAS THE MOST
TIC ONE OF THE
EVEN A SELECTI
NS TO CHOSE

THIS MORNING I WOKE UP in a castle. Actually it's been converted to a hotel. It's name is Bjertorp Slott. Even though now it's a hotel this place has been kept intact and it still looks like a castle. It has the winding, creepy staircases, a real working fireplace, candle chandeliers, and a stuffed moosehead—lots of them actually—and a stuffed wolf lying under an antique grand piano. There's also a stuffed bear, in the main hallway that leads to the dining area. This bear greets you when you enter in there, and he's holding a menu. The food is fancy. I came here for the breakfast. It was the most exotic one of the tour. There was even a selection of vitamins to chose from.

I wish the members of the Hymans were here this morning to eat breakfast with me. The Hymans are a Ramones-sounding band from Sweden. I met them once in Amsterdam around six years ago on the Leidseplein when I was walking around there one afternoon. They gave me some of their tapes and tried to explain themselves to me. Later on, when I was back home in my apartment by the Kaisergruft, and settled down a bit, I decided to give their tape a listen. This was when music in Europe was definitely changing to techno and it was getting hard to find any bands to listen to that I liked. After going to see Smash and those Animal Men, I started losing faith, so I was happy to find a punk tape to listen to. I was starving for it. I was amazed at what I was hearing. Whoever was writing the songs for the Hymans could have taken my place as song writer for the Ramones.

This band is named after Joey Ramone whose name in real life was

actually Jeffrey Hyman. He used to call himself Jeff Starship before he met me and adopted my surname, Ramone.

There's been a lot of bickering over this and that Ramones trivia, that's for sure. The truth is that I think they were doing fine after I left them and had a lot of courage to continue, but a lot of other people were beginning to wonder if they were becoming an act, the kind of a band that could be a TV sitcom, written by a Hollywood-type script writer.

CHAPTER 18

WE HAD TO GET UP EARLY
THE DRIVE TO STOCKHOLM
WONT BE TO LONG, MAYBE
HOURS BUT I HAD TO BE AT
HOTEL AT TWELVE OCLOCK
AND I AM EXPECTED TO DO
SERIES OF INTERVIEWS IN A
EXECUTIVE ORDER STARTING
SOON AS I AT THE
THERE WOULD BE TO
CONTINUE TILL A SOUND CHECK
THERE WOULD BE MORE AND
TILL I FINALLY CAME OFF

CHAPTER EIGHTEEN

BE SOMEONE IMPORTANT
MORE RIGHT AWAY
NOW FROM ME OUT
FUCKING PRIVACY MYSELF
SEEM TO JUST IN
DRESSING ROOM AS SOON AS

WE HAD TO GET UP EARLY TODAY. The drive to Stockholm wouldn't be too long, maybe four hours, but I had to be at the hotel at twelve o'clock noon and I'm expected to do a series of interviews in consecutive order starting as soon as I arrived at the hotel.

The interviews were to continue till the sound check and there would be more and more, till I finally came off stage dripping wet and there would be someone immediately demanding more right away, right now, from me. I don't have any fucking privacy. People seem to just burst into my dressing room as soon as I stop playing the show and they start heavily demanding attention and autographs. With all this to look forward to today, I'm not feeling too enthusiastic about playing in bands anymore. How could I?

It looks like a rugged day. My anger is intense. I didn't even get home from work till three o'clock last night.

When we left for Stockholm this morning, the promoter Stefan Nilsson from the Contan Club and Jari decided to hitch rides with us in our already overcrowded van. Wonderful! What this meant to us is that now none of us will get to semi-sleep in the van this morning and now we'll have to talk about the Ramones and business the whole time. And that every word I say will be written down by Jari so he could print it publicly on the Internet. That out of politeness, I have to talk and entertain the promoter who is a very big man and takes up a lot of space.

Everybody is pretty miserable about all this but we try to be good sports and put up with it and be fair. But it doesnt work. When we finally found our hotel in Stockholm, with no tangible help from this promoter, who is from there, and then could only find a parking space two blocks away, I started feeling myself lose my self-control. Still, Chase and I, trying to be professional, immediately after we somehow got the van parked, leaped out and without bitching started to unload the suitcases and guitars on to the sidewalk.

I had two bass guitars, two big suitcases, and two knapsacks to carry down the street and up to my room. Chris, Chase, and Minna had the same situation to deal with as Robert and I had three-fold. Plus, Chris' guitar is pretty heavy to carry and quite awkward as well. Jari and the promoter stood around out of the way, not offering to help us and sort of implying that it was enough that they had ordealed the ride. Ha! *What kind of men are these*, I thought! They saw what was going on. They see how hard we have it. Then they freeload to our inconvenience, bringing my morning and the band's down to the agony level. The promoter has been the usual fucking cheapskate type and he is only holding a briefcase. I'm not going to forget this, I noted, filing him on my shit list.

I had not been able to get ready for pictures this morning, to shower or shave. I was pounced on as soon as I struggled into the hotel lobby, before I even put my bags down.

"Can I just go to my room for a minute," I told whoever she was, the rep sent by Eagle Rock to herd me from one interview to the other throughout the day. As soon as I got through the door of my room I slammed it shut and went to the toilet to take a piss. Within a two-minute time span someone was knocking on my door as I was in mid-stream, to hurry me up.

In Holland they don't mosey into work on a Monday till after twelve o'clock and you can't call someone, especially at their home, and god forbid you call on a Sunday. These motherfuckers have a lot of rules relating to the respectful behavior they demand from outsiders (people who are not Dutch).

I really need to speak to my promoter, who must be avoiding me. He hasn't called the whole time I've been on tour to see how we were doing, offer any help, or give us any encouragement.

I borrowed the record company's rep's phone quickly when I was in the hotel lobby again, and called Paper Clip, fearing the worst.

LEGEND OF A ROCK STAR

"Rob can't come to the phone now," the receptionist answered me, sounding rehearsed.

"Well!" I steamed back. "Then I won't ever take a call from Paper Clip again. So be it. If I could get away with it I wish I could empty a clip into ya! Yeah, I'm like that. What did you expect. Saint Mary?"

14

CHAPTER 19

DONT KNOW HOW, BUT I GOT
EW THE REST OF THE DAY
NG AS LESS GROUCHY AS POSSIBL
STILL GROUCHY.
I MUST OF BEEN HORRIABLE
E PHONE TO PAPER CLIP, BUT
E I TAUGHT A FEW PEOPLE
SON ON COMMON SOCIOLOGIC
TERACTIVE COURTESIES. AN
CESSITIES OF GOOD MANN
TO STAY CIVILIZED
AL THING WEIGHING ON
NOW IS HOW TIRED I'A
ER AFTER DOING A

CHAPTER NINETEEN

SWEDEN GENERO
OF THE REST OF THE IN
WENT BACK TO THE HOTEL
TO THE MIRROR
I HAVEN'T SHAVED
RPOSE AND I'M
ST NIGHTS SHOW

I DON'T KNOW HOW, but I got through the rest of the day being the least grouchy possible, but still grouchy.

I must have been horrible on the phone to Paper Clip, but I hope I taught a few people a lesson on common sociological interactive courtesies, and the necessities of good manners for us to stay civilized.

The real thing weighing on me the most now is how tired I am. I got a break after doing a half-hearted sound check. The rep from Eagle Rock in Sweden generously called off the rest of the interviews. I went back to the hotel and looked into the mirror. I looked like shit. I haven't shaved on purpose and I'm still wearing last night's smelly T-shirt as a protest. The show at the Mango Rock Bar in Stockholm went off very well. In fact, it was fantastic. Maybe it has been one of the best ones so far. I had great monitors to sing through. The audience was completely there for us and they were on our side.

My bass was sounding very good, nice and mid-rangey. When I get it going right it makes a sound like a humming motor. I keep it steady and on an even keel no matter what obstacles I have to weather on stage.

Like the stage divers who come at the band tidal wave style. In Sweden I feel like I'm at an old Ramones show again. They have to separate the stage and the audience with steel fence barricades. After the show in Stockholm the situation backstage quickly turned chaotic. First to barge through the security into the dressing room was a huge, sexy Swedish girl shouting, "I know the Hymans." Right away she started stripping off her blue jeans, revealing that she was wearing silver panties. Then she arched her lovely butt at me and asked me to autograph her ass.

"Can you wait a minute till I change, huh?" I shouted back at her. "No girls allowed backstage! Okay?" In a few minutes she was back anyway, but I did what I had to do. At least I then got a minute to get out of my soaking-wet-with-sweat jeans and put something dry on. Well, I didn't know that the Hymans were so popular in Sweden. Congratulations, guys.

These girls know I am married, though, but they don't give two shits. If they like you, they want to fuck you. These babes are big here and strong. If one of these girls fancies you it's hard to get away.

The other night in Örebro a girl who had been in the support band that played there before me last year asked me, "Where's Barbara?"

"Why?" I suspiciously inquired.

"Because I wanted to see her play on stage," she answered me. "All the boys that saw her here last year fell in love with her. She's a rock goddess. I'd love to lick her pussy."

How could a modern punk-dyke lesbian who would disrobe and perform a nude private show later that night with six of her naked girlfriends for me Minna and Chris and Chase say anything so antiquatedly clichéd as "rock goddess?" I gasped to myself in disbelief, cringing at the same time at the thought of a whole audience of boys lusting after my wife Barbara.

"Oh, Barbara is never going to play in a band again," I said. It's too hard on her. She has to stay home now, we're going to have a baby," I added, lying through my teeth but hoping to unappetize her fantasies of licking my wife's pussy.

This is really a nightmare, I worried, as I excused myself, thinking about how enthusiastic Barbara would be about starting a new band with me when this tour was through.

After the show in Stockholm the backstage was packed with big Swedish guys that were feeling no pain and in a great mood, but I wasn't. Minna escorted me right out of there and back to the hotel. I have never been squeezed and hugged so much in my life. They really love me in Sweden. When these huge Swedish guys give you a hug it's pretty severe. They are all very strong and powerful men. They more or less crush you. But in a loving way.

LEGEND OF A ROCK STAR

As beer bottles were being knocked off tables and crushed on the floor, I moonwalked out the back exit door, putting on a poker face. I had had enough of the backstage ruckus and it wasn't going to get any better so I was heading to the street to where the van was waiting.

The girl who had come to see me in Eskilstuna was waiting for me by the van. When I saw her it depressed me. It was very cold outside. She was very dressed up for the show in her boots, miniskirt, and black monkey chubby. It was freezing and she was shaking with cold in the brisk night air. They didn't let her in because she was underage. She said her sister was in the club in the dressing room so I walked her back to the exit door and the security guard let her go in. I left and went back to the hotel.

I don't know what to say. When I got back to my room I felt about ninety years old. And very unattractive. But I am still not going to shave my new beard or dye my hair black, I thought to myself as I fell asleep.

Today is what Rob Berends calls a travel day off. The band and crew depart Stockholm and drive to Copenhagen, Denmark. The distance of the drive and the ferry ride is 620 kilometers. Travel time is estimated at nine hours.

When we get to Denmark it should be around eight-thirty in the evening. We don't have to play tonight so it's sort of a day off. Actually we're all thrilled and don't mind sitting in the van today. When we get to Copenhagen half of us will probably run to Hans Cristiana to buy weed.

This is Rob's address:

Paper Clip Agency
P.O. Box 1519
6501 Bm numegen
Holland

I put Paper Clip's address here not for you to write him and complain but because I know that a lot of people reading this are people who play in bands and want to get started. Well, this is what it's like, for better or worse, so if you want to do it, you have his address.

This is my tour:

<u>March 2001</u>
Wed 14 Travel day
Thu 15 Glasgow, King Tut's Wa Wa Hut
Fri 16 London, Garage
Sat 17 Liege, Soundstation
Sun 18 Amsterdam, Paradiso
Mon 19 Travel day
Tue 20 Salzburg, Rockhouse
Wed 21 Biella, Babylonia
Thu 22 Milano, Tunnel
Fri 23 Aarau, Kiff
Sat 24 Luzern, Sedel
Sun 25 Munchen, Kulturstation
Mon 26 Berlin, Knack
Tue 27 Berlin, Day off
Wed 28 Copenhagen, Stengade 30
Thur 29 Oslo, So What
Fri 30 Eskilstuna, BLA
Sat 31 Vara, Kronan

<u>April 2001</u>
Sun 1 Orebro, Contan
Mon 2 Stockholm, Mango Rock Bar
Tue 3 Travel day
Wed 4 Travel day
Thu 5 Dortmund, FZW
Fri 6 Zwickau, Alarm
Sat 7 Lingen, Schlachthof
Sun 8 Hamburg, Logo
Mon 9 Jena, Rosenkeller
Tue 10 Cottleus, Sudstadt
Wed 11 Freiburg, Atlantik
Thu 12 Weinheim, Cafe Central
Fri 13 Venlo, Day off
Sat 14 Venlo, Perron 55
Sun 15 Uttrech, Ekko

LEGEND OF A ROCK STAR

This is my set list for the tour:

1. Rockaway Beach
2. Lobotomy
3. Commando
4. Sheena
5. I Don't Care
6. Beat on the Brat
7. Chinese Rocks
8. Listen to My Heart
9. I Don't Wanna Walk Around With You
10. Cretin Hop
11. 53rd and 3rd
12. I Just Wanna Have Something To Do
13. Judy is a Punk
14. Loudmouth
15. Chain Saw
16. Sedated
17. Time Bomb
18. Come On Now
19. Pet Sematary
20. Pinhead
21. Blitzkrieg Bop
22. Basement
23. Havana Affair
24. Born to Lose
25. Do You Love Me
26. Mr. Postman
27. Locomotion

With Richard Hell at Max's Kansas City, 1976.

CHAPTER 20

[...]VE BEEN IN DORTMUND GERMA[NY]
[...] FOR TWO DAYS. WE'RE STATI[NG]
[...]SOME NICE HILTON LIKE HOTEL HER[E]
[...] IT'S NOT BEEN TO BAD. I'VE PRETT[Y]
[...]H NOT COME OUT OF MY ROOM. I'[M]
[...]AUSTED. MAXI DEX IS A HERO. HE
[...]NT US A PACKAGE WHICH WAS
[...]ITING FOR US WHEN WE CHECK[ED]
[...] TO THE HOTEL. THERE WERE
[...]ELEBRATIONS IN ALL [...]
[...]HE FIRST NIGHT. I B[...]
[...]AND TWO CASES O[F...]
[...]HEY DRANK IN THERE AND [...]
[...]EALIZED THAT THE [...]
[...]EER NOW EXCEPT FOR [...]
[...]KE ME IS SWORN OF[F...]
[...]NO [...]

CHAPTER TWENTY

[...]OUTRAGEOUSLY. HE [...]
[...]ICK BEFORE WE LEFT FOR EUROP[E]
[...] MADE HIM [...] DOCT[OR]
[...]E HAVE BEEN TRAVELLING A[ROUND]
THE WORLD FROM [...]
SOUTH AMERICA TO NORTH AMER[ICA]
THEN TO EUROPE WITH SO M[ANY]

I'VE BEEN IN DORTMUND, Germany, now for two days.
We're staying in some nice Hilton-like hotel here and it's not been too
bad. I've pretty much not come out of my room. I'm exhausted.

Maxi Dex is a hero. He sent us a package which was waiting for us
when we checked into the hotel. There were celebrations in all our
rooms the first night. I bought the band two cases of beer which they
drank in their rooms. I have realized that they have to have beer now,
except for Minna who, like me, is sworn off hard alcohol and lives very
happily without it. Chris has held out very courageously. He did get
real sick before we left for Europe and I made him go to the doctor. We
have been traveling around the world, from Japan to South America to
North America and then to Europe, with so many radical temperature
changes that it finally got to him. Chase works a regular job when we're
home and so does Chris. Neither one had a rest before we left on this
tour and Chris had no time to recover from being sick before we were
on a plane again. In the two weeks that we were home in Los Angeles
we had freak cold weather and torrential rain storms every day. I had
to move out of the new apartment I had gotten to paint in back to my
old apartment because as soon as I moved into the new one the ceiling
caved in from the rain.

I had an art show with Paul Kostabi before I left this year for my
European tour. All the paintings sold out before they went on display.
Paul, Barbara, and I had to make a slew of new ones before I left and
also get ready for our show in June.

Before I went to Japan, which was somewhere in between all this stuff, I did about six paintings with Mark Kostabi. After I left Japan they had a major earthquake.

After Japan, I played the Troubadour in L.A. and I hope I never have to see the bass player and the drummer, who I had to fire, again. Finally I got Chase back on drums after that Troubadour show and switched from guitar back to the bass. I also had to do lots of interviews about the Ramones every day and learn the bass again, which I haven't played since I've left the Ramones. I like playing the bass a lot.

I bought a brand-new black colored Jerry Jones short-scale bass for the tour. Schecter gave me a bass in Los Angeles. I could not bring it because I had too much to carry. I wish I had it with me. Too bad.

When I'm on tour in Europe I rent the amps and drums from:

Waterland Productions
Antoniusstraat 121
5912 Cjvenio
Holland

Contact: Johan Rutjens
Phone: 3177 35 49 420

I rent the van from:

Artist on the Road
3e Hugo de Grootstr 17 111
1052 LK Amsterdam
Holland

Contact: Doede Terveld
Phone: 3120 68 24 680

Where I am today, Dortmund, was the last date on my Euro tour last year. That tour was seven weeks long.

Before it started I had a three-stop connecting flight in Mexico to Los Angeles, then had to catch a plane right away from Los Angeles to Amsterdam. This was after two weeks of hell, playing all over Mexico. When

YOU MIGHT BE WONDERING
WHAT I'VE BEEN DOING
LATELY. USALY I JUST
SIT AT THE BUS STOPS
ARROUND TOWN TO REST
A WHILE AND THEN I WALK
ARROUND HOLLYWOOD AGAIN
FOR A WHILE AGAIN. THEN
ITS BACK TO AN OTHER BUS
STOP.

       I'VE BECOME SORT OF
AN OLD MEAN AND CRAFTY
STREET PERSON SINCE I'VE LEFT
THE RAMONES.
       MY ART CAME ABOUT
FROM STICKING UP KIDS
ARROUND HOLLYWOOD HIGH
SCHOOL AND FINDING ALOT
OF MAJIC MARKERS AND
STUFF IN THERE BAGS.
       AT FIRST I WAS JUST
AFTER THERE LUNCH AND
SOME SPARE CHANGE BUT
SOON I STARTED
DRAWING WITH THESE
KIDS SCHOOL SUPPLIES
THAT I HAD STOLEN FROM
THEM AND DOING
GRAFITI IN THE ALLEYS
ARROUND WEST HOLLYWOOD

I arrived in Mexico I was already beat from about a year of playing up and down the northwest coast. When I got to Amsterdam I checked into the Omega Hotel. I wanted to go walk around and see my city again but I couldn't make it and had to go back to the room because I almost blacked out from the jet lag and hit the pavement face first.

After the last seven-week tour I did in Europe, Artists World Wide, my agent in Los Angeles, sent me back to Mexico for three weeks, where it was a mess. I had to face riots and deal with bandit-like promoters. Finally I had a nervous breakdown and was hospitalized for a week in a funky hospital in Mexico City.

Somehow on this tour I found time to keep this writing up to date as it is. As like I say, "It's better to put it on paper than in your veins." I'm an ex-junky so I'm a very blessed person that I'm still alive. But this is pushing it, ain't it? It is common rock and roll folklore knowledge that it will kill you if you do it and kill you if you don't.

Today I'm off to Zwickav in Germany. I have never heard of this place but I imagine that it's a lot like Dortmund. But I can't even relate to where this town in Germany could be. "I feel sort of dead" would be the clichéd thing to say right now, but I don't. I'm sort of okay and I'm partying in the van now, smoking weed and drinking beer and, it's not even eleven o'clock. Yahoo! I am determined to get in a good mood despite the old-ladies-on-the-rag vibes I am getting from Chase and Chris.

CHAPTER 21

HE SIGN SAYS THIRTEEN KILOMETERS
ZWICKAU. THAT MEANS IT'S GONNA
LUCKY! I YELL OUT OVER THE SEATS.
IN MY ROW IN THE BACK OF THE VAN
OBODY IS OBVIOUSLY CONVINCED EVEN
AND I MAKE THE SIGN OF THE CROSS.
DRIVE UNDER A BRIDGE AND
THE OUTSKIRTS OF THIS SMALL TOWN.
NEVER SEEN EVERYBODY SO
AS THEY ARE TODAY. EVEN
WHO IS USUALY PRETTY LEVEL IS
BECAUSE WINNA HAS BEEN SO
OVER LATELY EVERY MORNING THAT HE
HAD TO TAKE OVER ON THE WHEEL. I AM
TO CHRIS BEING MISSERABLE NOW
CHASE HAS TAKEN THE LEAD, SLAMMING
DOOR OF THE VAN IN MY FACE. HE
AS THE FLU. THAT THEY ARE ALLWAYS
CK IS GETTING ON MY NERVES. THERE
RE NO PHONES
WANT TO DESPERTLY
ORLD WIDE TODAY TO MAKE SORE THAT
HERE
AFTER

CHAPTER TWENTY-ONE

THE SHOW IN DORTMUN LAST NIGHT
AS A LET DOWN. I
A JOKE
STERDAY TO THE MOSTLY SKIN HERE
THANK GOD WE'RE ANTI
JOKED. I WAS
WHICH USED TO BE
HORRIABLE AND
VER AND RESETTLED

"THE SIGN SAYS thirteen kilometers to Zwickav. That means it's gonna be lucky," I yell out over the seats from my row in the back of the van. Obviously, nobody is convinced, even me, and I make the sign of the cross as we drive under a bridge and enter the outskirts of this small town.

I have never seen everybody so miserable as they are today. Even Robert, who is usually pretty level, is pissed off because Minna has been so hung over lately, every morning, that he has had to take over the wheel. I'm used to Chris being miserable. Now, though, Chase has taken the lead, slamming the door of the van in my face. He has the flu. That they are always sick is getting on my nerves. There are no phones in the hotel today. I want desperately to call Artists World Wide today to make sure that they're not booking anymore shows. After this tour, I have to stop.

The show in Dortmund last night was a letdown. I made a joke in German yesterday to the mostly skinhead audience. "Thank god we're not in the East," I joked. I was meaning East Germany, which used to be Russia or something horrible, and has now been taken over and resettled by Germans.

Well, here we are in the middle of East Germany today, in a place called Zwickav. As soon as we checked into the Etap Hotel, with no telephones in the rooms, I started trying to look at the positive. Like the fact that there was no one else here but us and the lady at the reception desk, who was pretty friendly. I was happy that we were the only people at the hotel because I thought it would be more peaceful.

The Etap is also very clean but it's weird because it is prefabricated, like a trailer home but nicer. But!, it has one of those horrible coffee machines and no other services. So I decided to go to the sound check, which we're leaving for in ten minutes.

I told Chase that he didn't have to go because he had the flu and I would cover for him. Of course he had to go. "The fucking drums have to be done every day," he snapped.

At the sound check, Robert, Chase, and Chris started playing a Stiv Bators song from the Lords of the New Church, called "Russian Roulette." I got angry and told them off.

Chris, Chase, and Robert were embarrassed. I was even stunned momentarily by my rash behavior. "You Can't Put Your Arms Around a Memory." Damn straight you can't. It was obvious to all that I had exploded for reasons that had little to do with Chris and Chase and Robert playing a Lords of the New Church song.

Later, when we got back to the Etap Hotel, there was a lot of door slamming all around. I also heard the sounds of suitcases being bounced on the walls, and I also broke an ashtray on the floor of the dressing room, sending glass shrapnel in all directions.

I try to avoid kicking suitcases because you can really hurt your big toe if you're wearing basketball shoes and you kick the door of your car, a waste basket, or your suitcase.

You can kick a cat, but that's boring.

When I entered my room an *ieeeeedwowohwowa* was heard immediately throughout the hotel. Everyone then opened the doors of their rooms on cue to see what was happening. This loud, ear-splitting, horrible screeching wasn't coming from a hooker that some German pimp was beating up in his room in the Etap. It was a cat in agonizing pain that had been sitting on my bed when I entered my room. There was cat hair all over the bedspread and the animal made an unpleasant odor at me which really pushed my buttons from half-sane to the psycho level.

Staying somewhat calm I went into the bathroom and tightly rolled a towel into a cane and then I dipped it into the toilet to dampen it so I could use it as a weapon. These things are called twisters.

Then I took the can of hair spray out of my bag that Minna had gotten for me. "Air spray," I told him. He came back with hair spray.

"Air spray," I said.

"I thought you said 'hair spray'," he answered.

Now I could find a practical use for the hair spray. I was glad I hadn't chucked it out with the trash. First, though, I walked over to the window to make sure it was closed so that the cat couldn't escape. I was planning to make this poor little beast suffer. This will teach the bastard, I thought to myself, staring now at the cat with demonic hatred.

I attacked suddenly and without warning, snapping at the cat with my twister, causing it horrible and excruciating pain. It reacted frantically, trying to flee my wrath, and in desperation started flinging itself against the closed window, trying to escape.

Iiiieeowwooow, the cat shrieked as I snapped my twister at it, shredding the fur off its frail body. The cat was now jerking involuntarily and going into shock. Then it banged its head accidentally on the handle used to open and close the window and knocked itself out.

Seizing on the moment I took my lighter and, using the hair spray like a flame-thrower, started spraying flames all over the poor animal. It started roasting and when its carcass was good and burnt, and charred black, and it was stiff on its back with its legs sticking straight out, I hit it a few more times with my twister. To make sure it was dead. When I was convinced it was dead I picked its still-smoldering body up in a newspaper and left it in the shower stall. The smoke smell in my room was sickening so I opened the window that I had closed so the cat couldn't get out, to get some fresh air. When I opened the window I could see that everybody was outside, downstairs in the parking lot going to the van to go to the show. I grabbed a clean T-shirt and hurried after them, slamming the door to my room extra hard. I left the window open to let out the smell so the maid wouldn't come in and look around while I was gone.

The show at The Alarm went all right. They were good to us at the club but a little stingy with the weed. If you wanted to smoke, you had to do it in The Alarm's kitchen, and sit on a bench around a wooden table with these German people who had the weed. You never actually got to see the weed (this is not good). It was always already rolled into large cylinder spliffs, stuffed with tobacco and hash. This is Euro-style and no American person can smoke like this. It's just too hard up.

I prefer my drugs to be of the highest quality available, to keep all my drugs for myself; to get high alone, so I don't have to share my stash.

"Oh, no, I don't do drugs," I told them, lying through my teeth when they tried to pass me a spliff. I'm too much of a snob to sit on a wooden picnic table and smoke low-class hash joints with these country bumpkins.

"*Tchuss*," I said, interrupting a few of the frauleins that were eyeing me and sitting at the tables, having fantasies of having sex with an ex-Ramone in the broom closet or something, especially one of them, who had horrid metallic red-dyed hair and kept patting the empty seat next to her and motioning for me to sit down. "Tchuss" is what German and Dutch people say to excuse themselves from a pained situation, sort of a diplomatic way of saying "fuck you" with controlled reserve, like when a Spanish person says "thank you very much" to an American person and then says "No!" when the American person hopefully then asks them, "Do you speak English?" Even though the show at The Alarm was very professional, it didn't rock my socks off. German people who have corn rolls, dreads, and are vegetarians are not very sexy, like the Hollywood gym people, who have better teeth, but are most likely to be homosexual or some other type of pervert. There were about ten cuties up front at the show that were obviously looking for it. I think that they all made it back to the hotel that night after the show but they didn't turn me on and I hid in my room. They were so young I was afraid the police would come. I was happy alone in my room anyway because I'm sick of everybody and I'm sick of this tour.

I heard in the morning that the police didn't come, just the boyfriend of the best-looking girl in the bunch. He came looking for her at the hotel and was angry and made her go home. Who can blame him? She's lucky she didn't get murdered.

CHAPTER 22

LINGEN GERMANY, THIRTY
KILOMETERS FROM THE
NETHERLANDS TWO HUNDRED
KILOMETERS FROM AMSTERDAM
BUT HAS A FEELING LIKE VENLO
IN HOLLAND
          THE VENUE IS CALLED
THE SCHLACHTHOF
OR IN ENGLISH, THE
     SLAUGHTER HOUSE

CHAPTER TWENTY-
TWO

LINGEN, GERMANY, is thirty kilometers from the Netherlands, two hundred kilometers from Amsterdam, but has a feeling like Venco in Holland. The venue is called The Schlachthof or, in English, The Slaughter House. Lingen, lingen, *warum hast du nicht rauchen zum bringen. Idjoten dumbkopt, Netherlands ist thirty kilometers. Here ist meinen falschen nummer. Bitte ruff mich. Yha, hatt gute gesmacht aber nicht haben, du muss gehen, "tchuss."*

After the show in Lingen, which everybody liked but me, I was sitting on a bench in the dressing room with Chase. I was just changing my wet jeans and Chase was undressed and hadn't changed yet. All of a sudden three German girls burst into the dressing room. They were ugly drunk and wild. One of them grabbed Chase and wouldn't let go. In seconds, Minna was there and somehow got them to leave. How did they get in, I wondered. Wow, that was close! They almost saw me naked, I thought.

"Chase, are you all right?" I asked.

"No," he said. "My dick's kinda sore. She was really grabbin' on to me. I can't believe how hard I bit her hand to get her to let me go."

"Minna slapped her, too," I added excitedly. "He put her in a headlock, then rammed her skull into the wall. What's wrong with people?" I added.

"Well, why doesn't he ever put his pants on after a show anymore?" Minna butted in. "Last night, Chase," he then accused, "you even left to go back to the hotel in just your sneakers and leather jacket. You

shouldn't be surprised if someone grabs your ass if you walk around like that. And you also were walking around in the hallways in the hotel like that. What's up with you?"

"That fag who did the laundry in Eskilstuna didn't give me my pants back," Chase groaned. "I only have one pair left. I am sick with the flu, and I am soaking wet when I come off stage, and there's never any towels."

I gave him a pair of my frizzies when we got back to the hotel.

CHAPTER 23

CHAPTER TWENTY-THREE

THE REEPERBAHN IS THE RED LIGHT DISTRICT

of Hamburg. It's a mass of porno stores, peep shows, and side streets where prostitutes sit for sale in shop windows and an indoor three-story parking lot called The Sexual Paradise where the cheaper hookers can be found.

It is also where all the cheapest hotels in Hamburg are, like the dormitory-style Stern Hotel, which has no telephones in the room and is right next to the entrance to The Sexual Paradise (uggg). My room was right under a taxi stand and I had to listen to all these loud, laughing drunks all night, horsing around down there. And then at dawn the junkies, who flee to the Reeperbahn en mass, drove me nuts with their arguments with each other on their way to buying heroine from the street dealers at the S Bahn exit a half a block away from the hotel.

Being in this mood I don't want anyone backstage after the show, demanding from me. That's for sure. When we came off stage I did watch with great pleasure as Chase and Chris trashed the dressing room of the Club Logo. The dressing room is hideous and it provoked us. Robert brought one girl backstage. She wanted to exchange T-shirts with Chris. The girl took her T-shirt off right away and stood around topless for us all to see. This is not normal behavior. Her T-shirt was pretty cool though. It had some kind of tattoo design of a heart on it. She said that it was from a bar in Kreuzberg, in Berlin. She was also very cute, so Chris took off his smelly, wet T-shirt and they exchanged.

I can't say *tchuss*, so how about bye-bye, with a stiff upper lip and no hint of emotion whatsoever. I think you all know me well enough now to know that I wasn't angry at this girl. I have a good heart. But my heart's not in Berlin. It used to be. But that was long ago, dear. I feel sorry for her, for Berlin, for all of us.

When she left, I wasn't expecting anything else. Then for some reason Chase, who has a good heart, also let in five or six guys who publish a fanzine in Hamburg. Their fanzine looked good, like a cross between a magazine and a fanzine. I did a dreary interview with them. They liked the show. I've always had a hard time at the Logo in Hamburg. I told them how I felt. They agreed. This place is *scheiss* they all said.

Then they reminded me of when I played this same club for the first time seven years ago with my old band, I.C.C.C. I gave the audience a stern warning. "The guitars don't drink beer!" I bellowed into the mike. The next time I laid into one of them without warning as a show of force. Then I went on with the show.

All Americans who come here to this city wonder if the hamburger might have been invented in Germany, in Hamburg. I don't like that idea, but it might be true, I think suspiciously in the back of my mind.

CHAPTER 24

THE WAY I FEEL NOW IS THAT
[I D]ONT GIVE A DAMN IF I EVER COME
[BA]CK TO EUROPE OR GERMANY AND
[ES]PECIALY EAST GERMANY EVER
[AG]AIN. I HAVE NO DOUBTS IN MY
[MI]ND WHERE MY LOYALTIES ARE.
[T]HERE WITH MYSELF. I AM ALL I
[GO]T.

I USED TO FEEL SENTIMENTAL
[A]BOUT GERMANY. I GREW UP HERE.
[M]Y MOTHER IS GERMAN. MAYBE I
[D]ONT FIT IN, IN GERMAN THATS
[N]OT MY FAULT. WHAT 'AUSSLANDER
[D]OES.

WHEN WE GOT TO [ ] OF
[VIE]NNA WHERE I AM PLAYING TONIGHT
I WAS HOPING [ ] MAKE
[EV]ERY THING SO PERSONAL. THAT IT
[W]OULD BE JUST ANOTHER STOP ON THE

CHAPTER TWENTY-FOUR

[TO]UR [ ] SORT
[O]F LIKE LEEDS IN ENGLAND EXKLEPT
[T]HESE KRAUTS SEEM TO BE ALOT BETTER
[O]FF. ITS A BUNCH [ ] ELF ABSORBED
[N]OW IT ALL STUCK [ ]
[R]UNNING TO AND [ ] THEIR
[C]LASSES LIKE [ ]
[AN]D DADDY OR [ ]
[PA]YING THE B[I]D [ ]
[ ] THERES NO [ ]

THE WAY I FEEL NOW is that I don't give a damn if I ever come back to Europe or Germany, and especially East Germany, ever again. I have no doubts in my mind where my loyalties are. They're with myself. I'm all I've got.

I used to feel sentimental about Germany. I grew up here. My mother is German. Maybe I don't fit in, in Germany. That's not my fault. What *ausslander* does?

When we got to the town of Jenna, where I'm playing tonight, I was hoping I wouldn't take everything so personally. That it would be just another stop on the tour. It's a college town, sort of like Leeds, in England, except these krauts seem to be a lot better off. It's a bunch of self-absorbed, know-it-all students here, running to and fro from their classes like robots, and mommy and daddy or the state are paying the bills. I tried but there's no way I couldn't end up hating it here. I have always felt the sting of the upper-white-middle class. My only degree is in streetology. I'm uneducated. I had to leave school at sixteen and go to work in a supermarket to support myself. That's because I'm an honest person. I wouldn't know how to lean on society, or another person if I tried.

I had a feeling that, when I was playing the show at the college in Jenna, that the mostly student audience could tell how I felt. I could also tell how they felt. So I gave them a couple of Johnny Mathis-type versions of some Ramones songs to mimic their attitude. Oh, but careful, I'm in Germany, so I must be extra respectful. Ha. Ha.

When the East German government was in power they told these people every move they could make. Rock and roll music was forbidden. But I don't feel sorry for them. It's what they want. Now they might have a freedom of choice, but German peer pressure takes that away. Always. They have become so used to being American-haters that they hate rock and roll music. Okay! *Tuchuss*, you deserve the isolation that you have imposed upon yourselves. The audience in Jenna knows all this already. They knew that my concert there was a last-time kind of a thing. They tried to *macht show* but it wasn't good enough for me.

I'm not a punk, skin, Nazi, or snob. I'm defiant. I'm angry. You made me that way. So fuck you all. Yes, I'll want my turn in line. But if you want to give me dirty, impatient looks, to make tension or push your way in front of me because you don't think that trash like me belongs in the line, then you have got to expect trouble from me. What I had to end up becoming is an American fucking outlaw. So burn, Germany, burn. I'll light the fire.

CHAPTER 25

LAST NIGHT I HAD TO TELL IT
IS AND CALL A SPADE A SPADE
AS IN THE RIGHT PERFECT MOOD TO
GHT BUT THERE ISNT ANY REAL TH
IAM DO TO DEFEND MY SELF AGAINST
E UNPREDICTABLE WHAT EVERS TH
WITH TOURING IN A ROCK AND
BAND

THE GAME IS VERY MENTAL.
AGAINST THEM, MUSICIAN
BUSINESS MAN VERSUS ALL
AND POLITICAL BOUNDARIES
YOU YOU HAVE TO BE
OR IT WILL EAT YOU UP ALIVE
ROCK AND ROLL TRACK

THERE ARE PEOPLE ON T
OF YOUR CIRCLE WHO

CHAPTER TWENTY-FIVE

ADVANTAGE TO
PREPARE YOUR BELLION, YOU
CAN KILL THESE IDIOTS EVEN IF
YOU DO WISH THEM DEAD. ALL I
CAN REALY DO ABOUT THE CURRENT
THAT IAM IN IS TO
ING MUSIC I KNOW

CLUB SUDSTADT, Cottleus, East Germany.

There was a parade of drunken punks coming in and out of my dressing room doing as they will and demanding this and that. After my ten-hour van drive, and with no time to go to the hotel first to shower, I have to hop from the van to the stage. For dinner I had some cold potatoes and gravy. I felt lucky to find a clean plate and silverware.

Then I took my bass guitar and waded through the small audience of 150 people who had braved coming to this out of the way joint on a rainy Monday night, I guess to get their fuses lit. When I got to the small platform that served as a stage and was backed against the wall, with no exit out except straight through the crowd, again there were about five drunken punks and a big fat scary skin blocking me from getting on it.

They wouldn't move when they saw me. Instead the punks lay down on the stage on their backs with their feet hanging down off the edge and grinned at me like the fools that they are.

The big skin grinned a happy what-you-gonna-do-now look at me. I can't believe I did what I did and I'm still alive, but I did it. I automatically scoop-slammed him with the inside crook of my elbow across his face, knocking him off the stage, and then walked over the body of a punk still lying unconcerned on my stage. I then took my bass and plugged it in my amp and, counted "One, two, three, four," into my mike, and Chris and Chase and I went into the hardest version of "Rockaway Beach" that I have ever done in my life.

This woke everyone up. I don't think they were too impressed with me walking over them with my sneakers and slapping a skin, but they liked my sound. When the music started they formed a violent mosh-pit throughout the small club and took it up on stage with me and the band. They broke all the mikes right away.

Fuck this, I thought, I'm not going to risk being hurt by these animals. The only way we could play now was out of tune and instrumentally, so I said "Come on" to the guys, "We quit, let's go." It was scary pushing through the crowd back to the dressing room. I think the only thing that saved us was the people's disbelief that we weren't going to play anymore.

When we got back to the dressing room it was the first time that I could ever get the band to agree on anything. We all agreed that we were afraid. That this was an extremely dangerous, contagious situation, and that we'd better run for it. Oh, of course Minna couldn't agree. He wasn't up there on the stage with his back against the wall, though. Was he? But I don't really think he could believe what he was seeing. That wasn't registering.

I remember once a few years ago, in Spain, my tour manager and drummer decided to run for it and left Barbara and me on the street outside a club during a serious fracas. I was on my own and I could tell what was coming so I put a Coca-Cola bottle in a heavy canvas bag to use as a frail and fought it out on the street and then went to the hospital later to get stitched up. So how could I not trust my better instincts this time and not insist that we all leave together? I'm not an idiot. Once burned, forever learned.

If you have to fight, then you have to fight. Then so be it. But when the odds are so against you, what's the purpose? We wanted to get the hell out of there but Minna kept insisting that we do the show. That we had to get the money. So did the club. So did the audience. What money? I wondered. I've gotten six hundred dollars in five weeks.

So we were forced to go and try again to play. Of course, it was worse. The big fat skin was spoiling for a fight. He kept running at Chris and then at me, threatening us and flipping us the bird, and then retreating to a corner of the club to gather with his mates who obviously seemed to agree with each other that we needed to be taught a lesson. This action went on back and forth while we managed to get in about five songs. Whatever. We were playing great.

LEGEND OF A ROCK STAR

But then, as I watched the mosh pit take over the stage again I decided to let them have it, and Chase and Chris and I exited the stage through the crowd and retreated into the dressing room.

"There's going to be trouble, Minna," we pleaded.

"Oh, everything is going to be under control," he contradicted us. "We still need to finish the show. You guys have to go back up there."

After the set was over, things spilled out on to the street. The police had to come, and an ambulance. The only way that I can protect myself against all this is to stay home where it's safe, and to get out of the music business while I'm still in one piece.

FREIBURG THE ATLANTIK
...B. FREIBURG IS A BEAUTIFU
...WN IN GERMANY. IT LOOKS
...TE IT HAS A LOT OF SWISS
...FLUENCE OR A SWISS LOOK
...HINK MOST OF THE PEOPLE WH
...JE HERE HAVE A LOT OF MO
...IVE PLAYED HERE BEFORE
...E PROCTOR WHO RUNS THE
...LANTIC CLUB LOOKS LIKE
...[ ] MOTHER IN
...HAS NO TEET
...HART

CHAPTER TWENTY-SIX

FREIBURG, THE ATLANTIK CLUB. Freiburg is a beautiful town in Germany. It looks like it has a lot of Swiss influence, or at least a Swiss look. I think most of the people who live here have a lot of money.

I've played here before. The promoter who runs the Atlantik Club looks like my old grandmother in Berlin. He has no teeth left, is a diehard punk, and has bleached duck-yellow hair, like me, and like my grandmother in Berlin had.

If all this is sounding hopeful then please don't worry. It wasn't perfect, to say the least. Even though the owner of the Atlantik is a friend, we didn't get the royal homecoming treatment.

The Sport Park Hotel where he booked us sucked. This hotel had the usual, no phones, no TV, no bathroom in the room, and no heat. The mattress on the bed was caving in towards the floor. The first thing I thought when I saw this bed was that I wanted to urinate on it. We had just driven eleven hours to get here from our last gig at Cottleus in East Germany. Now we were sort of feuding, today, among ourselves. This is typical outlaw behavior.

When I entered my hotel room and saw where I would be spending the night I became incensed, and since a glass ashtray was the first thing within my reach I picked it up and threw it as hard as I could against the wall, sending glass all over the place. I then realized that I would have to sleep tonight in my sneakers so I wouldn't cut myself while walking around. Then I slammed the door off its hinges a few times, really making an impressive racket. Next, I kicked a garbage can to death. It was thin plastic and I destroyed it fairly easily. I heard Minna, Chase, Robert, and Chris doing likewise so I threw my suitcase against the wall a couple of times for effect, and to even things out.

We only had twenty minutes in the room anyway. Then we had to race over to the club. When I left, my room looked a mess. As I closed the door I was hoping that no one would come in there when I was gone and look around to see what all the noise was about.

When I got to the Club Atlantik I was in a fairly better mood than I had been in in days.

But then it changed. There was no hospitality spread to nibble on while we loaded in the equipment. That's pretty damn fucking disrespectful, because we were trapped at the club because of the schedule and had to drive straight to this gig without being able to stop at McDonald's to eat.

Things evened out again, though. We could forget about a sound check because the promoter had five other bands on the bill and he was letting them do their sound check first and it was obvious that we weren't going to get a sound check, even though we were the headliners and had sold the place out. We had raced here to Freiburg, risking a serious accident on the autobahn for nothing.

But!, we were served a wonderful *weiner schnitzel* dinner that they made us at the club, which also has a restaurant, so it wasn't really as big a deal as it seemed, but we appreciated it. The dressing room was communal but we appreciated that they did give us a private bathroom upstairs, which Chris, Chase, and I promptly trashed.

The show at the Atlantik was great. The audience was wild and was as much a part of everything as we were. That's how it should be. I imagined that it was what a Bill Haley and the Comets show would have been like in Germany in the late fifties.

They slammed and they jitterbugged and carried each other above themselves towards the stage. This is pretty freaky to watch. Sometimes they almost got human pyramids going, standing on each other's shoulders and riding someone around lifting him up on a sea of hands and passing him around the dance floor. Chris got caught after the show by the audience, who passed him around this way above their heads, till Minna got him free and he could escape into the backstage upstairs

LEGEND OF A ROCK STAR

toilet we were using as a dressing room. I don't know what gives here in Freiburg. The band on before us was a ska polka band. I have never heard this kind of music before but I liked it.

After the show a local tattoo artist came backstage to visit me. I knew him from before this tour and when I was playing tonight I was thinking about him and worrying if he was okay. When I saw him this time, he had a young girlfriend, brand-new teeth, and a pocket full of money. I guess that talk I had with him last year did him a lot of good.

I didn't like it that he and Chris got into a mock fight though. It didn't last too long, thank God, but it looked pretty grim and Chris can really hit hard, and so can this other guy. Chris was in a good mood though and nothing could break it. The show we did in Freiburg was one of the best ones I've ever done in Germany. So was the one at The Knack, in Berlin.

My friend's girlfriend kept trying to talk to me and kiss me. I don't know what she wanted, but I didn't like that, so I started trying to leave. But she made me listen to her.

She told me that when she was four years old her father killed her mother, who was then twenty-four years old. She told me that her mother had been a big Ramones fan and that all she had left her were two Ramones albums. She told me that, now that she had met me and seen me play, her life was complete. That I was her mother's favorite Ramone. Weird. I became so confused then by all this sadness and love and hate that all I could about do was panic.

CHAPTER 27 199

IN THE TOILET AT THE CLUB
ATLANTIK THEY HAD COPIES OF A
GERMAN POP MUSIC MAGAZINE CAL
BRAVO. THEY USE THIS MAGAZIN
HERE FOR THE TOILET PAPER. YO
SUPPOSED TO PICK UP A COPY O
THIS RAG OUT OF A CARDBOARD
NEXT TO THE BOWL, RIP OUT A P
AND WIPE YOUR ~~ASS~~ HOLE WITH
OUCH!

ROBERT CAME ACROSS
PINUP POSTER OF BRITNEY
IN ONE OF THE MAG'S S
SO PRETTY GOOD POSING
BEDROOM, LYING ASS U
HER BED AND MAKING A SEX

CHAPTER TWENTY-SEVEN

INSTEAD OF WIPING HIS AS
THIS POSTER   ACHE
FOR ANOTHER PAGE AND LEAN
HIMSELF WITH THAT
WE COULD ALL SEE WHA
WAS DOING BECAUSE WHEN H
WENT TO USE THE TOILET
DIDNT CLOSE THE DOOR. ACT

IN THE TOILET at the Club Atlantik they had copies of a German pop music magazine called *Bravo*. They use this magazine here for the toilet paper. You're supposed to pick up a copy of this rag out of a cardboard box next to the bowl, rip out a page, and wipe your asshole with it. Ouch!

Robert came across an old pinup poster of Britney Spears in one of the mags. She looked pretty good, posing in her bedroom, lying ass up on her bed and making a sexy pouting face for the camera. Instead of wiping his ass on this poster Robert reached for another page and cleaned himself with that.

We could all see what he was doing because when he went to use the toilet he didn't close the door. Actually, there wasn't one. What there was was a hole in the tile floor that you are supposed to squat over and take a shit. This is typical Euro-style crapping and they think this is normal. By now everyone had a serious case of "deli belly" from the meal at the Club Atlantik yesterday and we were all more squirting than shitting so no one was going to be to choosy about where they were going to crap—you just had to hope you didn't do it in your pants.

When Robert held up the poster of Britney for everybody to view it broke the tension from the smelly farts, bad hotels, and riding in the van, because she look so homey somehow. But then, without giving a warning for us to look away, he started to stroke his penis, getting it hard, then masturbating his hard-on and then shooting a load all over her pouting face.

"She's still a virgin," he remarked, zipping up. "That's the only way you can have sex with her. If that would have been a poster of Nina Hagen, I would have stuck my rod right up her asshole," he added, putting Britney's poster back in the cardboard box by the toilet hole.

I hope she was sixteen when they took that shot of her, I thought to myself, sort of stunned by what I had just witnessed, but despite myself, determined to snap out of my bad mood and stop being a bitch.

"Ho, ho, ho," I laughed, in that phony sort of a way that I do. "That was funny," I then remarked to the guys. Later on when we finally got back to the Sport Hotel we drank a few cases of wine and some beers, and got drunk out of our heads. Wine and beer is a knockout combination. When Chris finally passed out on his bed dead drunk, Chase painted his face like Paul Stanley from Kiss. He used White Out and a black jumbo permanent magic marker, and did a real good job of it.

The next morning, when Chris looked in the mirror and saw what they had done to him, he took what he was seeing with his usual good sense of humor. Later on he started getting more irritated about the Kiss makeup that Chase had painted on him, as he started realizing that the sanitary conditions in Europe were so primitive that he wasn't going to be able to wash this "guck" off himself till he was back home in Los Angeles.

He's going to have to finish the tour looking like Paul Stanley, oh well, I rationalized to myself, knowing better than to vocalize any of my opinions, for fear of instant rebuttal. *That's what he wanted. I'd hate to be in his shoes now,* I added as an afterthought to myself. Everyone is really getting on Minna's nerves already. He's getting more sour by the hour, and to steady himself he's been smoking one bowl of "H" after the other; in fact he's a registered dope fiend in Holland and can legally buy dope, but these stores for dope are for Dutch people only and you have to have I.D.

Minna's always in a deep fog now from smoking so much "H," so it's getting easier to run something by him once in a while. In the morning when he staggered down to breakfast Chase, Robert, Chris, and I shit a refried bean stew into a garbage pail that wasn't broken and then hid it in my room. After Minna came back up from having his breakfast he went inside his room and closed the door. The he came back out and put his bags in the hall and closed the door again so no one could get in there and spy on him and figure out what he does in there in private. He always does this routine, like clockwork.

Then he knocks on all our doors and expects us to come outside into the hallway with our luggage and stand there while he inspects the damage to each room. We know he's going to do all this because he always does. This time, though, we were creating a diversion so as to accomplish one last hideous act of debauchery on the Sport Hotel here in Freiburg.

When Minna pound-knocked on my door I came right out of my room with my luggage to put it down outside in the hallway, and tried to crowd him from slipping past me through the doorway into my room. I also stalled him a bit and jammed myself and my luggage in his way, and speaking to a wooden-faced Minna, impatient to inspect my room already, I said to him, "Hey Dude! Just a minute, I'm not ready. I forgot my key. I gotta go back inside my room a minute." That was our signal. Chris and Chase then lit the curtains in their room on fire, creating a diversion. Just as we figured, Minna momentarily forgot about my room, and inspecting it, and getting his jollies making me try to clean it up a little so that the hotel wouldn't call the police. He ran in to Chris and Chase's room to see what all the yelling and smoke was about.

"Fire! Fire!" Chris and Chase were yelling, putting on quite an act.

"Minna! Minna! Come quick," they were also yelling. Of course, Minna ran right in there and I was following right behind him with the garbage pail that was slopping with shit, with which I doused the flaming curtains and put out the fire.

"Aren't you glad the whole hotel didn't catch on fire?" I laughed heartily. "We better get going," Chase and Chris chorused.

"God gloeiende God yer domme!" Minna shrieked, his face turning purple with rage. "You guys get your fucking suitcases and get in the van right now! Under-fucking-stand?"

"Okay, okay," everyone agreed with him, trying to pacify him. There was diarrhea sprayed all over the walls where the curtains had burnt up, charring the carpet. The room smelled like hash and stale beer. It had a urine odor and a burnt-plastic and poop smell. There were still

some naked, underage girls in the room who had drunk beer spiked with Spanish fly, and had passed out and been molested. One of them had a banana in her twat.

There were banana peels and rubber gloves and a used-up tube of KY jelly lying about. Beer and wine bottles lay broken on the floor, and no one had used an ashtray. There was graffiti all over the walls written in magic marker and all the furniture was totaled. We had turned the place into a dump. We got out of there in a hurry. No one was arguing about leaving in a hurry this time.

"You look funny," I said to Chris, noticing his Kiss makeup for the first time this morning as we were getting back in the van.

"I'm back in the New York groove," Chris giggled, sounding exactly like Paul Stanley did in the *Detroit Rock City* movie.

As we were pulling out of the Sport Hotel's parking lot, I muttered out a "Let's get out of here," as I gave the place one paranoid last look.

CHAPTER 28

THE THREE HOUR DRIV
TO WEINHEIM WAS PRETTY
GRIM. NO ONE WANTED TO
LEAVE FREIBURG FOR THE
UNKNOWN. WE HAD SUCH
A GOOD TIME HERE.
THE
THE CAFE
WEINHEIM TURNED OUT T
BE
WHERE THE CAFE CENTRAL
WHERE
WEINHEIM

CHAPTER TWENTY-EIGHT

THE THREE-HOUR DRIVE to Weinheim was pretty grim. No one wanted to leave Freiburg for the unknown. We had had such a good time there. The promoter from the Cafe Central, where we were playing in Weinheim turned out to be a pretty level guy when we met him.

Who cares? By now everyone is completely disgusted with the main German promoter from IBD, Andrea Scholz. She's the worst ever, we all agreed, when we pulled up to a seedy dive called The Sea Hotel, which was where we were going to be staying for the night in Weinheim. This hotel was in the middle of nowhere again and it was thirty-four kilometers from the Cafe Central. This was really cutting into our time, making everything a lot more aggravating. Andrea Scholz had insisted that we stay there because she was getting off-season rates which are a lot cheaper than for a hotel in town and she could pocket the maybe 100 marks at the expense of losing me as a client and a friend forever.

The other promoter from the Cafe Central wanted us at a better hotel a half block from his club. It seemed like as soon as we got to Weinheim we had to do the show. I don't know what happened to about four or five hours of that day. The hours just disappeared into thin air and I was left a little disoriented.

I didn't like the support band that played with us at the Cafe Central. They were fat and ugly and they tried to steal our beer. These guys were given ten minutes to use our dressing room after their set. *Who are these assholes?* I wondered to myself as I watched them snake off the stage, all wet and sweaty, into the area reserved for me and my band.

Chris, thinking quick, tried to get a free T-shirt from them. They, in return, tried to get fifteen marks for it, bargaining among themselves to see if it was all right for them to give Chris a better price.

"No way!" Chris scoffed angrily. "You guys ain't worth shit for money," he added in a sort of mock-friendly way, trying not to escalate things, especially since we now only legally had to put up with them for seven more minutes.

They did go. But not too fast. First they boldly raided our refrigerator for some beer. We just wanted them to go, so we didn't challenge them.

Soon they got bored and left, probably to act out their adolescent rock-star fantasies elsewhere. I pissed over one of their guitars, a Fender Strat copy, when they left. Later on, after our show was over, they gave us ten minutes and then burst in on us in our dressing room on the pretense of retrieving their equipment, an old trick if there ever was one.

What they really wanted was beer and in an instant they were flocking around our fridge again and helping themselves to our beer, which we only drink after the show and was for us now.

"That's enough," I warned them. They reacted to my warning by laughing in my face. This provoked me to violently lurch at them, slapping the stolen beers out of their hands and on to the floor.

"Out! Motherfuckers!" I shouted, pointing to the exit door. They ran like sheep, mortified, out the door. They forgot to take their guitars so we took them so that no one would steal them. The band and I steal from the dressing rooms and hotel rooms all the time and we're always on the look out for valuables.

I've had to hit, kick, or slap someone on every day of this tour, from fans to security guards.

off the stage, all wet and sweaty, into the area reserved for me and my band.

Chris, thinking quick, tried to get a free T-shirt from them. Then, in return, tried to get fifteen marks for it, bargaining among themselves to see if it was all right for them to give Chris a better price.

them stupid. I would break my neck if I saw a dork like you laughing in my face. This provoked me to violently lunge at them, slapping the moldy beers out of their hands and on to the floor.

"Out Motherfucker!" I shouted, pointing to the exit door. They ran like sheep, mortified, out the door. They forgot to take their guitars so we took them, so that no one would steal them. The band and I steal from the dressing rooms and hotel rooms all the time and we always on the look out for valuables.

I've had to hit, kick, or slap someone on every day of this tour, from fans to security guards.

CHAPTER 29

CHAPTER TWENTY-NINE

I'M WORRIED ABOUT MONEY.

Friday the thirteenth is Good Friday. That's a religious holiday. We head back to Los Angeles on Monday the sixteenth. I dont know what time our flight is. We're going to be in Utrecht in Holland on the sixteenth. That's about an hour from Amsterdam, where we're flying home from.

If this is an Easter holiday weekend that might mean that the banks might not be open in Holland on Monday, or they might. That's why I'm worried. No one has gotten paid yet.

The guys could have gotten some of their money in Copenhagen. I nagged them to take it, but they didn't. They won't spend a nickel of their own money. They are trying to save their whole salaries to take home. How can I criticize them for that? They would have made Johnny Ramone proud. The thing is, though, that the financial strain of all this is on me, and it sucks. When we crossed the German border into Holland today we stopped at a money-changing place. Chase changed a few bucks and I had stashed a 150 to spend in Venlo.

We got to Venlo on Friday the thirteenth at around 3:30 P.M. Everything was still open and there were a lot of German tourists running around doing last minute shopping for the weekend, despite the heavy traffic at the border because the police are trying to crack down on drug smuggling. Venlo is definitely an outlaw town. I can vouch for that. It's where I used to live, raised Barbara, got hurt a lot, and hid out alone in the Rembrandt Hotel, a few blocks from the train station. This was a real dope addict place.

God is so good to me that I never did heroin here. It couldn't touch me then, and it still can't now. I'm free. I don't think I could have survived a heroin habit here in Venlo. This is a rough town. I used to have to carry a pistol. Every American lives by the gun. It's our right.

But being the only American in Venlo then, when I lived here, was foolish. I don't know how I got away with it. If I had been trying to maintain a dope habit I would have been killed for my money. I was always armed when I lived here. I carried a big, black-handled fisherman's switchblade that had more in common with a butcher knife than a stiletto. I also wore Doctor Martens and had my dog, Kessie, with me.

The Moroccans travel in groups of three here in this town, whirling themselves from one end of it to the other, scavenging the streets for victims to rob or rip off. "Don't fuck with them, Dee Dee, they're very tricky with the knife." That's what everybody told me. It was scary. They have no fear. Even if they're ten years old.

Once in Mechelen, in Belgium, Barbara and I were coming home from Amsterdam on the train. It was late at night. We had our Sparta motorbikes parked outside the station to ride home on. Both Barbara and I had a switchblade and a blackjack on us. We didn't have the dog. My bike wouldn't start. Barbara put-putted behind me as I pushed my bike through the dark streets of Mechelen. "Just go," I told her, but she wouldn't leave me. I was worried. There were groups of Moroccans coming out of the shadows and allies, and threatening us. Barbara and I are not pushovers and can survive Buenos Aires or a bad part of Berlin, but this was ridiculous. With God on our side again, we made it home without being attacked.

I was really upset and humiliated. These guys are rude to women and made remarks. I could never let anyone hurt her. Not on my life. We both had some kind of psychological wound from the experience though, compounded by all the other recent ones.

I leashed our dog Kessie when we got home. He was a very mean street dog and he seemed to have psychic intuition. I took Barbara with me back into the night to get some revenge. We waited in the bushes where we couldn't be seen, by a bus stop. When some unsuspecting Moroccans stopped to wait for the bus we let Kessie loose on them. "Get 'em," I whispered, and Kessie shot at them like a brawler. Biting low, chopping them up good. Messing the fuck out of them. The only thing I saw one of them do to defend himself was to hold his pant legs out straight. I guess he was hoping my dog would bite him through the pants material instead of his flesh.

When they were seriously injured enough and not too much of a threat, Barbara and I jumped out of the bushes with baseball bats and beat the motherfuckers to a pulp. We didn't even know them, and they hadn't done us any personal harm, but we had to do something to feel better.

Tonight it's snowing in Venlo and it looks beautiful. It's Easter Sunday eve. I feel like God is making a Christmas for me. I feel his love. And Barbara's love. I feel lots of it.

There's a lot of love in my heart wherever I go. And a lot of people love me. Today when I looked out my window I saw three sail planes gliding over the Dutch countryside. I think that God had me see that so I would feel a little sentimental. I mean, how could I deny that? I wonder if Chase and Chris and I will cry when we leave Amsterdam Monday for Los Angeles.

Once, about eight years ago, I was walking home with my old drummer Danny's brother. The dawn was approaching, the sun was coming up, and everything looked beautiful. We were taking a shortcut home through the park near the Venlo station, where there are hundreds of old-fashioned touring bikes and small 50 cc mopeds parked as best they could be in rows of bicycle-lot parking stands. I used to go to the station to look at bikes and watch people getting off the train to see the ones that had folding collapsible bicycles. After walking past all the bikes and the station and then entering into the park I was in a dreamy mood. I couldn't help but notice all the rabbits. They were wild ones. In a city park. It was weird. Maybe they all woke up at the same time. When they do, it's like they're coming out of hiding.

"They're the souls of all the junkies who died in this park," Danny's brother told me, commenting on the rabbits.

"Happy Easter," I said to the audience at the Personclub in Venlo last night. I also said, "I'd like to dedicate this song to Joey on this holy night."

I don't really remember which song it was. It probably was "Rock-away Beach," the first one I start my set with. I was trying to dedicate what I was doing to Joey out of respect to him, and to his contributions and his sacrifices that have kept me alive and made me into a somebody. Thank you Joey, and thank you John. I could feel he was going to leave us.

Now it's Easter Sunday morning. The church bells have been ringing since four in the morning. I've been in an odd mood. I didn't expect the show to go well last night, but it did. It went very well. It's hard to please anyone in Venlo so I'm sort of pleased now myself. But now it's eight o'clock in the morning at the Hotel Wilhelmina. The maids are making a lot of noise on purpose, banging brooms on the wall and vacuum cleaning outside my door, trying to drive me out of my room so that they can go in there, finish cleaning for the day, and then go home.

My wife Barbara just called. She told me that they said that Joey was dying in the hospital, on MTV. All I can say to both of them right now is Joey, I love you, and Barbara, I love you.

I'm thinking about death now. I'm afraid. I wonder if my old drummer Danny's brother is still alive. He couldn't have made it. He must be dead.

I remember his cheeky sense of humor and how funny it used to be to hear him say American slang words like "super" and "nature" in his growling, Dutch-Indo-Chinese accent. I want to hold on to my life. I'm so lucky that I'm still alive. But all the deaths of my friends haunt me. One of the first things Danny's brother said to me was, "I'm shocked you're still alive." If he's dead now, I'm not surprised in the least. I'm not happy about it. I don't want to take any more risks. Life is too precious. He reminds me of that.

The next morning, after the last show in Utrecht, I called up my wife Barbara. I was up early and was leaving for Los Angeles from Amsterdam in a few hours to go home.

"Hi Barbara," I said. "I'll be home in about twenty hours. How's everything going?"

"Joey's dead," Barbara's voice cracked on the telephone line. "I'm real sorry," she added. Then we both started crying.

I kept my emotions to myself after that. I stayed in my room so no one could see how sad I was.

When Minna came to my room later on to get me, I told him that

LEGEND OF A ROCK STAR

Joey died. That was about it. Then we drove to the airport. No one said anything. Everyone seemed to have their own troubles. Only Chase and I made it onto the plane. We didn't get seats next to each other.

CHAPTER 30

E BLANKET LIES CRUMPLED OVER
S. THE LIGHT ABOVE ME CAN BE TU
AND OFF FROM A SWITCH ON THE A
ST, WHICH FOLDS IN BETWEEN THE SE
THE BLANKETS ON THE PLANE
ATICALLY SMALL SO ARE THE PILL
R THE FLIGHT FROM ... TO LOS ANG
OM EUROPE, I HAD NICE PEOPLE S
EXT ... APPRECIAT
NO THAT THE TOUR IS OVER A
THAT I AM GOING HOME NOW AND
ASE AND I AM GLAD ... THE FLIGHT
... E CHRIS WHO LOST HIS TIC
NO THAT WAS ... R

CHAPTER THIRTY

DIE. I APPR
HIS ...
BUT THERE IS ALSO AN
N ME. THERE ALWAYS PE
WANT TO MUCH. THE SO
ITTLE IN RETURN. YOU CAN
ACK A THANK YOU A
SIGN OF RESPECT FOR
GET PEOPLE GATHERING

THE BLANKET LIES CRUMPLED over my legs. The light above me can be turned on and off from a switch on the armrest which folds in between the seats.

The blankets on the plane are small. So are the pillows. For the flight back to Los Angeles from Europe I had nice people sitting next to me, which I appreciated. Also that the tour is over, and that I'm going home now, and that Chase and I made the flight, unlike Chris, who lost his ticket, and that I wasn't the first Ramone to die. I appreciated all this.

But there is a lot of anger in me. There always is. People want too much. They give so little in return. You can give back a thank you. A smile. Or a sign of respect. For me, I get people gathering around me, nervously crumb-snatching from my very existence like a bunch of desperate pigeons, but since they're really humans and halfway intelligent they boldly hope that they're being clever. I'm forced, every time, to puff myself up. To spread my wings. Reassure myself that my claws can cut them down. So I can go in self-respect. Knowing that there's only one me.

Whatever these crumb-snatchers want, it isn't me. It's them. It's their life that's so important to them, unknowing as they are that there's a whole world out there to discover. You can only do that by your own personal standards. You need your own Ramones, that you can start for yourself, and live through. My Ramones are not a shortcut to your personal goals in life through.

That's why we have a God. He'll take you there if he wants to. If there are gods here on Earth, then can you expect that God to worship at your feet? To carry you on his back up a mountain and then chop it down for you with the edge of his hand so you don't have to climb anything too difficult yourself?

Your higher power, instead, wants you to make the effort yourself. He wants you to be strong. Unlike your enemies. I, in my human way, I would like you to be strong, so that you would be happy, so that you would get off my case. Move on. Be of use to others. God will admire you for that. For everything is already here right in front of us. As I pull the blanket restlessly over my head I try and force an automatic and simultaneous but weak smile out of myself, but inwardly, so as not to arouse any predators in this jungle of human animals that I'm caged in right now.

I have a right to survive. The way I want to. I lead a solitary existence for my own protection so when I show myself it will be more special and give me more power to distract the herd.

Clockwise from top left: Marky, Tommy, Arturo Vega, Legs McNeil. Still punks.

CHAPTER 31

DRAGONS .... IMAGINE ONE FLYING
OVER ONE OF THE MEADOWS HIGH ABOVE
NEW YORK CITIES CENTRAL PARK ONE
SLOWED SUNDAY AFTERNOON,
MAYBE THIS DRAGON COULD BE JOE
SOMEONE. I DONT SEE WHY NOT. HE
COULD BE A BEAUTIFUL GOLDEN
COLOR, CALORED ONE WITH A SILVER
RADIANCE RADIATING
FROM HIS WINGS.
FLASHING AND
EYES AND WOULD WINK
AT EVERY BODY STAIRING UP
AT HIM IN AMAZEMENT. THEN HE

CHAPTER THIRTY-ONE

FLY TOWARDS THE SUN TO
CALIFORNIA TO SURFIN AND
SOME FUN

I LIKE DRAGONS SO MUCH
I TRIED TO LOOK FOR
OUTSIDE THE WINDOW
PLANE THAT I AM IN NOW

DRAGONS. . . . . Imagine one flying over one of the meadows, high above New York City's Central Park, one crowed Sunday afternoon. Maybe this dragon could be Joey Ramone. I don't see why not. He could be a beautiful, golden-amber colored one with a silver lightning ambience radiating from his body and wings. He'd have two flashing and loving eyes and would wink down at everybody staring up at him in amazement. Then he would spread his fiery wings and fly towards the sun to California to go surfing and to have some fun.

I like dragons so much that I tried to look for one outside the window of the plane that I'm in now. I imagine that a dragon would love this part of the world that I'm flying through now. Dragons love to make it rain. I looked out the plane's window and scanned the clouds that are hanging so low in the sky because they're pregnant with rain water and sinking towards the ocean.

I spotted a dragon immediately. It was a sea dragon, disguised as the tip of a cloud framing itself in a beautiful gray sky. Then, when all I was seeing revealed itself to be an illusion, *what a beautiful sense of humor these creatures have,* I thought silently to myself.

Some of what I heard about how courageously Joey faced death and a horrible illness is truly amazing. He had faith until the end. Till they turned off his life support. All he wanted was to get better. He thought that he would only have to go through the cancer treatments that one last time.

He wanted to get out of the hospital and rock and roll some more. Whenever people used to ask me about him I would always say that Joey was a very tough guy. He had amazing courage to be so sickly and be in the Ramones. It was harder for him than the rest of us.

A couple of years ago I told him that this was going to kill him if he kept it up. I suggested to him that we both take off and go to Miami, and hide out, like when the Ramones first played California and we went to Huntington Beach. Joey just smiled when I said this. He didn't answer me, but I think he appreciated that I cared about him so much. The problem was that he was desperate for fame and success that he didn't think he'd achieved with the Ramones, and felt that the Ramones had held him back. He stayed in New York and I went to California. We never went to Miami.

I'm such a sentimental old bastard that I really don't want to stop playing music either. That's no good for me and I know that to do so would be seriously risking it. I know that I'm very lucky to be alive. That God blessed me. That I was very lucky to have started the Ramones and have been in the group.

My neighbor Chris, downstairs, is a guitar tech for a lot of big bands and is very much in demand. He also works part time for Schecter

Dee Dee's 44th Birthday at the Lakeside Lounge, NYC, September 18, 1996. It was the first time Joey and Dee Dee had shared a stage in years.

LEGEND OF A ROCK STAR

Guitars. I think he felt bad for me when I came home from the European tour. Joey died and that left me numb. I was freaked out by what happened to Jimmy Vapid. I wouldn't come out of the apartment or answer my door. After a week Chris finally just about broke the door to my apartment down and forced me to come out in the sunshine and go for a walk.

"Let's go over to Schecter and look around at the guitars," Chris suggested when we were at La Brea and Hollywood Boulevard.

"Sounds good," I answered.

They really like Chris over at Schecter. It's hard to believe how generous they are. I walked out of there later with a beautiful black Diamond series acoustic guitar and a black Telecaster. As beautiful as these two guitars are, when I got home with them and looked them over I started to worry. These two look dangerous, I thought to myself. They're just too nice. I'm going to have to play these guys, I realized.

Chris, Chase, and I got in a van on May sixteenth and drove up to somewhere on the outskirts of San Francisco. We're going to play six or seven more shows. Then we're going to stop for a while. My producer, Chris Spedding, who's even older than me and an even meaner old man than I am, will be available to do a new album in October. He's going to London this week for rehearsals with his old band Roxy Music, with Brian Ferry. He's doing fifty-five shows with them.

On June eighth I'm going back to New York. I'm having a private party for my new book the *Chelsea Horror Hotel*, which is just now being released and I'm also having an art exhibition with Paul Kostabi.

I won't be seeing Joey. That's hard. I also wish I could have played the Continental Divide one more time with my own band or the Remains, but that's never going to happen. I'm positive that everything will go well for me when I go back to New York again. It might even be the start of something new. I hope so and I don't hope so.

Today I was wondering what God was going to do with me now. Well, I know he's not going to refuse me into heaven, I'm not worried about that; more than anything, I just want to keep living. Please don't kill me now, God. I would love to be the last Ramone to die.

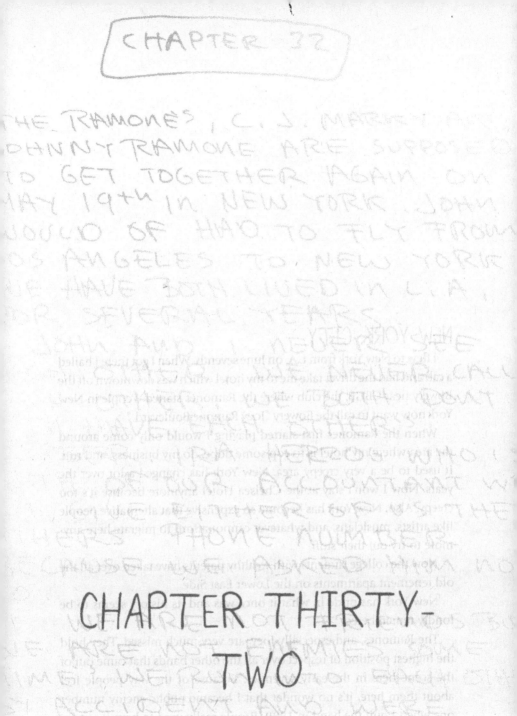

THE RAMONES, C.J., MARKY AND
JOHNNY RAMONE ARE SUPPOSED
TO GET TOGETHER AGAIN ON
MAY 19th IN NEW YORK. JOHN
WOULD OF HAD TO FLY FROM
LOS ANGELES TO NEW YORK
WE HAVE BOTH LIVED IN L.A.
FOR SEVERAL YEARS.
JOHN AND I NEVER GOT. WE
NEVER GOT. WE NEVER CALL
EACH OTHER. WE DON'T
HAVE OTHERS WHO
DO. OUR ACCOUNTANT. HE
HAS PHONE NUMBERS.
ON MY

CHAPTER THIRTY-TWO

ARE NOT ENEMIES. WE
WERE ACCIDENT AND WERE
POLITE. IN THE END WHEN I WASN'T INVITED
TO JOEY'S FUNERAL I GOT
VERY INSULTED.
I WASN'T INVITED

NEW YORK CITY.

I flew to New York from L.A. on June seventh. When I got there I hailed a cab and had the driver take me to my hotel which was downtown off the Bowery near CBGB, the club where the Ramones started. People in New York now want to call the Bowery "Joey Ramone Boulevard."

When the Ramones first started playing I would only come around the area where my hotel is to cop some dope, do my business, and run. It used to be a very creepy area. New York has changed a lot over the years. Now I won't stay at the Chelsea Hotel anymore because it's too creepy. Also, New York has become so expensive that alternative people like artists, musicians, and whatever cannot afford to migrate here anymore to try out their stuff.

Now the college students with wealthy parents have taken over all the old tenement apartments on the Lower East Side.

New York has pride in what it once was and its history seems to be fondly remembered.

The Ramones, and especially Joey, are very much missed. They hold the highest position of respect over all the other bands that came out of the scene here in the early seventies. Because of the way people feel about them here, it's no wonder that I became public enemy number one when I quit the band in 1989. People really used to have it out for me back then. Eventually I realized that I couldn't live in New York because I wasn't welcome there. My show at the Lakeside Lounge was a warm-up show for the one I'm doing at the Spa on the thirteenth.

What I'm doing is a book signing for the *Chelsea Horror Hotel* and an art show with Paul Kostabi, Barbara Zampini, and myself. I'm very interested in art. In New York the graffiti artists and taggers have felt the repression of the city's new zero-tolerance policies but then, when haven't they? Remember LL Cool J's "I was boomin on the subway, I would of got a summons but I ran away?" He might have been only sixteen when he wrote that rap. It's still the same deal here as it was back then, but worse. Iggy Pop said a while back that Los Angeles is a nice place to live if you have somewhere else to go. I feel the same way about New York. I love it, but I have to leave it. People come to New York for a lot of reasons. For fun, ambition, adventure, and other stuff, but not to settle down. Believe it or not, I came to New York to make a home for myself, but that didn't work out. I'm glad I can just come here now for a little while, have something to do, and then go back home to L.A.

The Spa, where I'm having my book signing and art show, is a carry-over of sin, decadence, and overindulgence, the kind that made New York City nightlife so famous long ago. The owners of The Spa are still loyal to the hedonistic moralities of the early seventies, but worse and more wicked.

As the name "The Spa" suggests, the club is designed as a sexual resort. In fact, the club made the cover of the *New York Post* yesterday. It

CBGB's on the Bowery, summer, 1977.

was raided. The police want to bust the place. The club is so popular that I don't think that the police will get away with it.

On the news this morning, the mayor was suggesting that patrons of the club be allowed to have sex inside a metal cylinder and not in public. Of course, there would be a video camera inside the metal cylinder taping everything that was happening and broadcasting the action throughout the club for all to see.

I can't imagine a jaded New York crowd getting into this. At CBGB, we used to just cheer drunken couples along as they fucked on the floor till the guy shot his load. Then we would all throw beer over them and the girl would be passed along to someone else.

The crowds of people that go out aren't what I imagine as a real New York kind of crowd, but they are. I just live in a time-warp sort of world. I have to get used to New York and to get familiar with it again.

I kind of like it but I can't hang with it. There are the same kind of people here now as in South Beach, a Lakers game (east, west, all the same), a Britney Spears concert, or a shopping mall—a nice one, but if I go into the store the detective is going to follow me around. You have to watch out on the street in New York on the weekends. It's best not to go out on Friday and Saturday, so as to avoid trouble. The sidewalks of the East Village will be crammed with muscular jocks from NYU, the college that has taken over my old neighborhood. These fellows will be drunk and have a rapist kind of mentality, so it's best to side-step them.

The women look very American Psycho-ish. It's also cool to be sexy. The girls around here are sticking out their butts and showing some tit as they walk down Second Avenue to go to the deli. It's all very sexual.

I'm not a party animal type but I'm still having a great time being here again and seeing all this.

On June thirteenth I met Paul Kostabi at his apartment over on Tenth Street. We thought it would be a lucky day. He had loaded a van already with paintings that we normally sell on the Internet at FollinGallery.com. Then we drove over to The Spa, on Thirteenth Street. By now there were too many thirteens for my liking. I felt very uptight, like I was a failure and had done something wrong again.

After we found a parking spot, I went inside the club anyway with Paul to hang the paintings. Then we were supposed to do a quick sound check which we decided to skip. I voted that we take off for the rest of the day and meet back at the club in five hours. Paul and Mike, who were playing with me, agreed that this was a good plan and I hid my bass in the coat check. Then I took a cab back downtown to my hotel.

I had been painting a lot besides everything else and the paint fumes from the spray cans were really fucking up my lungs. I felt like hell. I was in a daze when I got back to The Spa later. Things didn't go smoothly. Right away, they didn't want to let me into the club because I didn't fit the dress code. I had on ripped jeans, sneakers, and a T-shirt. "All right, no problem, you win, okay! I'll go," I protested and simultaneously started moonwalking backwards, looking for any excuse now that I could to get out of doing the book signing.

I didn't even make it a few steps when I was suddenly pushed forward again in a no-nonsense way. It was my old friend Hiroya doing the pushing. Hiroya is a madman Japanese artist who I know from the Chelsea and is someone who took an interest in me and helped me to learn about painting. He's like a modern-day Picasso but is the only old-school artist left on Twenty-third Street.

"Hey! This guy has to be here," Hiroya challenged The Spa's doorman in his thick Japanese accent, assuming a kung fu fighting stance and giving him an impatient look. He then frog-marched me past the confused doorman with evil stubborn determination and rushed me, before I could grasp what was happening, past the rows of salivating human debris lining up down the hallway that leads to the black heart of this decadent playground, where the stage sits, unlit, in the darkness, like an altar in this church of sin with its congregation of sexual deviates.

Instead of panicking I tried to focus somehow on what was going on around me and snap myself to attention. I noticed that the women for the most part were dressed in mail-order fetish gear. At first they looked great to me, very upscale. If you can imagine a bunch of beautiful young college girls dressed in leather and latex and showing a lot of skin, looking for a good time and looking to get laid with a sprinkling of glamorous high-fashion, hottie-type models desperate to get away from fag photographers and the gay male models that they're stuck with at photo shoots all day, and looking for a young college boy with a hard body and a hard dick, or an aging rock star to take home for the evening, this is the place.

LEGEND OF A ROCK STAR

In fact, right away I started feeling like I was the guy here tonight that had the best chance of scoring some pussy, pretty much because I'm Dee Dee Ramone.

Most of the guys seemed to be playing the role of masochists and had permanent erections begging to be attended to but not, not even by a fag, because of the AIDS epidemic in N.Y.C. That's why circle jerks are very popular late at night in the dorms around this area when the clubs close. The drugs of choice here are amphetamines, various date rape drugs, Viagra, Ecstacy, vodka, and tequila squirms, which are tequila cocktails that have live worms in them swimming around with the ice cubes in the glass.

I see people who are waiting around various sections of the club where it's known that they can connect with people of the same sexual preferences, like, say, people who hang around the bathroom are obviously looking for partners to join them in the toilet stalls for sessions of multiple penetration and good old-fashioned cocaine-snorting or a blow job. These kind of things will happen in a place like this.

"What about the book signing?" I questioned the woman from Thunder's Mouth Press, who had been sticking by me trying to keep things organized.

"There's no time for that now, Mr. Ramone," she yelled back at me through the roar of the crowd. There's three parties going on here at the same time. Just follow Hiroya, he's going to bring you to the stage. We're going to have to do the best we can, okay Dee Dee?"

"All right! All right!" I answered her, as all my shallow doubts that I had been harboring, and which were also completely justifiable, intensified.

Now I was completely unprepared and climbing up on to a stage in front of a jaded New York crowd expecting me to do a proper show that lived up to my reputation, if not as the king of punk rockers then as the craziest one.

Dee Dee, Marky, C.J. and Paul Kostabi perform at Book Expo America, May, 2002.

CHAPTER   33

THAT I AM STILL HERE AND
ALIVE MIGHT BE A MIRACLE
VERY LUCKY THAT THINGS
WENT ENDED UP MUCH WORSE
ESPECIALLY AFTER HOW MY LAST
ATTEMPT TO FORFILL MY TOUR
OBLIGATIONS WENT. IT JUST ABOUT
DID ME IN. MENTALLY AND PHYSIC
EVERYBODY WARNED ME NOT TO
THE SEATTLE DATE. THAT TH
WERE DOOMED ..... WE DID
THINK THAT I WAS GOING TO
THEM..... HOW?

WITH NO BAND
TO ME. CONFI
CHUCK OVER
AS POL

CHAPTER THIRTY-
THREE

WHAT
SAID
THE PHONE DURING ONE
LAST CONVERSATIONS
PLAY ALONE FOR EVERY ONE
MY BASS GUITAR
BE HORRIABLE

MIKE, who had played at the Lakeside Lounge with me, was up there with a guitar already and Paul was behind a drum tilt. Oh well, I thought to myself, and went up to the microphone and blurted out a "Hello, ladies and gentlemen, I'm Dee Dee Ramone and this ones called the Blitzkreig Bop."

I had already plugged in a bass guitar that I had found on the stage by the amps but it wasn't mine. It seemed to be somewhat in tune, so taking a chance, I counted "One, two, three, four" into the microphone expecting Paul and Mike to come into the Blitzkreig Bop with me.

"One! Two! Three! Four!" I shouted, turning first red, then purple, and making my bass go *blurrawwaaaawa* as I started the song on the note of A, which is where I think it starts itself.

"Hey, Ho, let's go, hey, ho, let's go," I sang the intro, making accents with my fist into the air like I'd seen the Bay City Rollers do when they used to do their song "Saturday Night," in the early seventies. How stupid I must have looked going through all this spell for nothing. This is how you do it. I don't know any other way, but it was horrible that Paul and Mike didn't come into the song when I counted off.

I immediately stopped playing when I realized what was going on. "Mike," I said turning around on one foot to confront him, "what happened?"

"I thought we were starting off with 'Loud Mouth'," he answered me. "So that's what started playing when you counted one, two, three, four."

"Oh!" I muttered out, a little stunned. *I didn't even realize your amp was on or that you were playing,* I telecommunicated to him amidst the crackle on the stage.

Then I shifted my eyes in the back of my head to see what Paul was doing. "Oh, Paul!" I whispered over in his general direction, still keeping my gaze on the audience as I looked now at Paul, who was behind me, next to my bass amp, surrounded by a borrowed drum set. All the while I was keeping a frozen, detached grin on my face for the audience, so as to be still entertaining them in a professional show-business like manner, much like ventriloquists do.

"What, Dee Dee?" Paul blankly penetrated the barriers of communication back to me as he started to pull the earplugs he uses when he plays live shows out of his ears.

"Oh! That's better," he remarked, quite poker-faced. "I couldn't hear a damn thing with these earplugs in my ears," he said, dangling two orange, foam earplugs from one of the circles attached to one of his antenna-like arms which he then promtly stuffed back into his ears, making it impossible to communicate with him again.

"God! It's really loud in here, Dee Dee," he yelled at me. "When are we going to start the show?" he added. "Are we still going to start with 'Loud Mouth'?"

"Yes! Yes!" I nodded my head frantically to answer him. Then, stepping up to the mike, I crooned, "You're a loud mouth, baby, and you better shut it up," and then counted "One, two, three, four," and went into the song. This time Mike and Paul were ready, but I think that Mike was playing "Blitzkreig Bop."

We did about five more songs and then that was it. One of the songs was called "Horror Hospital." It was a new one, the lyrics to it go:

"They say that I was taking dope and they could prove that I was, I was on the boulevard again. I was lookin' for some drugs. The dope is my only friend I guess It's just because

I feel awful
I feel awful
I feel awful
Horror hospital

After our "set" I ran off the stage and ducked through the crowded dance floor and into the coat-check room in the front area of the club that was also going to be my backstage dressing room, and flung myself on the floor, huffing and puffing and dripping wet with sweat.

There seemed to be a continuous stream of patrons coming and going in and out of the Spa. It was very horny, somehow. There was a hive of people now by my backstage area. They were checking their coats and taking them back to leave. Anybody who came up to the coat-check could see me lying crumpled up, shirtless, all sweaty and exhausted on the floor, and it was obvious that I had just done a show but I wasn't getting a break even to dry off (there also weren't any towels), and people were already starting to harass me and ask me for autographs.

"Hey! That's Dee Dee Ramone," one of the smarties who was leaning over the railing to collect his coat remarked to his over-sexy, slightly tipsy girlfriend.

"Oh yeah, let me see," she said, coming over to get a closer look. When she leaned over the railing to give me a look I was stunned by what I saw before me. This creature was drop-dead gorgeous. She could give Carmen Electra, Nikki Cox, or Jennifer Lopez a run for their money. All of a sudden I could tell that I had been faithful to my wife, who was back home in Los Angeles now, long enough. If this is what I get for being Dee Dee Ramone, then I'll take it, I decided right then and there.

"Hey beautiful," she said directly to me, snapping me back to reality. She was coming on strong, I could tell, this was going to be a full assault by her sexy, South American accent and her I-won't-take-no-for-an-answer way about her that was overwhelming. And that I could not withstand.

She was just too beautiful. What could I do? She was wearing a flimsy halter top and her two tanned, perfectly shaped breasts were practically popping my eyes out. Not backing off, she continued to command more of my attention.

"I thought you were playing here, tonight? I guess I missed you," she said.

"Yeah, the show's over," I answered, her not knowing what to do.

"I've always wanted to fuck you Dee Dee, since I was a little girl. I listened to all the Ramones CDs and I hoped I'd meet you someday. Now my dream can come true, she added excitedly, not caring that she was flipping out her "date," who thought he was going to take her home a few minutes earlier.

Then suddenly in an-all out effort, this South American bombshell exploded and started crawling over the coat-room counter, revealing her award-winning Brazilian butt as the micro-miniskirt that she was wearing hiked up her two brown curvy mounds, which were encased in a pair of brief white panties.

But this Brazilian babe was swiftly rescued from fulfilling her life-long fantasy of spending the night with me by her pissed-off boyfriend, who finally grabbed her by the heels and pulled her back over the coat-check counter, and then angrily ushered her outside into a taxi.

Well, I would have fucked her. To be honest I was at such a confusing time in my life that I needed a quick escape from it. She seemed like the perfect ticket to bliss, but I guess she had just been goofing on me.

Then I noticed that the coat check girl was only wearing a bikini and a pair of high-heeled, go-go dancer boots and she was bending over a bit so that I could get a good look at her ass. She was passable, but

Dee Dee with then girlfriend Connie and Arturo Vega, 1976.

starting to near thirty, and showing a little cellulite along the rims of her bikini bottoms near her thighs. She was thin and her figure was good, but then I noticed that her nose had been broken once and I didn't like the "Jose" tattoo that I could see written over half her left breast. Of course I'm too spoiled to go out with a mean old over-the-hill go-go dancer. I realized a long time ago that these women hate men. Their main mission in life seems to be to punish them.

I like women a lot. Life wouldn't be worth living without them. I couldn't imagine it.

I'm trying to like myself a little more. I'm a typical addict and I won't always be perfect. It's not that I'm too spoiled to be playing in rock and roll bands anymore. It's because I'm trying to be rational about the process of life, because I'm wearing out. I love rock and roll music a lot. I can't imagine life without it, but life is so precious that I have to take care of mine a lot better or it would be disrespectful. I'm writing this on July 4th, Independence Day, 2001. I can still sort of remember playing the Round House in London twenty-five years ago, on July 4, 1976. Wow.

Epilogue

A LOT HAS HAPPENED since I was in New York to do the book signings for *Chelsea Horror Hotel* and to play that chaotic show at the Spa with Paul and Mike. So many things have conspired to turn me away from New York. The twin towers bombing, the terrorist threat, the death of Joey Ramone. The city has lost its appeal for me. I can't imagine wanting to go back there again. For what? What's there for me? The best thing I can do for myself it to completely block out my past and move on with my life. But being a part of the Ramones family makes that pretty difficult. I will always have to pay the price for being me. It hasn't been easy. The current crisis I'm dealing with is that the Ramones have been inducted into the Music Hall of Fame. Quite an honor and one that insures that the Ramones will hold a legendary position in musical history, right there after the Beatles. This is a very nice thing but what comes along with it is scary. Like bringing the Ramones together again.

Marky Ramone called me on January 15, 2002 in Los Angeles from New York, where he still lives in Brooklyn with his high school sweetheart, Marianne Flynn. He had just returned from Japan where he'd been touring again with The Misfits. I'd been thinking of him lately and was hoping that I could speak to him, just the two of us, without the others around. Now he surprised me with a call, which really pleased me. Most of the Ramones crowd doesn't like Marky all that much. They have typecast him as being crazy and dangerous. I don't think Mark is crazy or dangerous at all. I like him very much. If he's crazy, then so am I and so is everyone else I know.

Anyway, I took the call, and this is what happened.

"Deeeeee Deeeee!" Marky announced his presence in that breezy Hollywood way of his.

LEGEND OF A ROCK STAR

"Marky. Hi, good bunny," I answered cheerfully, thrilled that he was calling me. But then I was put on guard by his obvious anger. He was trying to hold it in, but I could tell he was on the verge of insane rage.

I'd been worried about him. When he was in Los Angeles two months earlier he was playing two shows at the Key Club with The Misfits. This seemed like a fine gig for him. The Misfits were doing well. They looked like they were in the process of picking up some of the Ramones' old audience and getting back some of the game they'd had in the 80s. They were selling out shows all over the world. Their leader, Jerry Only, is spectacular on stage and a great bass player. I guess Jerry's the leader because he could probably kill someone with his bare hands.

Playing drums for The Misfits was a solid professional situation for Marky and I was happy for him, but I'd told Barbara that he'd come home from his mini-Euro tour in bad emotional shape. The tour had started early in December; The Misfit's tour that he'd been on when I saw him in L.A. had ended on December 2nd. Marky had flown to Belgium and met up with a local band to do a Paper Clip type tour: twenty-five shows in twenty-seven days. Driving in a van from the tip of Spain to the heel of Italy. A pretty rugged gig, in my opinion. I'd been there, I knew what he was going through. His last show was in Berlin in the bitter cold East German winter, on New Year's Eve. Then back to depressing New York City for a day or two of R&R before heading off to rejoin The Misfits in Toyko for ten shows in ten days.

Marky must feel like killing somebody right now, I thought as I talked to him on the phone. He had to be really worked up. Now that he was back home in his Brooklyn apartment and probably just wanting to chill, instead he had to deal with all his old wounds as a one-time Ramone. Old wounds reopening because the popularity of the Ramones was growing so much that we couldn't get away from each other. Couldn't put it all behind us once and for all. Couldn't start a new life.

Now that the Ramones had been inducted into the Hall of Fame we were expected to play a show together. And to pose for pictures. And to go to the ceremony and party together. We would have to meet in New York around mid-March. I knew how Marky must be feeling. I felt worries, fears, piling up inside of me. I just wanted to have fun now and not to do anything serious. But it's hard to get away with it.

All of this was causing me a lot of anxiety and part of me wanted to run for my life. But it seemed that Marky had come up with his own idea of a solution to our current dilemma.

"Dee Dee," he said, "you and I should play 'Sedated' and 'Blitzkrieg Bop' together with the orchestra at the induction ceremonies."

"You mean without Johnny Ramone?" I asked him.

"Yeah," Mark said.

"Marky—that's insane," I told him. "We can't do that. No way without Johnny."

"Well...I don't know," Mark pondered.

"Trust me, Marky, it can't be done without him."

I could see a whole lot of trouble ahead. We were one big dysfunctional family and it was unnerving. You had to factor in the Ramones' feud with Joey Ramone's brother Mitchell Hyman as an added unattractive bonus. This was a hate-you-to-the-death situation and it also involved Joey's mother Charlotte. I didn't want to have to confront all this unpleasantness, but now that I was talking to my old friend and partner in crime Marky Ramone the road ahead seemed unavoidable.

"We shouldn't take any pictures with Joey's mother," he said, his voice cracking, taking on an even crazier edge. He finished our conversation with a warning that he wasn't negotiating or making any deals.

Shit...I thought to myself when I hung up. I was overcome with a feeling of depression as I realized that Joey's mother and his brother were against the three of us—John, Mark and me—and I couldn't be on friendly terms with them.

I didn't expect a shouting match; I just didn't want to be anywhere near this aggravation. If I did have to be a part of the ceremony, then it would have to be a case of do what I have to do and get the hell out of there. I wasn't about to accommodate everyone's expectations of me. If the scene turned really bad I just might have to run for it.

I thought about Johnny Ramone. I had run into his girlfriend Linda at a new record store in Hollywood a couple of weeks earlier by accident. She spotted me first. I was shocked to see her and started to get nervous. I realized that if she was there then John must be somewhere around. Finally she broke the tension and edged over to me and said, "Hi, Dee Dee," in a natural, friendly way.

We made a little conversation. Then Johnny was suddenly looming over me. He'd seemed to come out of nowhere. He acted happy to see me. We started talking and the tone was friendly, easy. It cheered me up considerably to see him again and to sense the friendliness between us. Johnny is the undisputed leader of the Ramones. He wants it that way, and maybe I should be grateful that someone is overseeing the band's affairs. He told me that an album of old Ramones songs would be coming out in the summer.. They were being covered by some of today's biggest acts—Rob Zombie, The Red Hot Chili Peppers. I wished I could have helped with the record, maybe used one of my new songs like "Sheena," a surf punk piece that sounds like it could have been on "Rocket to Russia."

"Nobody knows about this new album but me," Johnny told me with a big smile.

Well, what about the bands playing with you, Johnny? I thought to myself. They know about it. I think what he meant was that everybody knew about this project but me. But I've already accepted all this stuff. I'm glad that Johnny is handling the business. John has much better taste musically in terms of what we both like and what a Ramones fan would like. We are both loyal to that vision. Neither of us is very experimental and we don't like too much musical change.

I don't think the Ramones—all of us playing together—will ever make another album of new stuff, especially with Joey gone. I don't ever want to go through another round with the music business. And I don't really care if I'm cutting off my nose to spite my face. Then I will be noseless—and so what? Maybe I'm sounding too negative here, but when I left the record store after seeing Johnny again and not exchanging phone numbers or making plans to get together, I still felt very happy. I was glad that I had seen John one more time and that Linda had been so friendly for once.

This is a pretty cool ending, I thought. I felt at peace. But I still couldn't imagine going to the awards ceremonies in New York City. I'm too rebellious. I was thinking that John, who would have to go, could just accept my award for me.

Another big instigator in my making an awards appearance was my publicist at Thunder's Mouth Press, the company that publishes my books. She called me up about the Hall of Fame ceremonies, shortly after Marky's call. We have a good relationship, but my wife is not too fond of her. Barbara's convinced that she is one of my secret girlfriends. I don't have any secret girlfriends, or public ones either, but no one believes me. All I can do is deny everything and keep trying to be my attempt at my perfect self. The publicist only called to try to take advantage of my being in New York to do press or a series of book signings.

"Dee Dee," she said, "I want to come to the party with you and also attend the Hall of Fame induction ceremony. And Neil [Neil Ortenberg, Thunder's Mouth Press's publisher] wants to come, too. Please get us tickets, okay? And my girlfriends—the ones you met at the Spa last time you were here? They want to come, too. Okay, Dee Dee? I need about six tickets."

She put me on a spot. What was I going to do? I realized that I had to do the dreaded thing and call my ex-management, Gary Kurfirst's office, and see what was happening. They still manage the Ramones' affairs. The receptionist, Josh, answered the phone.

"This is Dee Dee Ramone," I said.

"Yeah," Josh drawled insolently. "What do you want?"

I struggled to control my temper. "I was wondering if you could help me with the Hall of Fame awards."

"Here's their number," he said, cutting me off.

It was obvious they weren't going to lift a finger for me. Of course that pissed me off royally. I called the Hall of Fame people, and they were very nice, very polite.

"The tickets are two thousand five hundred each," the woman I was talking to told me. "Don't worry, though. Yours is taken care of. We'll fly you to New York for the day and return the next morning. Okay?"

"Great," I said, wondering how everybody else would get in.

A little later I got a call from Michael, a friend from New York who had just arrived in Los Angeles to interview Johnny Ramone, Phil Spector and to re-interview me for a Ramones documentary. "Can I come over to your apartment with my film crew to do some additional interviewing?" he said.

It was the last thing I needed—more Ramones business abuse. Fuck this, I thought as I reluctantly answered him, "Okay, Michael, come on over. I'll be here. Call me back later."

Goddamnit. Motherfuckers. I raged inside as I hung up the telephone.

LEGEND OF A ROCK STAR

So I submitted to the interview with Michael. He also interviewed Johnny Ramone at his house and at the NAM show, a guitar convention where John was endorsing Mosrite guitars.

When I talked to Marky again he sounded much better than the week before. He wanted to do a Remains tour of California with Barbara and me, but it was more of a nice thought than a reality. He was too busy, and I was so busy I was going nuts. I suffered a lot of grief because of Michael's interview and the Hall of Fame awards. But at the same time, I was elated to be entering the Music Hall of Fame. It feels quite prestigious.

The rumor was that the Ramones would be playing with Eddie Vedder, the singer from Pearl Jam. Okay, I'd be willing to do that, I agreed with myself, as I had no one else to talk it over with. The people from the Hall of Fame in Cleveland were calling me every day to make sure everything was all right. But then suddenly they stopped calling. I think it was because the Ramones' management probably told them not to call me about Ramones business. Shutting me out; it was so typical of them. Then Arturo Vega called me up. He runs the official Ramones' website. He's a real pain in the ass. He told me, and I guess that he would know, that Johnny would never play with the Ramones again. To forget it. No problem, I thought to myself. If the Ramones aren't playing I'm not going. It's too nerve- wracking and upsetting.

"Dee Dee, Dee Dee," Arturo nagged in that whiney Mexican accent of his. "You have to come to New York early and stay at my loft for two weeks. You can crash on the couch. Even though marijuana is eight hundred dollars an ounce in New York you'll be expected to pass around every joint you roll to my numerous guests who will be visiting at all hours, so you'll never have any privacy. I'm making this offer so you can paint non-stop while you're here."

"Hold it, hold it, Arturo, okay? I'm not going if the Ramones aren't playing.

"Dee Dee, listen to me," Arturo continued, ignoring my protests, "You have to write me a letter on how you feel about being in the Hall of Fame, and I need the lyrics to these Ramone songs—'Blitzkrieg Bop,' 'I Don't Wanna Walk Around With You,' 'Today Your Love, Tomorrow the World,' 'Poison Heart Glue,' 'Rockaway Beach' and '53rd and 3rd'."

"No! No! No way!" I shouted, feeling my face turning purple, like I was on the verge of a nervous breakdown. "I'm sick and tired of you giving me orders. You never do shit for me. No, I won't do it!" I screamed into the receiver and then hung up.

A few minutes later the phone rang again. I picked it up immediately, hoping it was Arturo and I could apologize.

"Chicken? . . . Chicken beak boy . . ." It was Marky's friendly voice greeting me. "How you doin'?"

"Marky, Marky. Jesus Christ, good bunny. You wouldn't believe what's going on here."

"Oh yes I would," he said. "It's been pretty wild here in New York. Arturo called."

"I just got off the phone with him."

"He wants me to write down how I feel about being inducted into the Hall." Marky groaned. "That guy always wants something. I mean, what the hell do you and I have to do with the official Ramones fucking website?"

Marky told me that he'd talked to John and John said that he refused to play the Hall of Fame as a tribute to Joey Ramone. He said that he loved the Ramones too much to insult their memory by playing in a watered down version of the band without the original lead singer.

"Hey, Dee Dee," Marky continued, "How about you and me playing some shows together with the Remains [?]."

"I can't," I said. "No bass player."

Des, who was playing with Mark and Jerry in The Misfits, had said that he might play with me. We could have rehearsed in California and I would have been willing to switch over to bass so that he could play guitar, but then he decided he was too busy playing with The Misfits. I told him I understood. I could certainly relate to being too overworked to take on anything else. I couldn't play with Barbara anymore. We had no time to rehearse, she had her own life now, and it didn't seem likely that I'd be finding anyone else. Stephen , Anthony, and Chris, who I play with in L.A., wouldn't play with Marky. There was nothing I could do but tell my old friend no. I didn't plan to play in New York again ever, and I'd already told Mark that a million times.

I said, "Mark, if we ever do get to play again it has to be here in California."

We said our goodbyes and then hung up.

LEGEND OF A ROCK STAR

My next call came about ten minutes later. "Hi, Dee Dee." The voice was familiar, though I couldn't place it. "It's Chris, from Artist World Wide," the voice continued quickly. "I just spoke to Marky Ramone. He told me you and Barbara want to come to New York and play Irving Plaza and a few dates around the city while you're here."

I can't believe this, I thought.

"No, Chris," I said. "I told Marky I never want to play New York again. I don't have a band, and even if I did have a band it would have to happen in California, after the Awards ceremonies. And anyway, I don't even know if I'm going to the Hall of Fame or not now. It looks like I won't. If I don't have the plane ticket to New York, then there's no way I'm going. I can't afford it.

Chuck was surprisingly calm. "It's okay, Dee Dee. "We'll work out something." And then he hung up.

The next Hall of Fame phone call came from the person who was in charge of the Hall of Fame Museum in Cleveland. They had already asked me for some personal items to exhibit and I'd told them I didn't have anything left from the old days. This person asked me if it was okay to get in touch with my mother or some other family member. I said, Sure, and good luck. Finally, this guy told me enthusiastically that he was sending someone over to my apartment in Hollywood to pick up five paintings that I had done of the Ramones. All the while he was insisting that the Ramones would have to play a show..

A week later, this same guy called me and said in haughty tones, "I don't want you to think I've been neglecting you."

"Well, call me back when you have more time," I rudely interrupted him. And then I hung up on him.

Next, the music director for the BBC called me from London. He was pretty snooty, too, and he also put me off.

"I have personal problems," I told him. "I'm not going to attend the Hall of Fame ceremony."

He didn't like that. He was adamant about the Ramones playing for the ceremony.

"It won't happen," I said. "I'd be willing to play but no one else from the Ramones will do it."

"Well, that doesn't seem right," he rebutted.

"You need to call Gary Kurfirst," I said. "He's in the charge of the

Ramones' affairs, you know. You have to call Gary," I said. "Okay?" Then I hung up on him.

I was so busy working on paintings that these phone calls were getting tiring.

I decided that I'd better call Ira Herzog after hearing from the BBC guy and see what he thought about all this.

"Everybody's buggin' me about the Hall of Fame thing," I told him when I got him on the line. "Everybody says we've got to play. It's making me miserable."

"Okay, okay," Ira said. "Just relax. I'm hearing all sorts of miserable things about this event. I'm going to have to step in. Call me back Monday, okay?"

"Sure, Ira," I said, feeling a little better.

On Monday, Gary Kurfirst's assistant called me. She sounded just like Faye at Eagle Rock in London, which wasn't the greatest omen in the world. "Gary would like to speak to you," she said. A moment later he came on.

"Dee Dee," he said, "congratulations on getting into the Hall of Fame. You were always something very, very special, and now you're certified as a bonafide rock-and-roll legend. You deserve it. I hope to see you at the Awards."

"Oh, you will." It was exciting hearing from Gary. I felt pretty happy. I hadn't spoken to Gary in at least ten years. It might be fun to meet up again with all my old cohorts—Ira, Gary, John, Marky. Sort of like a family reunion, I beamed to myself.

The next family member to call me was the mysterious Danny Fields. Danny was the Ramones first manager and also the manager for the Stooges. He had also been on the Rock-and-Roll Hall of Fame committee for the last ten years. I hadn't seen or spoken to him since 1980. I had no idea where Danny was living. Maybe a beach community in Long Island or somewhere like that. I knew for a fact that Danny, like my mother Trautel, had hidden his whereabouts from me. Well, if Danny didn't want me to visit him it was okay, but it was uplifting to have him come to my apartment. It was good to see him again.

He had gotten my phone number from Arturo Vegas and was in Los Angeles for the funeral of one of his old friends, Lance Loud.

"You mean Lance died?" I inquired.

LEGEND OF A ROCK STAR

"Yeah, Douglas," Danny answered me in an accusing manner with an edge of annoyance toning his voice, "Usually when there's a funeral it's because someone died."

I told him my address about a dozen times. He was writing it down and kept getting it wrong. Somehow he managed to find the apartment. He looked really good. I don't know how old he is—at least sixty—but he carried the years well and looked much younger.

He was writing a book about Joey Ramone and wanted to know if he could interview me. I said okay. We then switched to the subject of the Hall of Fame ceremonies. "Don't be a troublemaker," Danny warned me, wagging his finger. "I don't want it just to be Charlotte and Mitchell up there on that stage. Do you understand me? Huh?"

His 'huh?' was intended to snap me out of the daze I was in, my defense against all the stress I was feeling.

"Danny, can I bring Beverly and Trautel?"

"Only if you kill yourself first Dee Dee," Danny parried my answer impatiently. Danny got up from my living room couch and angrily swept the Jack Daniels and coke—his fourth in forty-five minutes—off the coffee table and drunkenly stormed out of my apartment.

"You better be there, man," he yelled at me, turning around to give me one last dirty look and then practically slammed the door off its hinges as he exited to the street.

Minutes later, another phone call.

"Hi, Dee Dee. Can you guess who this is? It's Daniel Rey. Do you remember me?"

Daniel was my old song writing partner in the Ramones. He also produced a lot of the albums for us. When people ask me about him, I say that he was sneaky but he was a good guy, and that the Ramones couldn't have existed without him. Strangely enough, before the phone rang I had just been talking about him with my wife Barbara. "I'll bet that damn fool's probably hiding from me now that Marky wants to play with him and me." Daniel would never play with me before. He was definitely Joey's man. I can't argue with that. After Joey died, his brother Mitch told Daniel not to play with me at Spa the last time I was in New York and to keep mixing Joey's solo album instead. Okay. I don't know how Daniel managed to make that record but he did, and it sounds really good. Many of the songs I wrote, like "Pet Cemetery," would never have come out as good if Daniel hadn't helped me with the writing. But he did it for the Ramones. I never dreamed he would ask me to play a show with him, not in a million years. He had always been a gentleman, but he chose his sides.

So when he called I was quite taken aback. He and Marky wanted me to play Spa with them and then do a tour in Brazil. I told Daniel I couldn't do it.

"I'm really sorry," I told him. "It's not because I don't love you guys. I do. But I have too much to think about right now."

As I talked to Daniel, I came to a decision. I would give Chuck and Chris a call and get some shows for my own band and play right here in L.A

When I hung up the phone, my eyes were rolling around in my head like the moving parts in a slot machine. I gave a long sigh of anguish.

Next, Mary Lambert came over with Gary Kurfirst to look at my paintings and to start a documentary on what I'm doing. If I did decide to go to the Hall of Fame I had already come to the conclusion that I couldn't take Barbara with me. We had reached the point where we argued every day and I needed a break. I thought that I might take Mary with me. She could get a lot of good footage on Paul's and my art projects in New York. Gary, though, is in charge and he seemed to have other ideas. He felt that it made more sense for me to go with Barbara. A nice gesture on his part—but how could he possibly know what it would be like for us to travel together the way things were? It would be too difficult for me. If I did attend the Hall of Fame awards, it would be like going into battle and I would need my wits about me. The main thing would be to keep myself in control and watch my back; it wouldn't exactly be a holiday.

On an even scarier note, if I stayed in L.A. for the summer it might be suicidal. The sister of the beautiful Swedish girl I met last year in Stockholm and never thought I'd see again had moved here to L.A. to attend college. I bumped into her on the street in Hollywood and she told me that her sister was coming to visit in July.

"Oh, great," I answered, cracking a sort of stupid smile out of myself somehow. Well, I guess that's something to look forward to.

LEGEND OF A ROCK STAR

• • •

I guess I'm still the same old Dee Dee. In a lot of ways, I'm still like a street kid and always will be. All I need is a city to roam around in and I'm okay.

I like how things are for me now. Getting to walk around Hollywood Boulevard with nothing to do. It's fun just being myself. I was in one of the world's best rock and roll bands. And one of the toughest ones. It took me, Joey, John, Tommy, and Marky to do it. We all paid a price for it. It was a lot. The Ramones accomplished a lot. No one can deny that. We did what we did together. It couldn't have happened if any of these people had not been in their predestined roles.

I just never thought it would mean so much.

It's not too bad being an old rock and roll star. It's like having a tear in your eye and a smile on your face at the same time.

Dee Dee Ramone, Pioneer Punk R...

By JON PARELES

Douglas Glenn Colvin, better known as Dee Dee Ramone, the founding bassist and songwriter of the pioneering punk band the Ramones, died on Wednesday in Los Angeles of an apparent heroin overdose. He was 50, and lived in Hollywood.

The Los Angeles County Coroner's Office said that his wife, Barbara, came home and found him unconscious on a couch with drug paraphernalia nearby. A rescue team confirmed that he was dead at 8:40 p.m. Capt. David Campbell of the

Closest thing Ra...

▶ RAMONE
From Page D1

than one of the group's pivotal songwriters: He epitomized its punk spirit. Joey, who died of lymphoma last April, played the sweet dweeb singer, Johnny adopted the role of stalwart guitarist, and Tommy and Marky did their duty as the self-effacing drummers. Dee Dee (real name Douglas Glenn Colvin) was hell on wheels, a rakish, goofball presence with a pixie's face and a demented pirate's heart. Punk girls loved his

told MTV News on Thur... "one of the great star bassists time — the model for all the bassists after him." Anyone d... ing that has only to check moves of Green Day's Mike ... or the Donnas' Donna F.

Dee Dee's death came at a ... when his life was, by his erratic standards, going well longtime heroin habit seemed to be in remission. He playing shows again, includi... scheduled appearance at Francisco's Pound SF tor... and planned to release a liv... here in the fall.

Rolling Stone

The Ramones Dark Heart

Bassist Dee Dee Ramone dead a... forty-nine from a drug overdos...

DEE DEE RAMONE WAS the dark side of the Ramones. If lead singer Joey

counted off the songs with trademark "One, two, three, fo... shout, but he was also the one w...

Punk Pioneer...

By Glenn Gamboa
STAFF WRITER

Dee Dee Ramone, the bass-playing co-founder of punk rock pioneers The Ramones, was found dead by his wife at their Hollywood home Wednesday night. The Los Angeles County Coroner's Office is investigating the death as an apparent drug overdose, after discovering drug paraphernalia, including a syringe on the kitchen counter He was 49.

His death comes as Ramone, born Douglas Glenn Colvin in Fort Lee, Va., had just begun to blossom into a rock-and-roll Renaissance man, with projects as an artist and fiction writer showing promise along with his ongoing music career.

giore, owner o... Hollywood age... mone. "I saw h... seemed in grea... seemed fine w... sober for years... thing. I just dor...

After a few to... reer was in the ... paintings are s... Pisa, Italy, and ... mand around t... "Chelsea Horro... seen as a succes... ed another nov... Press called "Le... he was set to p...

...EE from A7

thank myself, and give...

Ramone-ness from A to De...

By JIM FARBER
DAILY NEWS MUSIC CRITIC

Rock stars dream themselves up. They're self-conscious creatures, conceived in the neediness of youth, fired by imagination and ambition to create the looming image we all buy into once they've gained fame.

Every so often, though, there trundles by a rock star who doesn't seem to have been developed or tweaked at all, someone who seems to have arisen through spontaneous combustion.

These are what we call naturals. One of them was Dee Dee Ramone, who died, apparently of a drug overdose, in his Hollywood home last week at 49.

While the other Ramones crafted their cartoonish characters through larva and design, Dee Dee seemed like a Ramone by divine right. If his bandmates became Ramones, Dee Dee seemed to have had Ramone-ness thrust upon him — or at birth. No wonder fans considered him to be the heart of the group, the guy best perched to kick off each volley of riffs with his primal Queens cheer: "One, two, tree, faw!"

In youth, Dee Dee was also the band's gangly sex symbol, a rough-trade hustler type, exuding the danger and charm of an animal.

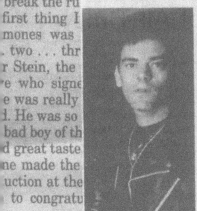

THE NATURAL: Dee Dee, right, with (from L) fellow Ramones Johnny, Joey and Marky

LIZ HAFALIA / The Chronicle

Dee Dee Ramone, who was t... appear at Pound SF tonight, died Wednesday.

had to a heartthrob

...ed an album, ...est," and he had ...is fifth book. His ... stab at litera-... "Chelsea Horror ...'s Mouth Press, ... a cult following ...obituary

band in 1989 but returned to write several tracks for the Ramones' final studio album, 1995's "Adios Amigos." He reunited with his faux brethren in 1997 for a Hollywood Palladium show and appeared with the Ramones a fi...

...mones as a whole when... MTV, "It's hard, you k... hard to hear about the... and finally realize — y... 'They're gone.'"

For fans in mourn... Dee Dee's death... e end of an era... mones now only e... pe and a continu... It's simply a lo... me, for rock's wa... it.

Neva Chonin at... onicle.com.

He was epitome of punk spirit

Star bassist ... Dee Ramone ... edgy lyricist

By Neva Chonin
CHRONICLE POP MUSIC CRIT...

...TO SEE GO

AP File Photo

... Ramone, co-founder of ... nones, had been branching

...e Dies

lived as fast as he pla... ut he was too tough to ... oung.

il he apparently overd... ntally at his Hollyw... Wednesday night, Dee ... e, 49, was a consum... list who transformed ... ence into punch-drunk ... hilarious poetry. The

The 50 Greatest Bands of All Time

The band is back. During the past year or so, the pop world has completed a cycle that began the mid-1990s. Back then, with grunge flannel on Macy's mannequins, the band model seemed a bit tired. Rappers, dancing teens, and DJs took ovet the pop charts, MTV, and magazines. Then, gradually, bands crept back. Groups like Creed, Incubus!, System of a Down, and, most notably, Staind and Linkin Park have spent serious time in the Top 10. Once again, the band dynamic—people interacting as musicians, friends, enemies, or fellow drug-addled lunatics—is capturing our imagination. So here's our look at 50 great bands from the 1960s forward. To qualify, these groups had to have a roof-raising, history-changing sound, presence, or hairstyle. They also had to clearly influence today's music in undeniable ways. Finally, they had to be bands that we care about deeply. We hope you will, too.

1

THE BEATLES

With John Lennon's legacy turned into an advertising fire sale, with Paul McCartney's 400 silly-ass love songs to wife Linda, with legions of babyboom Beatlemaniacs still pattering on about real music, why do these blokes remain so beloved? And why are they Spin's No. 1 band, more than 30 years after their last proper album? Well, check this scenario: Imagine if, over the course of about five years, 'N Sync (circa 'Bye Bye Bye) evolved into Radiohead (circa The Bends), into the Chemical Brothers (circa Exit Planet Dusty) and into Nirvana (circa In Utero). That was the Beatles from, say, 1964 to 1969. Their music didn't quite revolutionize the planet, but it blew up the world of pop culture and basically created the rock band statutes that all musical youth end up following, sooner or later. (For instance, they're the reason your favorite band is so annoyingly anxious to experiment. with its "sound.") They also made shaggy hair, acid-as-inspiration, and sampling (via the Mellotron) almost acceptable. And, oh yeah, they managed to break up before they started to suck (which cannot be said of most of their peers). After they disbanded, Lennon angrily sang, "I don't believe in Beatles," but the rest of us better recognize. P.S.: R.I.P., George. CHARLES AARON

Influenced: Beastie Boys, Blur, Oasis, the Chemical Brothers, Steve Earle, the Flaming Lips, Elliott Smith, Aimee Mann, Elvis Costello, Public Enemy, De La Soul, Jimi Hendrix, all boy bands—oh, forget it, everyone!
Classic albums: Revolver (Capitol, 1966) and Sgt. Pepper's Lonely Hearts Ciub Band (Capitol, 1967)

2

RAMONES

Punk exists because of the false assumption that the Ramones can be imitated. "1-2-3-4!" Three chords. "Second verse, same as the first." Technically speaking, it's simple. Legend has it that in every city where the Ramones played in support of their 1976 debut, a handful of punk kids started up bands, thinking that they could do it, too. But the Ramones' loud fast style masked a pop genius. Slow their tempos, and you've got Beach Boys melodies. Replace lyrics about sniffin' glue and eating refried beans, and you've got the Ronettes. Give everyone matching leather jackets, and you've got the punk rock Beatles. Just four lads from Queens who birthed thousands of bands, then blew each one away. Like sharks, they didn't evolve—they didn't need to. MARC SPITZ

TRIBUTE

One week before Dee Dee's death, Johnny Ramone spoke to *Rolling Stone* about his band's legacy. A week after his death, Johnny reflected on his former bandmate.

How did you get involved with the upcoming Ramones tribute album?

I was approached about it and I said, "Yeah I'll be involved, but I have to have full say." They said, "Yeah fine." So I said, "I can get Eddie Vedder, I can get Rob Zombie, and I can get the Chili Peppers and Marilyn Manson and Metallica." I told them right away who I could get, and they said, "Whoa, that's great, fine." So that's how it developed.

I heard you encouraged bands to come up with drastically different takes than the originals.

I tried whenever possible. Some bands are going to be more Ramones-like, but with other people I said, "Just try to pretend you wrote the song and you never even heard the Ramones' version." Rob Zombie's "Blitzkrieg Bop." Manson's "The KKK Took My Baby Away," those are pretty bizarre. You're going to have to hear them. I can't describe it. Rob Zombie sounds like Zombie doing "Blitzkrieg Bop." It doesn't resemble the same song. Eddie Vedder's version of "I Believe in Miracles" sounds like the version I wish we would have done. It's just a punk version. We were holding back. We were trying to make it commercial and this and that, and Eddie just did a punk version of it and sings it great. It's what we would have done if somebody wasn't saying, "It's got to be this speed—we've got to get to the click track and measure the right speed." They were looking at it as a single and doing it like that. The Pretenders' version of "Something to Believe In" is great. I never liked the song, but whatever they did to it is great.

Are you working on any other projects right now?

This is enough work. I hope I'm not involved in any more projects.

Talk about Dee Dee and his contributions to the Ramones.

Dee Dee was a very unique character, the most influential punk-rock bassist. He set the standard that all punk rock bassists look to. [His songs] weren't like anything else, just crazy, crazy stuff—like "Highest Trails of Above" on the *Subterranean Jungle* album, even "53rd and 3rd" and things like that. Just everything, the whole structure of the song, the whole lyrical content, I don't know of anything else like it. He was a great lyricist. I'd write something like, say, "Wart Hog," and I'd give it to Dee Dee and go, "Here's a song called 'Wart Hog.'" And he'd have the lyrics down and he'd just open up his book and just start singing a page out of his book of lyrics. He was really prolific as far as coming up with the lyrics constantly, and I think he influenced every bassist who came to see him play.

Dee Dee continued writing songs for the Ramones right until the end, the final album. I think he might have written about six songs for the Ramones after he left. His songs were always my favorites. Anything I co-wrote, I co-wrote with Dee Dee.

Had you been in touch with him recently, and did you have any sense he was having problems?

I saw Dee Dee about two weeks before it happened. I saw him on Hollywood Boulevard. We had spoken a few times. We went out for lunch before the Rock and Roll Hall of Fame [induction ceremony, in March] and I convinced him to go to it. I ran into him a couple times at Amoeba Records [in Los Angeles]. We would see each other here and there. As far as I knew everything was fine, and I didn't know anything was wrong. I'm starting now to look into it a little bit and see if anyone else knows anything. I'm trying to speak to people who were a little closer. I've been working on that for the past couple of days. Of course, there were different periods of time where you could have expected something like this to happen, but Dee Dee was always a survivor and so it came as a shock.

Colin Devenish, June 24, 2002

✝ ✝ ✝

The first time I met Dee Dee was by Birchwood Towers in Forest Hills, Queens. I was 17, and Johnny and I were checking out this new kid who had just moved into the neighborhood. We found out that Doug Colvin, just like us, was into music and was a musician. He got us all excited when he started talking about the Vox "Super Beatle" amplifier that he had in his bedroom. We did not know anyone in the neighborhood who had such a magnificent amp. Somehow, we never got to see this piece of equipment of his but we did become acquainted with one of the most lovable, unique, and imaginative individuals we had ever met.

Dee Dee was the romantic one in the Ramones—he was the poet. He was also one of the major architects of punk rock. His songs set the rules and made the blueprint. I had never heard songs like the ones he wrote—they were totally original and powerful.

He knew how good he was and he must have been frustrated by his mistaken impression that people did not fully appreciate his gift. The people who knew these things knew what a genius he was. We were in awe of his gifts.

For a while in the mid-seventies, Dee Dee and I shared an apartment on the Lower East Side. It was somewhat of an odd-couple situation. I was somewhat on the practical side and Dee Dee was quite restless and energetic. He thought it was amazing that I could cook and feed myself, even though I was only making hamburgers and scrambled eggs.

Even then he had plans to be a writer—his idols were Hunter S. Thompson and William Burroughs. He felt we had something in common because we had both grown up in Europe, and he wanted us to collaborate on a book about our origins.

Dee Dee was loved by so many people because of his unpretentious and friendly personality. It is so sad to have such a treasured person taken from us at such a young age. We are truly fortunate to be left with the bounty of his works. And feel blessed to have been lucky enough to have known him.

Tommy Ramone, June 2002

† † †

I met Dee Dee at Arturo's in 1989 or 1990. He was wearing a suit and tie and said he'd quit drugs.

Straight off, we got along. He gave me an idea for a logo for my band, Youth Gone Mad, that Arturo was designing for me in exchange for Kostabi art. "A safety pin going through the globe, so this way the world will be a safe place." This was the beginning of our relationship. I used the logo and always credited Dee Dee. He felt I used him but all the time he wanted to "help" people. He felt like he would always come to the rescue and aid of people who were down and out, which he actually did. A couple years later, about 1992, Dee Dee was doing rap music. He would call me at Kostabi World and play me the mixes. I would pump them through the entire building sound system on speakerphone because I wasn't patient enough to listen to an hour of mixes, so I would leave the speakerphone on and do other work. This was actually some of his best work, I think. "EMERGENCY calling Mr. Dee Dee!"

I never hero-worshipped the guy and never really was into the Ramones. I never saw the Ramones with Dee Dee in the band. I was more into groups like the Germs and Weirdos. I saw them a few times with C.J. on Bass because I was an art dealer and was always invited by

Arturo to the local shows because then he could pay me for paintings by Mark Kostabi that he bought. "Here's another thousand dollars direct from the Ramones' money-making machine, be back in fifteen minutes with another." This was at the Ritz.

A few years later, I met Joey Ramone's mom at an art expo in New York. Her gallery was called Gallery Ramona and she was showing an artist named Ramana. Somehow we got to talking and she said her son is a rock star named Joey Ramone.

A month later, they were eating at a café on Nineth Street and I re-introduced myself to Joey's mom and she said, "This is my son Joey." We got along fine and Joey said to call him and maybe we could write some songs because he had heard of Youth Gone Mad and there was one song in particular he enjoyed, "Peanut Butter Sandwich." We wrote words for it and changed the name to "Meatball Sandwich."

Joey told me he was looking for "new blood to work with," and wanted "a new sound similar to the early Rolling Stones." I would sit for hours at Joey's house and write New/Old songs with him. "Brick Wall" was good and "Pelican Pie" was nice, too.

This had to be about 1995. I started a group called Psychotica and had no more time for Joey because things were starting to happen for the band. Psychotica and the Ramones ended up touring one summer in Lollapalooza 1996 with Metallica.

I don't know how this happened, but Joey called and wanted Mark Kostabi to do the last Ramones CD cover design for *Adios Amigos*. I spoke to the manager Gary Kurfirst and struck up a deal and delivered a painting with two dinosaurs wearing pointed hats. Gary wanted to change the pointed hats to sombreros; I said that would be fine. He told me not to tell the band but it was "supposed to be Johnny and Joey as dinosaurs." Apparently, Johnny and Joey completely hated the cover but Gary pushed it through somehow because Ramones were impossible to deal with.

Around this time I was also helping run Posh Boy Records with my friend Robbie Fields. A&R and producing was my position. In between Psychotica sessions I would be flying off to L.A. to produce OC punk bands and to Germany to try and get the latest act together for Posh Boy. Robbie and I were in front of CBGB one night for some reason and we ran into Dee Dee and I believe he was married or about to be to a very young Barbara Zampini. He said he had some demos to listen to and maybe Posh Boy could release them. We went to this house on Thirty-fourth Street and listened, but Robbie was too distracted with the young Barbara and the pit bull wanted to bite my head off. We left.

Dee Dee called, he heard I was painting and wanted to collaborate on some paintings. He gifted me a giant canvas of *Chelsea Horror Hotel*, a book he was writing. I accepted the piece mainly because he was moving upstate and didn't have room for it. In the next few months he would come to the city, and we recorded songs for Youth Gone Mad because he really liked the band and wanted to make a full-length CD and tour with me. He said he liked the BIG sound of Psychotica and Youth Gone Mad and wanted to be involved.

We produced about three hundred collaborative paintings and sold them all. When he would give me solo paintings Heidi Follin, of Follin Gallery, tried to sell them as fine art, but quickly discovered a huge market for Ramones fans that could afford the more illustrious work. Eventually his work became stronger and stronger and we produced solo exhibitions for him that he was very insecure about. He always wanted the "team" (Paul Kostabi/Dee Dee Ramone). I guess it felt more like a band to him.

The solo work traded for about three hundred dollars each and I would split the money with Dee Dee, as we were operating under the name Follin Gallery. At this time, Arturo was becoming jealous and wouldn't join the "punk rock art group" that Dee Dee so wanted to be the next big thing.

Dee Dee and I spoke every day, up until his unfortunate and abrupt passing, about the future and all we had done in such a short time and how much we had planned.

All was well that morning; I DON'T KNOW WHAT HAPPENED!

I produced a few singles for him and, yes, we finally did get the full-length Youth Gone Mad CD he always wanted finished. I hired his last and best drummer, Tony Mann, for the drum work and it will be released by the end of 2002 on Trend Is Dead records. An appropriate label title for the end of an era.

Dee Dee was loved by many from afar, yes. But the people closest to him always hustled him and took advantage of him. It was sad. He knew this and it bothered him. I am sure that he even thought that Heidi and I were hustling him, too, at times. We were building a strong future; we bought land together and were planning on building retirement homes in the hills of Southern California.

R.I.P. Douglas, we love you.

Paul Kostabi

✝ ✝ ✝

A Letter To Dee Dee

Dee Dee,

I don't even know where to begin. I have lost a very good friend and that makes me very sad. There have been so many times when I have wanted to pick up the phone just to say "Hi" and talk about nothing, make plans to go record shopping, go to Melrose, go to the art store, just drive around doing nothing or eat lunch at Swingers to check out the hot waitresses. I will really miss those times and I already do. I will never forget how generous you were with your time and your friendship. I am a huge fan of the Ramones who became a very good friend of a Ramone. On many occasions you even called me your best friend, even when I wasn't around! That meant a lot to me and it always will. I remember you saying one day that since I didn't have a family anymore we could be each other's family. I thought that was really cool.

About twelve years ago, long before we became friends and after you quit the Ramones, I ran into you in front of the Space at Chase in Manhattan. Johnny Thunders had just died and you were walking around the Village, just hanging out. You stopped in front of the club and we started to talk about music or the show you had just played with your post-Ramones rock band. You were really nice to stop and talk to my

201

LEGEND OF A ROCK STAR

friends and I as we waited for the False Prophets to play. We were having a great time until some stupid squatter punk, who happened to be a real popular guy on the Lower East Side scene and was revered as some type of squatter punk hero, opened his big mouth and said something to the effect of "Stiv Bators hit by a bus, Johnny Thunders dies . . . these things always happen in threes, who's next?" and he looked right at you. Your smile turned into a frown and you walked away. I felt really bad. That guy was just a fucking creep. We wanted to tell you we were sorry, but you were already gone.

I never told you that story as I felt it wasn't worth repeating until now. They were your friends and you were sad when they were gone. You were my friend and I am sad you are gone, but your spirit will always live on, as will theirs.

Gabba Gabba Good-bye,

A.P.

✝ ✝ ✝

Dee Dee was one of a kind.
Innocent and street wise.
A fearless talent with a pure heart.
He was the soul of the Ramones and the prototype for the entire punk rock scene.

Daniel Rey, producer and co-songwriter with the Ramones

✝ ✝ ✝

Dee Dee was the best punk. Once, in 1977, when Talking Heads were supporting the Ramones on a tour of Europe, the Ramones blew out the power to an entire quarter of the city of Marseilles during their sound check. The police were called to disperse the upset fans and the gig was cancelled. We went back to our hotel in the Old Port, where we ran into Dee Dee, who wanted to take a walk around the city. So, we joined him. Dee Dee revealed to us that he wished his band would get out and see the sights more, but that they only wanted to stay in their hotel and watch TV or go to McDonald's.

So we walked and walked around Marseilles, window shopping and stopping in cafés for beer or coffee. Dee Dee was happy to have a night off and so were we. He seemed very comfortable walking, considering he had recently been stabbed in the ass by his jealous girlfriend. We repeated our walks with Dee Dee in Amsterdam and London.

Once, when the tour bus was headed back to London after a gig in Penzance, the tour manager arranged for us to make a stop at Stonehenge. Johnny Ramone was annoyed and had no interest in stopping to see "a bunch of old rocks!" But Dee Dee said, "No, Johnny, I want to see them." This was in the days when you could still walk up and touch the stones, before the fence was built around them. Dee Dee and the members of Talking Heads visited Stonehenge while the rest of the Ramones stayed on the bus.

We always felt close to Dee Dee. He had a noble heart. It was a pleasure to have him sit at our table when, twenty-five years later, we were all inducted into the Rock and Roll Hall of Fame. After the ceremony, he gave his award to the man who had managed both of our bands, Gary Kurfirst. He gave the tie he wore that night to our son Egan.

Shortly after that, we played a show for Publisher's Group West at Roseland in New York City with Tom Tom Club and Dee Dee's new band. Dee Dee was rocking so hard and sounded so good to us that it seemed he was going to burn up our psyches all over again. We were very moved when he was joined onstage by Marky Ramone and C.J. Ramone.

The news of Dee Dee's death was terribly saddening to us. We had hoped that with his new band and his new careers as both an author and a painter he would become the Renaissance Man of Punk. If only he could have resisted the temptation to take that one last hit. We always believed that Dee Dee was the best punk and we always will.

Chris Frantz and Tina Weymouth

† † †

Eddie Vedder's Speech at Rock and Roll Hall of Fame

Good evening. Hey. Ho. Let's go. Y'know, if it weren't for Johnny Ramone, I would have come here not knowing who Brenda Lee was. But that's part of the story you'll get in a bit. And yeah, I do have a Mohawk. No, I didn't get it to pose up here as a punk rocker for this exalted occasion. It actually stems from my frustration with world events and bombings and things like that. I took it out on my own hair. Sometimes you feel powerless and you do sometimes silly things.

Two days after it was done, back in November, I walked in a shop to buy Christmas gifts and I was accused of shoplifting. So even though the Ramones are being inducted into the Hall of Fame, it doesn't mean punk rockers, or looking like a punk rocker, has become respectable.

The Ramones didn't need Mohawks to be punk. They never had one. I don't think anyone in the band ever had one. They were visually aggressive. They were four working-class construction worker delinquents from Forest Hills, Queens who were armed with two-minute songs that they rattled off like machine-gun fire. It was enough to change the earth's revolution, or at least the music of the time. It was an assault. Someone asked Johnny Ramone once why the songs were so short. He said, "They're actually fairly long songs played very, very quickly."

First time I saw the Ramones I was pretty young. Before the show even started, I was trying to get closer and closer and got up to the stage. I got up there packed and ready and even a little bit nervous. The crowd was intense, the look of the crowd. Outcasts one and all. They were hardcore punkers with spikes on their jackets, chains on their boots. Skinheads, horror film fans, nerds and geeks and outcasts, they were all ready to get out all of their aggression in the next hour and fifteen minutes. As I was getting closer I saw something really strange about the microphone stand in the middle. It was about ten feet high. There was something really strange about that. I saw a roadie put the set list down. He stood up and he was half the size of the microphone stand. I thought, "Who the fuck is going to sing at that microphone stand?" It was very unsettling. Then looking at the amount of amps that they had symmetrically placed at either side, and knowing that there was a huge amount of volume that was going to come out of that, it was very unsettling. Then the lights go out and they start playing "The Good, the Bad, and the Ugly." The crowd starts getting into third and fourth gear. Then they come out. One-two-three-four! Into the first song. All hell broke loose. It was complete chaos. The guy with the boots and the chains . . . all of a sudden they were right in front of your face, swinging by. It was terribly frightening and totally blissful at the same time.

I think of the amount of intensity in that show and in that one night, and then I think of how many times that happened. The Ramones played 2,269 shows. J. Lo's got a lot of catching up to do!

Speaking of J. Lo, disco was huge in the seventies. Disco took over the clubs and the airwaves, along with the indulgent guitar solos and seven-minute songs that were the musical landscape of 1976. The Ramones made a record in 1977. There's a black and white photo of four guys in leather jackets all with the same last name, Converse shoes, and jeans standing against a brick wall. This became a beacon for anyone who ever wanted to be in a band, those disenfranchised by the dynasties of giant rock bands.

They obliterated the mystique of what it was to play in a band. You didn't have to know scales. With the knowledge of two-bar chords, you could play along with their records. That's what people did. They sat in front of their parents' hi-fis and played along with *Road to Ruin* or *It's Alive*. Within weeks, they were starting bands with other kids in town who were doing the same thing.

LEGEND OF A ROCK STAR

You could be on stage, getting it out, saying what you feel, singing about sniffing glue, and not be a virtuoso or genetically gifted with Elvis' cheekbones, either. You could look like an outcast and still be cool. Talking Heads were the same thing in a different way. It's a big night.

The Ramones were a blueprint, a blueprint so necessary at the time. That fact alone is so important for everything that came after. Thurston Moore from Sonic Youth was saying that he can't think of a band or a musician these days where the Ramones weren't a very important part of their life. John McBain, a great musician from Seattle that I know, said something—and I think he spoke for the whole Seattle community when he said, "The Ramones were our Beatles."

Going back to that time at CBGB and the New York scene, Patti Smith said it was a reclamation of rock 'n roll, but we created it and we're gonna take it back. Let's take it over. I'm up here for a bit . . . I need to . . . It may have to happen again, because Thurston and I were talking, and now it's Disney kids singing songs written by old men and being marketed to six and seven year olds. So some kind of change might have to happen again soon. But that's a whole 'nother thing.

After the initial surge of the late '70s, commercially the Ramones were never embraced. Bands around them were, but never them. Virtually ignored by radio, eighties MTV, and even other artists, they never stopped and regardless have a following worldwide that's as devoted as ever.

I went with them once to South America. There were 50,000 people. Riots for tickets. People screaming outside. It was the reaction I always thought they deserved.

When punk finally broke in '91, the Ramones still weren't brought along for the ride, even though the bands Nirvana, Rancid, and Green Day wouldn't have existed without them. Punk bands' first or second records now sell ten times the amount of records the Ramones did throughout their career of twenty-something records. That's why I go over to Johnny Ramone's house and do yard work three times a week, just to absolve some of the guilt. A bunch of people do it. Bono and Edge do their windows. Kirk Hammett, the guitarist from Metallica, he dusts, house cleans, makes French toast . . . that's a true story. Even Kurt Cobain wanted to be as good as the Ramones. The list is endless. Turn page.

They never had a top ten hit. You know it's crazy when Phil Spector produces your record and you still don't have a top ten record. But it's really circumstantial. It doesn't alter the fact that they were one of the most important bands in rock 'n roll. They accomplished a lot for a punk band. Most of the others, like the Sex Pistols, crashed and burned. Most punk bands pretty much crashed and burned. In the Sex Pistols 'case, thank you Malcolm McLaren for being an ego-driven fool (or fuck, for the non-edited version of this VH1 televised event).

They existed for twenty-two years with the same level of intensity the whole time. They may not have gotten along the whole time, but that was touring for twenty-two years in a van, for fuck's sake, so you have to understand . . . it's a highly respectable thing to travel in a van and not go up to a tour bus, not get your separate planes because you don't get along with the other guys in your van. It's torturously insane to stay in a van for eight years, but they did it. Even after Dee Dee left the band— and he was such a huge part of the band—he still wrote songs for them, which I think speaks to the brotherhood they had, an intense brother-hood of sorts.

After Dee Dee left, there were some intense Converse shoes to fill. The guy who did it, his name was C.J. For whatever reason, the Rock and Roll Hall of Fame chose not to include him with those being inducted. It's a Hall of Fame thing, I wouldn't understand. But he played eight hundred-something shows, he participated in three or four records, wrote a lot of songs and really importantly, he was accepted by the hard-core Ramones fans. The Ramones kept playing and were able to play for another generation because of C.J. C.J.'s been working twelve-hour days cleaning pollution out of the air ducts down around the World Trade Center. He's here tonight. He might not get up here, but I was going to ask him to stand up and be recognized. C.J. Ramone! [Applause.]

I'll mention that Johnny Ramone's been an extremely great friend. His wife and he have been such great friends to me and taught me a lot about music I was too young to see. Going back to the Brenda Lee com-ment, and Gene Pitney . . . I was introduced to them by John. He's been a tutor of sorts. The guy saw Hendrix and was sitting down. The whole crowd was sitting down. He saw the Who open for the Doors. He him-self has more information than probably the institution into which he's being inducted tonight.

Okay, at this point I've spoken long enough: We could have heard three or four Ramones songs. And after this, I'm sure the evening will

LEGEND OF A ROCK STAR

move quickly. But it's the Ramones and it's punk rock and I'm just about finished and I hope you're okay with that. Apparently you're not. Fuck you. Take it easy, Eddie. All right.

The last thing I was going to say was about when the Ramones' manager, Gary Kurfirst, first talked to me. He said there was a night back in December of the year 2000. He got a phone call from Joey Ramone. Joey had had an accident in front of his apartment. He slipped and fell on some ice. I guess he was just lying there for a bit, tangled up. He ended up breaking his hip. He wasn't getting any help. People were just walking by, either side of him. He was pretty upset by it. At the end, I guess he called Gary and he said, "The worst thing about it was that no one would help me. I was down and nobody would help me."

Maybe they didn't know it was Joey Ramone. He was tangled in black hair and they thought he was a bum or whatever. But in a way, it's only mentioned because it's analogous to the Ramones' career. It's hard. Then obviously Joey died on Easter of 2001, less than a year ago. I'm sure he would have loved to be here tonight.

The only reason I mention that is that's why tonight's really important and special. Because I'm sure there's a number of bands and people who never get to be up here and never get to be brought up before all you people and applauded. I thought that would probably happen with the Ramones. Something very unusual is happening here tonight, and that is that this industry is paying some respect to the Ramones. So with the power invested in me, I'd like to induct Joey, Johnny, Dee Dee, Tommy, Marky, C.J., which we've talked about. The Ramones.

† † †

The first time I heard the Ramones, I was about five years old. I remember hearing "Blitzkrieg Bop" on my father's car stereo and losing my mind. This was probably around 1982 or 1983. At the time, I think Michael Jackson was burning up the charts. As time went by, I realized that this was the greatest music I had ever heard. Of course, it was loud, fast, and rebellious, but there was also a sincerity to it that you knew had to have come from the heart.

The Ramones got me into rock 'n roll at an abnormally early age. I loved hearing Dee Dee count off the songs. I wished that some day I could be as cool as him. You could imagine my excitement when I got the most important phone call in my life. The phone rang and it was my friend Stefan Adika. "How would you like to be Dee Dee Ramone's guitarist?" I think it may have been the happiest day of my life. I was lucky enough to be a member of Dee Dee's band during the last years of his life. More than that, I was honored to have him as a friend. His music was the blueprint for my youth and gave me something to believe in. His songs spoke for all of us who felt like outcasts and gave us hope when we all needed it most.

Although I had listened to the Ramones my whole life, my real relationship with Dee Dee began when I was twenty-two years old. Somehow, I felt like I already knew him. I had never been in a professional band situation before and I couldn't believe that it would be with someone I had looked up to my whole life. We clicked instantly and had so many things in common. I was so much younger than him, but really felt like he understood me. We would sit together in hotel rooms and talk for hours upon hours about anything and everything. After a while, it turned into a mentor/father figure kind of relationship. I soon forgot that he was the same guy on all my posters and records. To me, he was just Dee Dee. Having no family in L.A., we would spend our holidays together and eventually he became my upstairs neighbor. His wife, Barbara, and my ex-girlfriend Leah, became very close and we all felt like a family. We would play shows and I remember singing and looking over at him in amazement. I thought it was the coolest thing in the world.

I will always miss the way he listened to me in my times of need, and gave the best advice. Dee Dee was no angel by any means, but if you understood him, he understood you. Even in our darkest moments on tour, he still managed to give 100 percent on stage every night and I couldn't help but admire that. He was a lot of fun to travel with too. Even when he would do things like yell at promoters and scream at border patrol workers. When I was sitting next to him on the bus in Europe, I remember him writing this book and laughing his ass off. A lot of people had a hard time accepting his sense of humor. Like when he would dedicate songs to himself on stage. I'll always miss hearing that "1-2-3-4" and then blasting through a set of my favorite songs with my amigo. This is the side of Dee Dee I wish he could be remembered by.

Drugs are powerful things. More powerful than us sometimes. Dee Dee knew this and as far as I could tell, he was over them. So what happened? None of us will ever know. Maybe some people are just too fucking talented for this world. So Dee Dee, in the hearts of all of us, including your band (Stefan, Anthony, and myself) you will be missed eternally.

Christian, a.k.a "Chris the Creep," 6/13/02

† † †

To say that Dee Dee Ramone could be very negative would be like saying that Lizzie Borden's parents split up because they had trouble controlling their temperamental daughter. Another understatement is that he was important to rock 'n roll. He wrote and co-wrote some of the greatest rock 'n roll songs of all time, with many (like "53rd and 3rd," "Poison Heart," and his signature song, "Wart hog") reflecting his dark side perfectly. I photographed him onstage and off various times, but I know him best through his music and writing. He was a work of art, a great talent who, sadly, often seemed to view the world as a war zone, his adoring admirers as predators and—at his worst—himself as an object to be destroyed. I once took a photo of him in concert in which, eyes shut and head slightly back, he had the most uncharacteristic expression on his face of perfect peace. I never showed him the photo. He'd have hated it. And not just because he looked dead. Regardless, I loved that image of him because I'd like to think that—up there on stage—maybe he'd really felt that peaceful at the moment I'd taken the photo. I hope he's finally resting in that kind of peace now. For him, I titled that photo *"Der Warthog Schläft Heute Abend."* Why? He liked German. The translation? "The Warthog Sleeps Tonight."

John Nikolai

† † †

I met Dee Dee in 1973. He used to come into the building where I lived to see a girl he was dating. The door to my loft was always open and he would come in and talk to me while I painted. He only talked about girls. When I asked him what he did for a living, his answer was that he didn't like what he did, but did it anyway because he met a lot of girls.

After a few months of these casual encounters he came in one day as I peeled off the masking tape I used to outline the images on the canvas, suddenly revealing a finished piece. He seemed surprised by the process as if I had performed a magic trick. He stared at it for a few seconds and said, "These are paintings right?" So I said, "Yes they are. What do you think?" His immediate answer was, "Oh, art is okay, but it's not that important."

Up to that point I was feeling very good, high on a feeling of self-importance, proudly admiring my just-finished work. His words brought me back from that place a person goes when he gets carried away by his intuition, selfishness, and paranoia. I felt as if he had cut my wrists and slowly but surely my blood was dripping out of my body. I tried to tell myself he didn't know what he was talking about, that he probably was a sales clerk at a ladies' shoe store, but I asked him to explain what he meant and without thinking about it he assumed for the first time in front of me the posture I would see many more times throughout the years to come. Extending his arms and showing the palms of his hands like a child stating the obvious he said: "Well, art is not necessary."

That was the first sign that Dee Dee was only interested in what was truly essential. Then, as if trying to compensate for the negativity of his pronouncement, he added, "Me and my friends are going to put a band together. We're going to be very good. Maybe you'll want to do art for us."

Twenty-five years and over twenty-five hundred shows later (the Ramones did 2,263, of which I missed two, and Dee Dee started to tour solo almost as soon as he quit the band) I found out that Dee Dee was playing a tiny club in New York City. I had refused to go and see him play again, thinking I couldn't possibly enjoy it, and he never insisted that I did, but this time I decided to surprise him. I had not seen him for some time and I was excited about it.

The day of the show I couldn't wait to go. I had passed by the club (really just a bar) where he was playing many times but had never been inside. As soon as I saw the room I could not believe he was playing such a small place.

I approached him and when he saw me he gave me a big smile and a hug and said:

"You're here."

We talked for about fifteen minutes and it felt good, then he said he had to get ready for the show and went to the corner where the "stage" was. The guys in his band didn't know what to do to set up or they were afraid to do the wrong thing and waited for DeeDee to make all the decisions. The result was confusion if not chaos. Then they started to play. It was bad. I listened for three songs and decided I had enough and walked outside. I was leaning on a car parked right in front of a window, and Dee Dee was right on the other side. I could not hear very well but I was able to watch him perfectly so I continued observing for the rest of the show. The new perspective changed everything. On one side, I saw a crowd with expressions of curiosity, and on the other side, to my amazement, I saw a man doing exactly what he wanted to do, completely oblivious to the bewildered faces in front of him. He had no problem with his working conditions, the problem was all mine. He had left one of the greatest rock 'n roll bands ever because he valued his freedom above anything else. Dee Dee was in total control because there was no self-pity and absolutely no regret in his demeanor. He knew what he had to do and he was man enough to do it. I walked away thinking I had never been more proud of him.

Arturo Vega, New York City, September 18, 2002

✝ ✝ ✝

Musician Dee Dee Ramone Found Dead
Coroner's office says member of punk band the Ramones may
have died from drug overdose
By Jeff Wilson, Associated Press Writer

Dee Dee Ramone, a founding member of the pioneer punk band the Ramones, was found dead of a possible drug overdose in his Hollywood home, the coroner's office said today. He was 50.

Ramone, whose real name was Douglas Glenn Colvin, was found dead on the couch by his wife when she returned home at 8:25 P.M. Wednesday, said Craig Harvey, operations chief for the coroner's office. Paramedics were called and he was declared dead at 8:40 P.M.

"The investigator noted drug paraphernalia, including a single syringe on the kitchen counter, and we are handling it as a possible accidental overdose," Harvey said. An autopsy was planned later Thursday.

The death comes eleven weeks after the band was celebrated with an induction into the Rock and Roll Hall of Fame.

"I'd like to congratulate myself, and thank myself, and give myself a big pat on the back," Ramone joked at the time. "Thank you, Dee Dee, you're very wonderful."

He had often feuded with his fellow band members, eventually quitting the group in the late eighties to launch a career as a rapper under the name Dee Dee King.

Lead singer Joey Ramone, born Jeffrey Hyman, died in April of last year of lymphoma, a form of cancer. He was 49. The other two members are Johnny and Tommy Ramone; the four adopted the common last name after forming the band in 1974 in New York City.

The Ramones' best-known songs reflected their twisted teen years in Queens: "Beat on the Brat," "I Wanna Be Sedated," "Now I Wanna Sniff Some Glue," "Teenage Lobotomy," "Sheena Is a Punk Rocker."

Dee Dee Ramone was one of the band's major songwriters, and among his better-known songs was "Chinese Rock"—a tale of going on the street to score heroin, co-written by punk rock icon and overdose victim Johnny Thunders.

Despite their influence and critical acclaim, though, the Ramones never cracked the Top 40.

While British bands such as the Sex Pistols and Clash received the media attention once punk rock exploded, both were schooled by the Ramones' tour of England that began on the U.S. Bicentennial—July 4, 1976.

"They're the daddy punk group of all time," Joe Strummer, lead singer of the Clash, once told *Spin* magazine.

Dee Dee Ramone was the band's bassist. The Ramones recorded their first album in February, 1976. The band then earned a loyal cult following with a seemingly endless string of tours, where they would crank out thirty songs in ninety minutes.

The Ramones disbanded in 1996 after a tour that followed their final studio album, *Adios Amigos*. A live farewell tour album, *We're Outta Here!*, was released in 1997.

The coroner's office did not say what drug was suspected of causing

Ramone's death. In his autobiography, *Lobotomy: Surviving the Ramones*, he had written of his struggle with drug and alcohol abuse.

Associated Press Writer Larry McShane in New York contributed to this report

† † †

New York Honors Dee Dee
Former bandmates, friends salute late Ramones bassist

New York punks old and new paid tribute to Dee Dee Ramone on Tuesday with a concert at the downtown club the Continental, where the legendary Ramones bassist had gigged frequently in recent years. The Toilet Boys, Star Spangles, and Charm School appeared on the bill along with the trio of Marky Ramone (drums), C.J. Ramone (bass), and Ramones producer Daniel Rey (guitar), who played Ramones covers with help from an array of guest singers, including the Dictators' Handsome Dick Manitoba, the Heartbreakers' Walter Lure, and Black Flag's Dez Cadena. Proceeds from the event went to UNICEF.

Dee Dee, known for his propulsive basslines and trademark "One, two, three, four!" count off, died June fifth of an apparent drug overdose in his Los Angeles home. His death came barely a year after the passing of singer Joey Ramone from lymphatic cancer, and just months after the Ramones were inducted into the Rock and Roll Hall of Fame.

"He was probably the greatest punk rock songwriter of all time," said C.J., who replaced Dee Dee when he acrimoniously left the group in 1989. And besides penning Ramones classics like "Rockaway Beach" and "53rd and 3rd," Dee Dee was a novelist and painter; several of his chalk drawings and paintings fill the walls in the downstairs green room at the Continental. He was working on his third book, *Legend of a Rock Star*, at the time he died. "He was always compelled to create," Rey said. "Without it he went crazy."

"His influence as an individual—it spread everywhere," said Marky. "When Sid Vicious was in New York, we'd be hanging out at CBGB, and the first thing he would say was, 'Where's Dee Dee?'—because the guy would follow Dee Dee around, and he would imitate him."

In addition to the performers, several Ramones associates showed to honor Dee Dee. Both Monte Melnick, the band's former tour manager, and "Trigger," the Continental's owner, gave heartfelt tributes from the stage. The surprise guest of the night was Tommy Ramone, the band's original drummer, who sang "I Wanna Be Your Boyfriend." After Tommy's performance, the evening's performers crowded the stage for a sing-along of "Blitzkrieg Bop."

CHRISTIAN HOARD, July 3, 2002

✝ ✝ ✝

Dee Dee Ramone
1952–2002
By John Holmstrom

Dee Dee Ramone (born September 18, 1952 as Douglas Colvin) died on June 5, 2002, at his home in Los Angeles. Dee Dee was the most important musician in the history of punk rock, and probably the most overlooked.

There was something authentic about the Ramones. If there hadn't been they would have been dismissed as poseurs, fakes, and pretenders. In fact, too many "rock journalists" dismissed them as a joke, but they didn't realize that the Ramones wrote songs from their life experiences: sniffing glue, mental hospitals, growing up in Germany, being an army brat, working the streets. That idiotic term "street punk" that so many rock critic mediocrities like to throw around has been used to describe everyone in rock 'n roll: Bruce Springsteen, Patti Smith, Bob Dylan, John Lennon, Steven Tyler, and other nice kids from the suburbs. But only Dee Dee was the real thing. And he wasn't just a guy in the band—he and Joey wrote most of the music.

Not that Dee was a tough guy or an asshole. He was genuinely nice. He was like a little kid, very naive. He was incapable of putting on an act. His one scene with dialogue in *Rock 'n' Roll High School* needed more takes than any other in the movie because Dee Dee couldn't deliver his lines about pizza.

Johnny was The Boss of the Ramones—a right-wing conservative who beat up hippies when he worked as a construction worker. Joey was the nice guy of the band who loved rock 'n roll music more than anything else in the world. Tommy was the brains of the group and an accomplished musician with credentials (like working on "Electric Ladyland"). But Dee Dee was the punk. He was the guy who had a girl-friend who stabbed him in the ass with a broken beer bottle. He worked on 53rd and 3rd. The other three guys in the band you could figure out, you knew where they came from. But Dee Dee was completely unpre-dictable. Even Dee Dee didn't seem to know where Dee Dee came from.

Legs McNeil's *Please Kill Me* started out as an autobiography of Dee Dee because Legs thought that punk rock began with Dee Dee. Oddly enough, when the book turned into an oral history of punk rock, Dee Dee became determined to write his own life story. He seemed unable to figure it all out. Dee Dee's own account of his life (published as *Poison Heart* and *Lobotomy*) was somewhat unreliable because Dee Dee had a lot of difficulty telling reality from fantasy.

Dee Dee and Joey wrote most of the Ramones songs together on a two-string acoustic guitar. They'd painstakingly experiment with each simple riff over and over, until a song sounded just right to them. Because of their limitations the Ramones never sounded like anything but the Ramones. The joke at CBGB used to be that it would be use-less for any record label to sign them to a contract because all their records would sound exactly the same. But this turned out to be their strength.

Niagara once suggested to me that someone should publish a book of Dee Dee stories because they would all be so weird and funny, and anyone who knew or even met Dee Dee would have one. You could call it: *Dee Dee Says The Darnedest Things!* He'd say something so off the wall or strange that you'd have to laugh. He really was one-of-a-kind and all of us miss him.

† † †

Fan Tributes:

Dee Dee's death is another great loss, coming so soon after Joey's. They dared to challenge the establishment and go against the grain of stadium rock that had taken over in the late seventies, and make some fantastic tunes in the process. Their legend will live on.

Dan Martin, U.K. (BBC News, 6/10/02)

Joey Ramone may have been the voice of the Ramones, but Dee Dee was the heart and soul. He had the look, the attitude, and the humor. If Dee Dee Ramone hadn't helped to invent punk rock then punk rock would have never invented and reinvented so many who came after him. God bless you, Douglas Glenn Colvin.

Mark Z., U.S. (BBC News, 6/10/02)

I remember a show almost twenty years ago, Dee Dee kicked a girl off stage for sitting on his amp . . . then let me crawl up there and spend the rest of the show sitting on the edge of the stage in front of it. I'll never forget that . . . it was the height point of my eighteenth year. I cried when I heard about his death—he'll always have a special place in my heart. "Four-five-six-seven, all good cretins go to heaven. . . ."

Anonymous

My condolences to Barbara and all of Dee Dee's close friends and family. I am very sad about this. Dee Dee was someone who touched my soul like no other songwriter. I once saw the Ramones play here in my hometown of Lexington, Kentucky, and it was in

this crappy club that usually had Chippendale dancers and honky-tonk bands. I was up front by the stage and I was getting crushed throughout the night. I was slumped over the barricade, which was actually a table that had been propped on its side. About halfway through the show Dee Dee came over to me and started to hand me a guitar pick. About twenty people tried to snatch it from him and he pulled it back and stuck it right in my face. I still have that pick. It is one of the best memories I have of a musician being totally cool and dedicated to his fans. Whatever problems the Ramones, and Dee Dee in particular, had they always took care of their fans. I hope Dee Dee found the peace that he never seemed to have in life.

Yours truly,
Kevin Martinez

Dee Dee (real name Douglas Glenn Colvin) was hell on wheels, a rakish goofball presence with a pixie's face and a demented pirate's heart. Punk girls loved his unpredictable aura; punk boys used him as a template of geekdom. He was the closest thing the Ramones had to a heartthrob.

San Francisco Chronicle, 6/8/02

Mr. Ramone also had a volatile personality and a long history of drug use, though in recent years his friends thought he had left heroin behind. "He was really the ultimate punk," said Arturo Vega, the Ramone's art director. "He always did what he wanted, and he never settled for anything. He should be remembered as somebody that showed us how much fun it was and how much it hurt to be a real punk."

The New York Times, 6/7/02

Legs McNeil, who started *Punk* magazine in the 1970's, said yesterday: Dee Dee was very charming, he was cute. . . . But you never knew when

LEGEND OF A ROCK STAR

he was going to go off. I think it takes really disturbed people to make great rock and roll, and Dee Dee was a greatly disturbed person. I don't think he had a peaceful day on the planet."

The New York Times, 6/7/02

"The first thing I ever heard from The Ramones was Dee Dee saying, 'One...two...three...four,'" said Seymour Stein, the influential record executive who signed the Ramones. "Dee Dee was really the sex symbol of the band. He was so great onstage. He was the bad boy of the band, but he always had great taste."

Newsday (New York), 6/7/02

Stein said he was proud of Ramone's speech. [Referring to Dee Dee's speech at the Ramone's Rock and Roll Hall of Fame induction] "I kept thinking, 'I hope they realize what he's saying,'" Stein said, choking back tears. "He clawed his way back. He had grown into a new career. He deserved to be proud."

Newsday (New York), 6/7/02

"When you hear a Ramones song, you know it's Ramones," Mr. Kristal said. [Hilly Kristal owner of CBGB's] "You can't say that about bands like the Sex Pistols and the Clash."

The New York Times, late edition, 6/7/02

[Fan, Wallis Meza's] favorite bit of Dee Dee Ramone wisdom, from the song, "Poison Heart": 'I just wanna walk right out of this world because everybody's got a poison heart.' "It's simple, but it was perfect," she said. "Everyone can relate." Ms. Meza said that the band continues, and will continue, to speak to people young and old. Just a few days ago, she saw a little girl with a stick-on tattoo of Joey Ramone's head. Almost as powerful as his music, these fans said, was Mr. Ramone's attitude, which was rooted in the belief that he could do anything.

The New York Times, 6/7/02

"Rock stars dream themselves up. They're self-

conscious creatures, conceived in the neediness of youth, fired by imagination and ambition to create the looming images we all buy into once they've gained fame. Every so often, though, there trundles by a rock star who doesn't seem to have been developed or tweaked at all, someone who seems to have arisen through spontaneous combustion. These are what we call naturals. One of them was Dee Dee Ramone, who died, apparently of a drug overdose, in his Hollywood home last week at 49. While the other Ramones crafted their cartoonish characters through savvy and design, Dee Dee seemed like a Ramone by divine right. If his bandmates became Ramones, Dee Dee seemed to have had Ramone-ness thrust upon him—at birth. No wonder fans considered him to be the heart of the group, the guy best pitched to kick off each volley of riffs with his patented Queens cheer: "One, two, tree, faw!" In youth, Dee Dee was also the band's gangly sex symbol, a rough-trade hustler type, exuding the danger and charm of an animal.

Daily News (New York), 6/11/02

And, it should be noted, Dee Dee was more than just an idea made flesh. He was also a hilarious writer, a true believer in rock 'n' roll and, ultimately, a star so bright, he couldn't shine any higher or, seemingly, tone it down. If that insured his life would end in a clichéd burnout, at least he gave music an original charge in his prime.

Daily News (New York), 6/11/02

Ramones anecdotes from their early club days were too numerous to count, but one good-natured memory stands above the others for Hilly Krystal. "He had this girlfriend at that time, Connie," he recounted. "She was tough, and prone, after a couple drinks to haul off and whack him. He wouldn't hit her back, so we'd pretty regularly have to pull her off him. He was a big kid then, and I guess he always was."

LEGEND OF A ROCK STAR

Music journalist Gil Kaufman said, "I spoke to the two producers of the album, Johnny, their manager, Marky . . . and of all the people I spoke to, he had the clearest memories of the [Ramones' heyday]. He remembered everything about the old days, especially the Malibu Diner Deli, where they used to eat regularly. They would always order shrimp cocktails, even for breakfast, just because they could." "Sometimes I wish I could go back in time and have a nice dinner with the band," Ramone told Kaufman, who noted that Dee Dee was probably the most well-liked among the bandmembers. Johnny and Joey couldn't stand each other, Kaufman said, and Marky could be distant, but everyone (almost) always loved Dee Dee and he always loved them, to the end.

mtvasia.com, 6/10/02

The last time I spoke to Dee Dee Ramone—in March, just before the Ramones were inducted into the Rock and Roll Hall of Fame—he reminded me of one of the first conversations we ever had. "We were talking about metaphors," he said with a laugh, recalling an interview from over 25 years ago in which he was trying hard to explain the meaning of some of the songs he wrote. "Take 'Now I Wanna Sniff Some Glue,'" he told me back then. "It isn't really a song about getting high. The next line is 'Now I wanna have somethin' to do.' See it's about being a kid and being bored." The glue sniffing, then, was really a metaphor? "I guess so," he said, and then broke into one of his goofy bug-eyed stares—as if his head had started to hurt from too much brain drain."

The Village Voice, "Dee Dee Ramone, 1952-2002"
by Billy Altman, 6/7/02

The club's owner, Hilly Kristal, later recalled: "The first time they played they were terrible. They didn't get good for a few months; but when they did, they played 20 songs in 17 minutes without stopping, and that caused a sensation."

The Daily Telegraph (London), 6/8/02

"Dee Dee was a true friend and an amazing person," said Neil Ortenberg of Thunder's Mouth Press, which published *Lobotomy*. "You could be having the most mundane conversation and Dee Dee would suddenly say something off the top of his head that would make you realize the kind of genius that he was. We'll miss him."

The Houston Chronicle, 6/7/02

"None of them really lived it or died it the way that Dee Dee did," Bessman said. "What is essentially one of the most recognizable bits in rock and roll history was Dee Dee yelling out '1,2,3,4' before every song . . . That was as much a trademark of the Ramones sound as anything else."

***The Guardian*, 6/7/02**

"He was a star and the most influential punk rock bassist," Johnny Ramone said in a statement. "I believe he has influenced every kid playing bass that saw him perform . . . He was my friend and I will always miss him."

"I'll never forget Dee Dee's classic acceptance speech at the Rock and Roll Hall of Fame ceremony," Ramones manager Gary Kurfirst said in a statement, "when he walked up to the microphone and said, 'I would like to thank myself, and congratulate myself, and if I could, I would pat myself on the back.' That was Dee Dee, direct and to the point. . . . Dee Dee Ramone was punk rock. I am really going to miss him. He was truly a unique individual and there will never be anyone like him."

"He was sort of a wacky guy who wrote great songs," said Deborah Harry, whose band Blondie, like the Ramones, emerged from New York's CBGB scene. "He was a really good songwriter, though a little self-destructive. He was always nice to me, and we always had a good time together. He was a lot of fun." "He had this manic energy," she added. "I always thought that the Ramones were this tactical force, like the Marines jumping out of a plane or something. They had focus that I really admired."

223

LEGEND OF A ROCK STAR

I was still working out the final details on Joey's headstone when I got the shocking word that another brother in our extended family was gone," said Mickey Leigh, Joey Ramone's brother. "For me, he was one of the greatest rock and roll songwriters alive. Today, sadly, another life becomes legend. My heartfelt sympathies go out to his wife, family and friends."

MTV.com News, 6/6/02

No question, Dee Dee was a major guiding force in the Ramones. He was the group's resident punk icon and proved a major guiding force in the Ramones . . . His trademark rapid-fire 'one-chew-fee-fowa' count-offs—sometimes translated into German—signaled the very pulse of the music. It continues to be recited by punk bands to this day.

He often took credit for holding up the tough, street-wise end of the Ramones' sound and image, and indeed supplied some of their best and grittiest tunes.

The guy tried so hard. He really had some demons to wrestle with. [Jan Haust]

The Toronto Sun, 6/7/02

So glad we got to share the stage with him at Roseland. You know, we'd been doing shows together since 1975. He was an old friend. It's such a shame.

Chris Frantz and Tina Weymouth, 6/6/02

"Dee Dee was the epitome of what punk rock was all about," the Ramones' long time manager Gary Kurfirst said. "He lived it; he lived dangerously."

Los Angeles Times, 6/7/02

"He was the guy living the life," said Dictators' bassist Andy Shernoff, who played with Mr. Ramone occasionally. "I think he was a brilliant songwriter. Intuitive. He'd just write stuff down and you'd pick up the paper and there was the song. Those songs were bold and brash, often employing cartoonish imagery along with visions that were equally humorous and grim."

The Boston Globe, 6/7/02

Johnny Ramone said it "took about 12 hours" before Joey's death sank in last year, and he figured there'll be a similar lag in processing Dee Dee's departure. "It's hard, you know? It's hard to hear about these things and finally realize . . . you know: They're gone."

MTV news.com, 6/6/02

Like Dennis Wilson, the only Beach Boy who actually surfed, Dee Dee was the Ramones' resident gut check, and remained that symbol even after his departure from the group in 1989: You could take the Dee Dee out of the Ramones, but you could never take the Ramones out of Dee Dee.

The Village Voice, Dee Dee Ramone, 1952-2002
by Billy Altman, 6/7/02

HORROR HOSPITAL

This is A true story. it takes place in NYC AND starts At the Chelsea Hotel where X Sex Pistol Sid Vicious lives with his girl friend NANCY.

By Dee Dee Ramone

LEGEND OF A ROCK STAR

SID VICIOUS SNEAKING OUT OF HIS ROOM AT THE CHELSEA HOTEL 1978

He took the stairs INSTEAD OF the elevator so that the Hotel MANAGER WOULDN'T see HIM AND ASK About the rent. then He HEADED DOWNTOWN to the EAST VILLAGE.

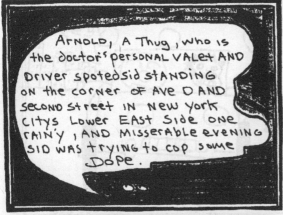

LEGEND OF A ROCK STAR

LEGEND OF A ROCK STAR

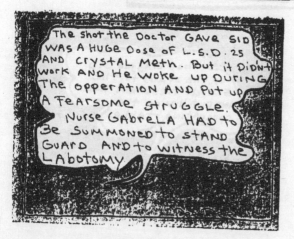

LEGEND OF A ROCK STAR

The Ramones

Studio Albums:

RAMONES May 1976
(Sire 7520) 'Blitzkrieg Bop'; 'Beat on the Brat'; 'Judy is a Punk'; 'I Wanna Be Your Boyfriend'; 'Chainsaw'; 'Now I Wanna Sniff Some Glue'; 'I Don't Wanna Go Down to the Basement'; 'Loudmouth'; 'Havana Affair'; 'Listen to My Heart'; '53rd and 3rd'; 'Let's Dance'; 'I Don't Wanna Walk Around with You'; 'Today Your Love, Tomorrow the World'.

LEAVE HOME January 1977
(Sire SA-7528) 'Glad to See You Go'; 'Gimme Gimme Shock Treatment'; 'I Remember You'; 'Oh Oh I Love Her So'; 'Carbona Not Glue' ('Replaced by Sheena Is a Punk Rocker' in later pressings); 'Suzy Is a Headbanger'; 'Pinhead'; 'Now I Wanna Be a Good Boy'; 'Swallow My Pride'; 'What's Your Game'; 'California Sun'; 'Commando'; 'You're Gonna Kill That Girl'; 'You Should Never Have Opened That Door'.

ROCKET TO RUSSIA November 1977
(Sire SR-6042) 'Cretin Hop'; 'Rockaway Beach'; 'Here Today, Gone Tomorrow'; 'Locket Love'; 'I Don't Care'; 'Sheena Is a Punk Rocker'; 'We're a Happy Family'; 'Teenage Lobotomy'; 'Do You Wanna Dance?'; 'I Wanna Be Well'; 'I Can't Give You Anything'; 'Ramona'; 'Surfin Bird'; 'Why Is it Always This Way?'.

ROAD TO RUIN September 1978
(Sire SRK-6063) 'I Just Wanna Have Something to Do'; 'I Wanted Everything'; 'Don't Come Close'; 'I Don't Want You'; 'Needles and Pins'; 'I'm Against It'; 'I Wanna Be Sedated'; 'Go Mental'; 'Questioningly'; 'She's the One'; 'Bad Brain'; 'It's a Long Way Back'.

END OF THE CENTURY January 1980
(Sire SRK-6077) 'Do You Remember Rock 'n' Roll Radio?'; 'I'm Affected'; 'Danny Says'; 'Chinese Rocks'; 'The Return of Jackie and Judy'; 'Let's Go'; 'Baby, I Love You'; 'I Can't Make It on Time'; 'This Ain't Havana'; 'Rock 'n' Roll High School'; 'All the Way'; 'High Risk Insurance'.

PLEASANT DREAMS July 1981
(Sire SRK-3571) 'We Want the Airwaves'; 'All's Quiet on the Eastern Front'; 'The KKK Took My Baby Away'; 'Don't Go'; 'You Sound Like You're Sick'; 'It's Not My Place'; 'She's a Sensation'; '7-11'; 'You Didn't Mean Anything to Me'; 'Come on Now'; 'This Business Is Killing Me'; 'Sitting in My Room'.

SUBTERRANEAN JUNGLE February 1983
(Sire 9238001) 'Little Bit o' Soul'; 'I Need Your Love'; 'Outsider'; 'What'd Ya Do?'; 'Highest Trails Above'; 'Somebody Like Me'; 'Psycho Therapy'; 'Time Has Come Today'; 'My-My Kind of a Girl'; 'In the Park'; 'Time Bomb'; 'Everytime I Eat Vegetables, It Makes Me Think of You'.

LEGEND OF A ROCK STAR

TOO TOUGH TO DIE October 1984
(Sire 25187) 'Mama's Boy'; 'I'm Not Afraid of Life'; 'Too Tough to Die'; 'Durango 95';
'Wart Hog'; 'Danger Zone'; 'Chasin' the Night'; 'Howling at the Moon'; 'Daytime
Dilemma'; 'Planet Earth 1988'; 'Humankind'; 'Endless Vacation'; 'No Go'.

ANIMAL BOY May 1986
(LP Sire 25433) 'Somebody Put Something in my Drink'; 'Animal Boy'; 'Love Kills';
'Apeman Hop'; 'She Belongs to Me'; 'Crummy Stuff'; 'My Brain Is Hanging Upside Down
(Bonzo Goes to Bitburg)'; 'Mental Hell'; 'Eat That Rat'; 'Freak of Nature'; 'Hair of the
Dog'; 'Something to Believe In'.

HALFWAY TO SANITY September 1987
(Sire 2-25641) 'I Wanna Live'; 'Bop 'Til You Drop'; 'Garden of Serenity'; 'Weasel Face'; 'Go
Lil' Camaro Go'; 'I Know Better Now'; 'Death of Me'; 'I Lost My Mind'; 'A Real Cool Time';
'I'm Not Jesus'; 'Bye Bye Baby'; 'Worm Man'.

BRAIN DRAIN May 1989
(Sire 2-25905) 'I Believe in Miracles'; 'Zero Zero UFO'; 'Don't Bust My Chops';
'Punishment Fits the Crime'; 'All Screwed Up'; 'Palisades Park'; 'Pet Sematary'; 'Learn to
Listen'; 'Can't Get You Outta My Mind'; 'Ignorance is Bliss'; 'Come Back, Baby'; 'Merry
Christmas (I Don't Want to Fight Tonight)'.

MONDO BIZARRO September 1992
(Radioactive RARD-10615) 'Censorshit'; 'The Job That Ate My Brain'; 'Poison Heart';
'Anxiety'; 'Strength to Endure'; 'It's Gonna Be Alright'; 'Take It As It Comes'; 'Main Man';
'Tomorrow She Goes Away'; 'I Won't Let It Happen'; 'Cabbies on Crack'; 'Heidi Is a
Headcase'; 'Touring'.

ACID EATERS December 1994
(Radioactive 7243 8 27676 1) 'Journey to the Center of the Mind'; 'Substitute'; 'Out of
Time'; 'The Shape of Things to Come'; 'Somebody to Love'; 'When I Was Young'; '7 and
7 Is'; 'My Back Pages'; 'Can't Seem to Make You Mine'; 'Have You Ever Seen the Rain?'; 'I
Can't Control Myself'; 'Surf City'; 'Surfin' Safari' (Bonus track not included on U.S.
release).

ADIOS AMIGOS July 1995
(Radioactive 11273) 'You'; 'Oh Oh I Love Her So'; 'Sheena Is a Punk Rocker'; 'Suzy Is a
Headbanger'; 'Pinhead'; 'Now I Wanna Be a Good Boy'; 'Swallow My Pride'; 'What's Your
Game'; 'California Sun'; 'Commando'; 'You're Gonna Kill That Girl'; 'You Should Never
Have Opened That Door'; 'Babysitter'; 'California Sun' [live]; 'I Don't Wanna Walk
Around with You'.

ALL THE STUFF (AND MORE)-VOL 2 July 1991
(CD Sire 2-26220) 'Cretin Hop'; 'Rockaway Beach'; 'Here Today, Gone Tomorrow';
'Locket Love'; 'I Don't Care'; 'Sheena Is a Punk Rocker'; 'We're a Happy Family'; 'Teenage
Lobotomy'; 'Do You Wanna Dance?'; 'I Wanna Be Well'; 'I Can't Give You Anything';
'Ramona'; 'Surfin' Bird'; 'Why Is It Always This Way?'; 'Slug'; 'I Want You Around'; 'I Just
Wanna Have Something to Do'; 'I Wanted Everything'; 'Don't Come Close'; 'I Don't Want
You'; 'Needles and Pins'; 'I'm Against It'; 'I Wanna Be Sedated'; 'Go Mental';
'Questioningly'; 'She's the One'; 'Bad Brain'; 'It's a Long Way Back'; 'I Don't Want to Live
This Life (Anymore)'; 'Yea, Yea '.

RAMONES MANIA 2 1999
(EMI 65233) 'Censorshit'; 'Poison Heart'; 'Strength to Endure'; 'It's Gonna Be Alright';
'Take It As It Comes'; 'I Won't Let It Happen'; 'Touring'; 'Journey to the Center of the
Mind'; 'Substitute'; 'Somebody to Love'; '7 and 7 Is'; 'My Back Pages'; 'Have You Ever Seen
the Rain?'; 'I Don't Wanna Grow Up'; 'The Crusher'; 'Life's a Gas'; 'Take the Pain Away';

'I Love You'; 'Cretin Family'; 'Have a Nice Day'; 'Got a Lot to Say'; 'She Talks to Rainbows'; 'Spiderman'; 'Anyway You Want It'; 'R.A.M.O.N.E.S.' [C.J. vocals].

HEY HO LET'S GO!: THE ANTHOLOGY July 1999
(Rhino 75817) 'Blitzkrieg Bop'; 'Beat on the Brat'; 'Judy Is a Punk'; 'I Wanna Be Your Boyfriend'; '53rd and 3rd'; 'Now I Wanna Sniff Some Glue'; 'Glad to See You Go'; 'Gimme Gimme Shock Treatment'; 'I Remember You'; 'California Sun'; 'Commando'; 'Swallow My Pride'; 'Carbona Not Glue'; 'Pinhead'; 'Sheena Is a Punk Rocker'; 'Cretin Hop'; 'Rockaway Beach'; 'Here Today, Gone Tomorrow'; 'Teenage Lobotomy'; 'Surfin' Bird'; 'I Don't Care' [Sire Single Version]; 'I Just Wanna Have Something to Do'; 'I Wanna Be Sedated'; 'Don't Come Close'; 'She's the One'; 'Needles and Pins' [Sire Remixed Single Version]; 'Rock 'n' Roll High School'; 'I Want You Around'; 'Do You Remember Rock 'n' Roll Radio?'; 'I Can't Make It on Time'; 'Chinese Rocks'; 'I'm Affected'; 'Danny Says'; 'The KKK Took My Baby Away'; 'She's a Sensation'; 'It's Not My Place (in the 9 to 5 World)'; 'We Want the Airwaves'; 'Psycho Therapy'; 'Howling at the Moon (Sha-La-La)'; 'Mama's Boy'; 'Daytime Dilemma'; 'I'm Not Afraid of Life'; 'Too Tough to Die'; 'Endless Vacation'; 'My Brain Is Hanging Upside Down'; 'Somebody Put Something in My Drink'; 'Something to Believe In'; 'I Don't Want to Live This Life'; 'I Wanna Live'; 'Garden of Serenity'; 'Merry Christmas (I Don't Want to Fight Tonight)' [Sire Single Version]; 'Pet Sematary'; 'I Believe in Miracles'; 'Tomorrow She Goes Away'; 'Poison Heart'; 'I Don't Wanna Grow Up'; 'She Talks to Rainbows'; 'R.A.M.O.N.E.S.'

Compilation Albums:

L.A. AND ABERDEEN 1979
(Dragonfly)

HIGH SCHOOL CONFIDENTIAL 1979
(Sire)

RAMONES MANIA May 1988
(Sire 2-25709) 'I Wanna Be Sedated'; 'Teenage Lobotomy'; 'Do You Remember Rock 'n' Roll Radio?'; 'Gimme Gimme Shock Treatment'; 'Beat on the Brat'; 'Sheena Is a Punk Rocker'; 'I Wanna Live'; 'Pinhead'; 'Blitzkrieg Bop'; 'Cretin Hop'; 'Rockaway Beach'; 'Commando'; 'I Wanna Be Your Boyfriend'; 'Mama's Boy'; 'Bop 'Til You Drop'; 'We're a Happy Family'; 'Bonzo Goes to Bitburg'; 'Outsider'; 'Psycho Therapy'; 'Wart Hog'; 'Animal Boy'; 'Needles and Pins'; 'Howling at the Moon (Sha-La-La)'; 'Somebody Put Something in My Drink'; 'We Want the Airwaves'; 'Chinese Rocks'; 'I Just Wanna Have Something to Do'; 'The KKK Took My Baby Away'; 'Indian Giver'; 'Rock 'n' Roll High School'.

END OF THE DECADE 1990
(Beggars Banquet)
--cannot find more info online--

ALL THE STUFF (AND MORE)-VOL 1 June 1990
(Sire 26220) 'Blitzkrieg Bop'; 'Beat on the Brat'; 'Judy Is a Punk'; 'I Wanna Be Your Boyfriend'; 'Chainsaw'; 'Now I Wanna Sniff Some Glue'; 'I Don't Wanna Go Down to the Basement'; 'Loudmouth'; 'Havana Affair'; 'Listen to My Heart'; '53rd and 3rd'; 'Let's Dance'; 'I Don't Wanna Walk Around with You'; 'Today Your Love, Tomorrow the World'; 'I Don't Wanna Be Learned/Don't Wanna Be Tamed'; 'I Can't Be'; 'Glad to See You Go'; 'Gimme Gimme Shock Treatment'; 'I Remember You'; 'Oh Oh I Love Her So'; 'Sheena Is a Punk Rocker'; 'Suzy Is a Headbanger'; 'Pinhead'; 'Now I Wanna Be a Good Boy'; 'Swallow My Pride'; 'What's Your Game'; 'California Sun'; 'Commando'; 'You're Gonna Kill That Girl'; 'You Should Never Have Opened That Door'; 'Babysitter'; 'California Sun' [live]; 'I Don't Wanna Walk Around with You' [live].

LEGEND OF A ROCK STAR

ALL THE STUFF (AND MORE)-VOL 2 July 1991
(CD Sire 2-26220) 'Cretin Hop'; 'Rockaway Beach'; 'Here Today, Gone Tomorrow';
'Locket Love'; 'I Don't Care'; 'Sheena Is a Punk Rocker'; 'We're a Happy Family'; 'Teenage
Lobotomy'; 'Do You Wanna Dance?'; 'I Wanna Be Well'; 'I Can't Give You Anything';
'Ramona'; 'Surfin' Bird'; 'Why Is It Always This Way?'; 'Slug'; 'I Want You Around'; 'I Just
Wanna Have Something to Do'; 'I Wanted Everything'; 'Don't Come Close'; 'I Don't Want
You'; 'Needles and Pins'; 'I'm Against It'; 'I Wanna Be Sedated'; 'Go Mental';
'Questioningly'; 'She's the One'; 'Bad Brain'; 'It's a Long Way Back'; 'I Don't Want to Live
This Life (Anymore)'; 'Yea, Yea'.

RAMONES MANIA 2 June 1999
(Japan: Toshiba-EMI 65233) 'Censorshit'; 'Poison Heart'; 'Strength to Endure'; 'It's
Gonna Be Alright'; 'Take It As It Comes'; 'I Won't Let It Happen'; 'Touring'; 'Journey to
the Center of the Mind'; 'Substitute'; 'Somebody to Love'; '7 and 7 Is'; 'My Back Pages';
'Have You Ever Seen the Rain?'; 'I Don't Wanna Grow Up'; 'The Crusher'; 'Life's a Gas';
'Take the Pain Away'; 'I Love You'; 'Cretin Family'; 'Have a Nice Day'; 'Got a Lot to Say';
'She Talks to Rainbows'; 'Spiderman'; 'Anyway You Want It'; 'R.A.M.O.N.E.S.' [C.J. vocals].

HEY HO LET'S GO!: THE ANTHOLOGY July 1999
(Rhino 75817) 'Blitzkrieg Bop'; 'Beat on the Brat'; 'Judy Is a Punk'; 'I Wanna Be Your
Boyfriend'; '53rd and 3rd'; 'Now I Wanna Sniff Some Glue'; 'Glad to See You Go';
'Gimme Gimme Shock Treatment'; 'I Remember You'; 'California Sun'; 'Commando';
'Swallow My Pride'; 'Carbona Not Glue'; 'Pinhead'; 'Sheena Is a Punk Rocker'; 'Cretin
Hop'; 'Rockaway Beach'; 'Here Today, Gone Tomorrow'; 'Teenage Lobotomy'; 'Surfin'
Bird'; 'I Don't Care' [Sire Single Version]; 'I Just Wanna Have Something to Do'; 'I Wanna
Be Sedated'; 'Don't Come Close'; 'She's the One'; 'Needles and Pins' [Sire Remixed Single
Version]; 'Rock 'n' Roll High School'; 'I Want You Around'; 'Do You Remember Rock 'n'
Roll Radio?'; 'I Can't Make It on Time'; 'Chinese Rocks'; 'I'm Affected'; 'Danny Says'; 'The
KKK Took My Baby Away'; 'She's a Sensation'; 'It's Not My Place (in the 9 to 5 World)';
'We Want the Airwaves'; 'Psycho Therapy'; 'Howling at the Moon (Sha-La-La)'; 'Mama's
Boy'; 'Daytime Dilemma'; 'I'm Not Afraid of Life'; 'Too Tough to Die'; 'Endless Vacation';
'My Brain Is Hanging Upside Down'; 'Somebody Put Something in My Drink';
'Something to Believe In'; 'I Don't Want to Live This Life'; 'I Wanna Live'; 'Garden of
Serenity'; 'Merry Christmas (I Don't Want to Fight Tonight)' [Sire Single Version]; 'Pet
Sematary'; 'I Believe in Miracles'; 'Tomorrow She Goes Away'; 'Poison Heart'; 'I Don't
Wanna Grow Up'; 'She Talks to Rainbows'; 'R.A.M.O.N.E.S.'.

YOU DON'T COME CLOSE [live] May 2001
(Burning Airlines 79) 'Teenage Lobotomy'; 'Blitzkrieg Bop'; 'Don't Come Close'; 'I Don't
Care'; 'She's the One'; 'Sheena Is a Punk Rocker'; 'Cretin Hop'; 'Listen to My Heart';
'California Sun'; 'I Don't Wanna Walk Around with You'; 'Pinhead'.

BEST OF THE CHRYSALIS YEARS April 2002
(EMI 538472) 'Pet Sematary'; 'Don't Bust My Chops'; 'Ignorance Is Bliss'; 'Sheena Is a
Punk Rocker'; 'Teenage Lobotomy' [live]; 'Surfin' Bird' [live]; 'Poison Heart'; 'Anxiety';
'Take It As It Comes'; 'Cretin Hop' [live]; 'Rockaway Beach' [live]; 'I Wanna Be Sedated'
[live]; 'Out of Time'; 'Somebody to Love'; 'Do You Remember Rock 'n' Roll Radio?' [live];
'Blitzkrieg Bop' [live]; 'I Don't Wanna Grow Up'; 'Got a Lot to Say'.

Live Albums:

IT'S ALIVE April 1979
(Sire 26074) 'Rockaway Beach'; 'Teenage Lobotomy'; 'Blitzkrieg Bop'; 'I Wanna Be Well';
'Glad to See You Go'; 'Gimme Gimme Shock Treatment'; 'You're Gonna Kill That Girl'; 'I
Don't Care'; 'Sheena Is a Punk Rocker'; 'Havana Affair'; 'Commando'; 'Here Today, Gone
Tomorrow'; 'Surfin' Bird'; 'Cretin Hop'; 'Listen to My Heart'; 'California Sun'; 'I Don't

Wanna Walk Around with You'; 'Pinhead'; 'Do You Wanna Dance?'; 'Chainsaw'; 'Today Your Love, Tomorrow the World'; 'I Wanna Be a Good Boy'; 'Judy Is a Punk'; 'Suzy Is a Headbanger'; 'Let's Dance'; 'Oh Oh I Love Her So'; 'Now I Wanna Sniff Some Glue'; 'We're a Happy Family'.

LOCO LIVE October 1991
(Sire 2-26650) 'The Good, the Bad, and the Ugly'; 'Durango 95'; 'Teenage Lobotomy'; 'Psycho Therapy'; 'Blitzkrieg Bop'; 'Do You Remember Rock 'n' Roll Radio?'; 'I Believe in Miracles'; 'Gimme Gimme Shock Treatment'; 'Rock 'n' Roll High School'; 'I Wanna Be Sedated'; 'The KKK Took My Baby Away'; 'I Wanna Live'; 'My Brain is Hanging Upside Down (Bonzo Goes to Bitburg)'; 'Chinese Rocks'; 'Sheena Is a Punk Rocker'; 'Rockaway Beach'; 'Pet Sematary'; 'Carbona Not Glue' (hidden track); 'Judy Is a Punk'; 'Mama's Boy'; 'Animal Boy'; 'Wart Hog'; 'Surfin Bird'; 'Cretin Hop'; 'I Don't Wanna Walk Around with You'; 'Today Your Love, Tomorrow the World'; 'Pinhead'; 'Somebody Put Something in My Drink'; 'Beat on the Brat'; 'Ignorance is Bliss'; 'I Just Wanna Have Something to Do'; 'Havana Affair'; 'I Don't Wanna Go Down to the Basement'.

GREATEST HITS LIVE June 1996
(Universal/Radioactive RARD-11459-1) 'Durango 95'; 'Blitzkrieg Bop'; 'Do You Remember Rock 'n' Roll Radio?'; 'I Wanna Be Sedated'; 'Spider Man'; 'I Don't Wanna Grow Up'; 'Sheena Is a Punk Rocker'; 'Rockaway Beach'; 'Strength to Endure'; 'Cretin Family'; 'Do You Wanna Dance'; 'We're a Happy Family'; 'The Crusher'; '53rd and 3rd'; 'Beat on the Brat'; 'Pet Sematary'; 'R.A.M.O.N.E.S.'; 'Anyway You Want It'.

WE'RE OUTTA HERE! November 1997
Packaged with a videocassette of The Ramones' final concert, interviews and past band performances
(Universal/Radioactive RARD-11555) 'Durango 95'; 'Teenage Lobotomy'; 'Psycho Therapy'; 'Blitzkrieg Bop'; 'Do You Remember Rock 'n' Roll Radio?'; 'I Believe in Miracles'; 'Gimme Gimme Shock Treatment'; 'Rock 'n' Roll High School'; 'I Wanna Be Sedated'; 'Spider Man'; 'The KKK Took My Baby Away'; 'I Just Wanna Have Something to Do'; 'Commando'; 'Sheena Is a Punk Rocker'; 'Rockaway Beach'; 'Pet Sematary'; 'The Crusher'; 'Love Kills'; 'Do You Wanna Dance?'; 'Somebody Put Something in My Drink'; 'I Don't Want You'; 'Wart Hog'; 'Cretin Hop'; 'R.A.M.O.N.E.S.'; 'Today Your Love, Tomorrow the World'; 'Pinhead'; '53rd and 3rd'; 'Listen to Your Heart'; 'We're a Happy Family'; 'Chinese Rocks'; 'Beat on the Brat'; 'Anyway You Want It'.

Miscellaneous Audio:

'Howling at the Moon (Sha-La-La)' [Swedish Remix] 1985, Sweden:
Tandan.

JUDY'S IN THE BASEMENT - THE 914 SESSIONS 1975 (10 inch EP)
(Germany: Hit and Run Records) 'I Don't Wanna Go Down to the Basement'; '53rd and 3rd'; 'I Wanna Be Your Boyfriend'; 'Judy Is a Punk'; 'Loudmouth'.

RAMONES TALKIN' MONDO BIZARRO PROMO CD 1993
Interview with Joey; 'Strength to Endure'; 'Anxiety'; 'Tomorrow She Goes Away'; 'It's Gonna Be Alright'; 'Cabbies on Crack'; 'Censorshit'; 'Touring'; 'Take It as It Comes' [live]; 'Censorshit' [live]; 'Poison Heart' [live]; 'Strength to Endure' [live].

RAMONES - YOU DON'T COME CLOSE 2000 [live]
(NMC Music) 'Rockaway Beach'; 'Teenage Lobotomy'; 'Blitzkrieg Bop'; 'Don't Come Close'; 'I Don't Care'; 'She's the One'; 'Sheena Is a Punk Rocker'; 'Cretin Hop'; 'Listen to My Heart'; 'California Sun'; 'Don't Wanna Walk Around with You'; 'Pinhead'. Video footage can been seen using a computer.

LEGEND OF A ROCK STAR

Video:

ROCK 'N' ROLL HIGH SCHOOL 1979 (New World Pictures).

GET CRAZY 1983 (D&P Production).

RAMONES: LIFESTYLES OF THE RICH AND RAMONES 1990 (Warner-Reprise Video 38178-3)
Interviews, guest appearances, and videos: 'Do You Remember Rock 'n' Roll Radio?'; 'Rock 'n' Roll High School'; 'We Want the Airwaves'; 'Psycho Therapy'; 'Time Has Come Today'; 'Howling at the Moon (Sha-La-La)'; 'Something to Believe In'; 'I Wanna Live'; 'I Wanna Be Sedated'; 'Pet Sematary'; 'Merry Christmas (I Don't Want to Fight Tonight)'.

RAMONES: WE'RE OUTTA HERE! November 1997 (Radioactive Records).

RAMONES: AROUND THE WORLD October 1998 (Rhino Home Video).

12" singles:

'Something to Believe In'/'(You) Can't Say Anything Nice' (year TK), U.K.:

'Howling at the Moon'/'Smash You'; 'Street Fighting Man' (1985), U.K.:

'Bonzo Goes to Bitburg'/'Go Home Ann' (year TK), U.K.:

'Real Cool Time'/'Life Goes On'; 'Indian Giver' (1986), UK:

'Crummy Stuff'/'She Belongs to Me'; ' I Don't Wanna Live This Life (Anymore)' (1986) U.K.:

"I Wanna Live'/ 'Merry Christimas (I Don't Want to Fight Tonight)' - Extended (1987), U.K.:

'Somebody Put Something in My Drink'/'Something to Believe In'/'Can't Say Anything Nice' (1986)

'Pet Sematary'/'All Screwed Up'/'Zero Zero UFO' (1989)

'Live Poison Heart'/'Chinese Rocks'/'Sheena Is a Punk Rocker'/'Rockaway Beach' (1992)

7" singles:

'Blitzkrieg Bop'/'Havana Affair' (1976), Sire SAA 725; U.K.: Phonogram 6078 601; France: Philips 6078 503.
'I Remember You'/'California Sun' [live]; 'I Don't Wanna Walk Around with You' [live] (1976), U.K.: Phonogram 6078 603.
'I Wanna Be Your Boyfriend'/'California Sun' [live]; 'I Don't Wanna Walk Around with You' [live] (1976), Sire SAA-734.

'Blitzkrieg Bop'/'California Sun' [live]; 'I Don't Wanna Walk Around with You' [live] (1977), Holland: Philips 6078 504.
'Baby, I Love You'/'High Risk Insurance' (1977), Germany: Sire 101 399-100; Holland: Sire 17 589; Portugal Sire SRE 49182 NP9.
'Do You Wanna Dance?'/'Babysitter' (1977), SIRE 1017.
'Do You Wanna Dance?'/'Rockaway Beach' (1977), Italy: Sire SRE 1008.

'Glad to See You'; 'Babysitter'/'California Sun' [live]; 'I Don't Wanna Walk Around with You' [live] (1977), Italy: Sire SAA 734.
'Rockaway Beach'/'Locket Love' (1977), Sire SRE 1008; Italy: Phonogram/Philips 6078 517; Canada: Sire/GRT 1147-1008.
'Rockaway Beach'/'Teenage Lobotomy'; 'Beat on the Brat' (1977), U.K.: Sire 6078 611.
'Sheena Is a Punk Rocker'/'Commando'; 'I Don't Care' (1977), U.K.: Sire 6078 606.
'Sheena Is a Punk Rocker'/'Commando' (1977), France: Philips 6173 525.
'Sheena Is a Punk Rocker'/'I Don't Care' (1977), SIRE/ABC SA 746; Germany: Phillips 6078 511; Italy: Sire SAA 746.
'Sheena Is a Punk Rocker'/'Swallow My Pride' (1977) Spain: Philips 60 78 513.
'Swallow My Pride'/'Pinhead' (1977), Sire SA 734.
'Swallow My Pride'/'Pinhead'; 'Let's Dance' [live] (1977), U.K.: Phonogram 6078 607.

'Don't Come Close'/'I Don't Care' (1978), Italy: Sire 15 868 AT.
'Don't Come Close'/'I Don't Want You' (1978), Sire SRE 1025; U.K.: Sire/Warner SRE 1031; Germany: Sire 101399-100.
'Do You Wanna Dance?'/'It's a Long Way Back to Germany'; 'Cretin Hop' (1978), U.K.: Phonogram 6078 615.
'Do You Wanna Dance?'/'It's a Long Way Back to Germany' (1978), Holland: Philips 6078 521.
'Do You Wanna Dance?'/'Rockaway Beach' (1978), Italy: Sire SRE 1008.
'I'm Against It'/'Needles and Pins' (1978), France: Pathe Marconi/EMI 2C 008-62.042.
'Needles and Pins'/'I Wanted Everything' (1978), Sire SRE 1045.
Promo cut from Road To Ruin album (1978), U.K.: Sire J. Ramone Promo 1
'She's the One'/'I Wanna Be Sedated' (1978), U.K.: Sire SIR 4009.
'She's the One'/'Sheena Is a Punk Rocker' (1978), Italy: Sire 100 394-100.

'Come on Let's Go' (The Paley Brothers and The Ramones)/'Magic Power' (The Paley Brothers) (1979), U.K.: Sire SIR 4005; Italy: Sire 100 018-100.
'Rock 'n' Roll High School'/'Do You Wanna Dance?' [live] (1979), Sire SRE 1051.
'Rock 'n' Roll High School'/'Rockaway Beach'; 'Sheena Is a Punk Rocker' (1979), U.K.: Sire SIR 4021.

'Baby I Love You'/'Do You Remember Rock 'n' Roll Radio?' (1980), Italy: Sire SRE 1012/ JKAS 33245.
'Baby I Love You'/'High Risk Insurance' (1980), Sire SRE 49182; U.K.: Sire SIR 4031; Holland: Sire/Warner WBN 17-589; Italy: Sire 101 399.
'Baby I Love You'/'Rock 'n' Roll High School' (1980), Spain: Sire/Hispavox Vox 45-1951
'Do You Remember Rock 'n' Roll Radio?'/'I Want You Around' (1980), U.K.: Sire SIR 4037; Holland: Sire/WEA WBN 17-642.
'Do You Remember Rock 'n' Roll Radio?'/'Let's Go' (1980), Sire SRE 49261; Spain: Sire/Hispavox Vox 45-2003.
'Do You Remember Rock 'n' Roll Radio?'/'Rock 'n' Roll High School' (1980), Germany: Sire 101 871.
'Do You Remember Rock 'n' Roll Radio?'/'Sheena Is a Punk Rocker' (1980), France: Pathe Marconi/EMI 2C 088-63.717.
'I Just Wanna Have Something to Do'; 'Here Today, Gone Tomorrow'/'I Wanna Be Your Boyfriend'; 'Questioningly' (1980), U.K.: Sire SREP 1.
'I Wanna Be Sedated'/'I Don't Want You' (1980), Holland: Sire SRKS-602.
'I Wanna Be Sedated'/'The Return of Jackie and Judy' (1980), U.K.: RSO 70; Spain: RSO 20 90 512.
'Rock 'n' Roll High School'/'Danny Says' (1980), Holland: Sire/Warner WBN 17-568.
'We Want the Airwaves'/'All's Quiet on the Eastern Front' (1981), Sire SRE 49812.
'We Want the Airwaves'/'You Sound Like You're Sick' (1981), U.K.: Sire SIR 4051; Spain: Sire/Hispavox Vox 45-2131; Belgium: Sire/WEA WB 17-850 A.

'Time Has Come Today'/'Psycho Therapy' (1983), U.K.: Sire W 9606.

LEGEND OF A ROCK STAR

'Howling at the Moon (Sha-La-La)'/'No Go' (1984), France: Closer 730.
'Howling at the Moon (Sha-La-La)'/'Wart Hog' (1984), Spain: Ariola A-107136.

'Bonzo Goes to Bitburg'/'Daytime Dilemma' (1985), U.K.: Beggards Banquet 140.
'Chasing the Night'/'Howling at the Moon (Sha-La-La)'/'Street Fighting Man'; 'Smash You' (1985), U.K.: Beggards Banquet 128D.
'Howling at the Moon (Sha-La-La)'/'Smash You' (1985), U.K.: Beggards Banquet 128.

'Crummy Stuff'/'Something to Believe In' (1986), U.K.: Beggards Banquet 167.
'Somebody Put Something in My Drink'/'Something to Believe in' (1986), U.K.: Beggards Banquet 157.
'Something to Believe In'/'Somebody Put Something in My Drink; (1986), Spain: Ariola A-108-287; France: Barclay 885-249-7.

'I Wanna Live'/'Bye Bye Baby' (1987), Germany: Teldec 6.14958 TS.
'I Wanna Live'/'Go Lil' Camaro Go' (1987), France: Barclay 887-135-7.
'I Wanna Live'/'Merry Christmas (I Don't Want to Fight Tonight)' (1987), U.K.: Beggards Banquet 201.
'I Wanna Live'/'Real Cool Time' (1987), Holland: Torso 70045.
'Real Cool Time'/'Life Goes On' (1987), U.K.: Beggards Banquet 198.

'I Wanna Be Sedated' [LP Version]/'I Wanna Be Sedated' [Ramones on 45 Mega Mix] (1988), Sire 9 27663-7.

'I Believe in Miracles'/'All Screwed Up' (1989), Germany: Chrysalis 112-792.
'Pet Sematary'/'All Screwed Up' (1989), U.K.: Chrysalis 3423.
'Pet Sematary'/'Don't Bust My Chops' (1989), Germany: Chrysalis 112-489.
'Pet Sematary'/'Merry Christmas (I Don't Want to Fight Tonight)' (1989), U.K.: Chrysalis 3483.
'Pet Sematary'/'Sheena Is a Punk Rocker' (1989), Sire 9-22911-7.
'Sheena Is a Punk Rocker'/'Baby I Love You' (1989), U.K.: Old Gold 9909.

'Poison Heart'/'Censorshit' (1992), U.K.: Chrysalis 3917.
'Poison Heart'; 'Do You Remember Rock 'n' Roll Radio?' [live]; 'Chinese Rocks' [live] (1992), U.K.: Chrysalis 0946 3 23917 2 8.
'Poison Heart'; 'Sheena Is a Punk Rocker' [live]; 'Rockaway Beach' [live] (1992), U.K.: Chrysalis 0946 3 23917 2 7.

'Substitute' (1993), U.K.: Chrysalis CDSUB1; France: EMI SPCD 1701

'I Don't Wanna Grow Up'/'She Talks to Rainbows' (1995), Holland: Chrysalis 8-82324-2.

'I Wanna Be Your Boyfriend'/'Judy Is a Punk' (1997), Norton 45-065

'Blitzkrieg Bop'; 'Do You Remember Rock 'n' Roll Radio?'; 'Sheena Is a Punk Rocker' [single version]; 'Rock 'n' Roll High School' (2001), Spain: Warner Bros. SPO56W
'Judy Is a Punk'/'Human Being' (New York Dolls) (2001), Germany: Musical Tragedie MT-509.

Unreleased & Demo Songs:

Mondo Bizarro Sessions - 'Perfect Day'.
Adios Amigos Sessions - 'Tomorrow Never Comes'.
End of the Century Sessions - 'Please Don't Leave'.
Pleasant Dreams Sessions - 'Sleeping Troubles'; 'Baby Say You Beg'; 'Touring'; 'I Wasn't Looking For Love'.

Too Tough to Die Sessions - 'You're Not Fooling Me'; 'Working It Over'; 'Chasing the Night' (Richie vocals); 'Danger Zone' (Dee Dee vocals); 'Humankind' (Richie vocals).
Unknown Sessions - 'Drinking'; '(There's) Nothing New to Try'.

7" Bootlegs:

ALL REVVED UP OCTAGON CENTRE SHEFFIELD
November 15, 1987
'Psycho Therapy'; 'Blitzkrieg Bop'; 'Do You Remember Rock 'n' Roll Radio?'; 'Bop 'Til You Drop'; 'Chinese Rocks'; 'Weasel Face'; 'Rockaway Beach'; 'Garden of Serenity'; 'Loudmouth'; 'Pinhead'; 'I Wanna Live'; 'Somebody Put Something in My Drink'; 'Bonzo Goes to Bitburg'.

BABYSITTER
Fake Australian Philips Single 6528-712
'Babysitter;' 'I Don't Wanna Be Learned'; 'No, It Gets Me'.
Tracks are from a John Peel Session, recorded Dec. 12th 1977.

CARBONA NOT GLUE
Fake Sub Pop Single SP 666
With comics and sticker.
'Carbona Not Glue'/'I Can't Be'.

CRETIN HOPPERS
'Psycho Therapy'; 'Dangerzone'; 'The KKK Took My Baby Away'; 'Too Tough to Die'; 'Chinese Rocks'; 'Wart Hog'.

EARLY DEMOS
Recorded in New York City, summer of 1975.
'53rd and 3rd'/'Judy Is a Punk'.

HERE TODAY, GONE TOMORROW
Fake Japanese Philips Single SLF-2188
'Here Today, Gone Tomorrow'/'I Can't Give You Anything'; 'Let's Dance'.

HOLLYWOOD
Hollywood Palladium, Los Angeles, October 15, 1992.
'Take It As It Comes'; 'Censorshit'/'Poison Heart'; 'Strength to Endure'.

JOEY & FRIENDS
The Ritz, New York City, April 1, 1988
'I Had Too Much to Dream (Last Night)'; 'For Your Love'; 'Sonic Reducer'; 'The Wind Cries Mary'/'Go Lil' Camaro Go'; 'I Wanna Be Sedated'; 'Loudmouth'.

LIVE AT THE CBGB'S
CBGB's, New York, May 15, 1976
'I Don't Wanna Go Down to the Basement'; 'Now I Wanna Sniff Some Glue'; 'Blitzkrieg Bop'; 'Swallow My Pride'/'Let's Dance'; 'Judy Is a Punk'; 'I Don't Wanna Walk Around with You'; 'Today Your Love, Tomorrow the World'.

LIVE, FAST & PUNK OVER DEUTSCHLAND
(Germany: Play Loud! LK 004) 'Chinese Rocks'; 'Somebody Put Something in My Drink'/'Rockaway Beach'; 'Do You Wanna Dance?'.

LIVE IN LA SPEZIA
Recorded live in La Spezia, Italy, July 6, 1991.

LEGEND OF A ROCK STAR

(Italy: Mosrite Recordings) 'I Wanna Be Sedated'; 'The KKK Took My Baby Away'/'I Wanna Live'; 'Bonzo Goes to Bitburg'.

RAMONES
Paradisio, Amsterdam, September 15, 1978.
(Fake Sire SRE 1033) 'Needles and Pins'; 'Surfin' Bird'; 'Cretin Hop'; 'Listen to My Heart'/'California Sun'; 'I Don't Wanna Walk Around with You'; 'Pinhead'.

R.A.M.O.N.E.S. 2001
(Desire DES 701) 'R.A.M.O.N.E.S.' [Joey Vocals]; 'Spiderman'/'Got Alot to Say'; 'Anyway You Want It'.

TEENAGE LOBOTOMY
Recorded at a Long Beach appearance, September 25, 1987.
(Hey Ho Let's Go Records)
'Teenage Lobotomy'; 'Psycho Therapy'; 'Blitzkrieg Bop'; Interview with Johnny Fenders.

WE ARE PUNK GENERATION
(Fake Japanese Philips SLF 2340)
'Havana Affair [Live Palladium N.Y.C 1977]; 'Commando [Live Palladium N.Y.C 1977]; 'Beat on the Brat' [Live Philadelphia 1977]/'Don't Come Close' [O.G.W.T., U.K. 1978]; 'She's the One' [O.G.W.T., U.K. 1978]; 'Go Mental' [O.G.W.T. , U.K. 1978].

WE'RE A HAPPY FAMILY!
Recorded live in Los Angeles, December 9, 1984.
'Teenage Lobotomy'; 'Psycho Therapy'/ 'I Wanna Be Sedated'; 'Beat on the Brat'/ 'Chinese Rocks'; 'Wart Hog'/ 'Pinhead'; 'We're a Happy Family'.

WE'RE GETTING OUT OF HERE!
(NPP 025)
'Working It Over' [Demo from the Too Tough To Die session 1984]/ 'Please Don't Leave' [Demo from the End Of The Century session 1979]; Promotional announcement for End of The Century.

Full-Length Bootlegs

ADIOS RAMONES
River Plate Stadium, Bueno Aires, Argentina, March 16, 1996
(Verano Al Rojo Records) 'Durango 95'; 'Teenage Lobotomy'; 'Psycho Therapy'; 'Blitzkrieg Bop'; 'Do You Remember Rock 'n' Roll Radio?'; 'I Believe in Miracles'; 'Gimme Gimme Shock Treatment'; 'Rock 'n' Roll High School'; 'I Wanna Be Sedated'; 'Spider Man'; 'The KKK Took My Baby Away'; 'I Don't Wanna Grow Up'; 'I Just Wanna Have Something to Do'; 'Sheena Is a Punk Rocker'; 'Rockaway Beach'; 'Pet Sematary'; 'Strength to Endure'; 'Cretin Family'; 'Do You Wanna Dance?'; 'Somebody Put Something in My Drink'; 'Surfin' Bird'; 'Wart Hog'; 'Cretin Hop'; 'Ramones'; 'Today Your Love, Tomorrow the World'; 'Pinhead'; 'The Crusher'; 'Poison Heart'; 'We're a Happy Family'; 'My Back Pages'; '53rd and 3rd'; 'Beat on the Brat'; 'Chinese Rocks'; 'Have You Ever Seen the Rain?'

PACO RAMONES POUR HOMME
N.Y. Palladium, January 1, 1978
'Rockaway Beach'; 'Teenage Lobotomy'; 'Blitzkrieg Bop'; 'Sheena Is a Punk Rocker'; 'Havana Affair'; 'Command'; 'Pinhead'. New Pop Festival September 7, 1980, Rotterdam, Holland: 'Gimme Gimme Shock Treatment'; 'Rock 'n' Roll High School'; 'I Wanna Be Sedated'; 'Do You Remember Rock 'n' Roll Radio?' British TV "Old Grey Whistle Test," September 19, 1978: 'Don't Come Close'; 'She's the One'; 'Go Mental'. New York City July 20, 1982: 'Surf City'; 'I Don't Want You'; 'Go Mental'. Minneapolis, First Avenue, July 27, 1986: 'Cretin Hop'; 'I Don't Wanna Walk Around with You'; 'Today Your Love, Tomorrow the World';

SHEENA TRYING TO COMFORT ME
I'AM MISSERABLE (11)
BECAUSE BARBARA
WONT COME BACK
TO L.A. SHES
GOING TO HONG
KONG TO BE A
MODEL TILL I
WRITE A NEW
RECHORD FOR US!

BARROES BYRDS

CHASE MANHATTEN DRUMMER
FOR DEE
DEE
RAMONE

IT WAS
OKAY. BUT
NOW'S HE'S
LEFT ME
TO JOIN

BUGS ORCHARDS

CHRIS THE CREEPS GROUP
TOKYO 本 ♡
KONG!

WHIST! ME
WORRY!
NEIN!

NO! NO! NO! NO! NO! NO! DONT GO TO HONG KONG

WE, ME BARBARA AND CHASE ⑨
WENT TO THE
ASTRO HALL TO
SEE SHEENA AND
THE ROCKETS PLAY
AND THEY ASKED
US TO JAM.

WE PLAYED
FOR TWO
HOURS.
THE FIRST
THREE RAMONES
ALBUMS AND
TEN JOHNNY
THUNDERS
SONGS,
EVERY BODY
LOVED IT.

THEY GAVE
ME A JOHNNY
RAMONE
MOSRITE
MODEL
GUITAR IN
JAPAN FOR
FREE! . .

OUR PROMOTORS
SONNY
AND
MICHIKO

OKAY!!

THE TOYKO ~~YUMI~~ HOP SUMMER 2001 ⑫

PLEASE SAY HELLO TO MY FRIENDS IN JAPAN

TO MICHIKO YOKOTA

SHEENA AND THE ROKKETS

THE KENT HOTEL

BOSTER DRAGON BILLY DOLL HOUSE BEFORE CHRIST BUTTERFLY BARBARA ZAMPI

YES YES OKAY

LEGEND OF A ROCK STAR

'Pinhead'; 'Chinese Rocks'; 'Somebody Put Something in My Drink'; 'Rockaway Beach'; 'Do You Wanna Dance?'; 'California Sun'; 'We're a Happy Family'.

BONZO GOES TO GOTHENBURG
Gothenburg, Sweden, March 28, 1990
'Durango 95'; 'Teenage Lobotomy'; 'Psycho Therapy'; 'Blitzkrieg Bop'; 'Do You Remember Rock 'n' Roll Radio?'; 'I Believe in Miracles'; 'Gimme Gimme Shock Treatment'; 'Rock 'n' Roll High School'; 'I Wanna Be Sedated'; 'Beat on the Brat'; 'I Wanna Live'; 'Bonzo Goes to Bitburg'; 'Go Mental'; 'Sheena Is a Punk Rocker'; 'Rockaway Beach'; 'Pet Sematary'; 'Don't Bust My Chops'; 'She's the One'; Interview with Joey Ramone; 'Mama's Boy'; 'Animal Boy'; 'Wart Hog'; 'Surfin' Bird'; 'Cretin Hop'; 'I Don't Wanna Walk Around with You'; 'Today Your Love, Tomorrow the World'; 'Pinhead'; 'Chinese Rocks'; 'Somebody Put Something in My Drink'; 'California Sun'; 'Ignorance Is Bliss'; 'Judy Is a Punk'; 'We're a Happy Family'; 'I Just Want to Have Something to Do'; 'Listen to My Heart'. France 1980: 'I'm Against It'; 'This Ain't Havana'; 'Commando'; 'I Wanna Be Your Boyfriend. Finland, June, 5, 1988: 'I Don't Want You'; 'Garden of Serenity'; 'Do You Wanna Dance?'.

SUBTERRANEAN B.A.
Sanitarias Stadium, Buenos Aires, September 17, 1992
'The Good, the Bad and the Ugly'; 'Durango 95'; 'Teenage Lobotomy'; 'Psycho Therapy'; 'Blitzkrieg Bop'; 'Do You Remember Rock 'n' Roll Radio?'; 'I Believe in Miracles'; 'Gimme Gimme Shock Treatment'; 'Rock 'n' Roll High School'; 'I Wanna Be Sedated'; 'Censorshit'; 'I Wanna Live'; 'Bonzo Goes to Bitburg'; 'Commando'; 'Sheena Is a Punk Rocker'; 'Pet Sematary'; 'I Wanna Be Well'; 'Glad to See You Go'; 'Take It As It Comes'; 'Animal Boy'; 'Wart Hog'; 'Cretin Hop'; 'California Sun'; 'Judy Is a Punk'; 'Today Your Love, Tomorrow the World'; 'Pinhead'; 'Chinese Rocks'; 'Somebody Put Something in My Drink'; 'We're a Happy Family'; 'Los Ramones Es Un Sentimiento'; 'Main Man'; 'I Just Want to Have Something to Do'; 'Havana Affair'.

AT YOUR BIRTHDAY PARTY (released 1979)
The Roxy Theatre, Los Angeles, CA, August 12, 1976
(Dansker Fanklubbe) 'Loudmouth'; 'Beat on the Brat'; 'Blitzkrieg Bop'; 'I Remember You'; 'Glad to See You Go'; 'Chain Saw'; '53rd and 3rd'; 'I Wanna Be Your Boyfriend'; 'Havana Affair'; 'Listen to My Heart'; 'California Sun'; 'Judy Is a Punk'; 'I Don't Wanna Walk Around with You'; 'Now I Wanna Sniff Some Glue'; 'Let's Dance'.

KGA LIVE 1977
Whiskey a Go-Go in Los Angeles, CA, November 24, 1977
'Loudmouth'; 'Beat on the Brat'; 'Blitzkrieg Bop'; 'I Remember You'; 'Glad to See You Go'; 'Gimme Gimme Shock Treatment'; 'You're Gonna Kill That Girl'; 'Oh Oh I Love Her So'; 'Commando'; 'I Wanna Be Your Boyfriend'; 'Havana Affair'; 'Listen to My Heart'; 'California Sun'; 'Judy Is a Punk'; 'I Don't Wanna Walk Around with You'; 'Pinhead'.

IN CONCERT N.Y. 1982
New York, 1982
'Do You Remember Rock 'n' Roll Radio?'; 'Do You Wanna Dance?'; 'Blitzkrieg Bop'; 'This Business Is Killing Me'; 'All's Quiet At the Eastern Front'; 'Gimme, Gimme Shock Treatment'; 'Rock 'n' Roll High School'; 'I Wanna Be Sedated'; 'Beat on the Brat'; 'Needles and Pins'; 'I'm Affected'; 'Chinese Rocks'; 'Rockaway Beach'; 'Teenage Lobotomy'; 'Surfin' Bird'; 'We Want the Airwaves'; 'I Just Want to Have Something to Do'; 'We're a Happy Family'.

RAMONES—LIVE AT THE ROXY 1976
(Cat and Dog 516) 'Loud Mouth'; 'Beat on the Brat '; 'Blitzkrieg Bop'; 'I Remember You'; 'Glad to See You Go'; 'Chainsaw'; '53rd and 3rd'; 'I Wanna Be Your Boyfriend'; 'Havanna Affair'; 'Listen to My Heart'; 'Hang Ten'; 'Judy Is a Punk'; 'I Don't Wanna Walk Around with You'; 'Let's Dance'.

BACK STREET PARTY
Leysin Festival, Switzerland, July 10, 1991
(Luxembourg: Swingin' Pig Records Tsp-Cd-165) 'Durango 95'; 'Teenage Lobotomy'; 'Psycho Therapy'; 'Blitzkrieg Bop'; 'Do You Remember Rock 'n' Roll Radio?'; 'I Believe in Miracles'; 'Gimme Gimme Shock Treatment'; 'Rock 'n' Roll High School'; 'I Wanna Be Sedated'; 'The KKK Took My Baby Away'; 'I Wanna Live'; 'Bonzo Goes to Bitburg'; 'Commando'; 'Sheena Is a Punk Rocker'; 'Rockaway Beach'; 'Pet Sematary'; 'Go Mental'; 'Glad to See You Go'; 'Mama's Boy'; 'Animal Boy'; 'Wart Hog'; 'Surfin' Bird'; 'Cretin Hop'; 'I Don't Wanna Walk Around with You'; 'Today Your Love, Tomorrow the World'; 'Pinhead'; 'Chinese Rocks'; 'Somebody Put Something in My Drink'; 'We're a Happy Family'.

BLITZKRIEG BOP (Audio & Video CD) 1995
Bremen, Germany, September 13, 1978
(U.K.: Master Tone MM 5119)
'Rockaway Beach'; 'Teenage Lobotomy'; 'Blitzkrieg Bop'; 'Don't Come Close'; 'I Don't Care'; 'She's the One'; 'Sheena Is a Punk Rocker'; 'Cretin Hop'; 'Listen to My Heart'; 'California Sun'; 'I Don't Wanna Walk Around with You'; 'Pinhead'.

BLITZKRIEG IN ATHENS
Rodon Club, Athens, Greece, March 13, 1989
Same recording as "European tour summer '89"
(Italy: insect Records IST 10) 'Durango 95'; 'Blitzkrieg Bop'; 'Teenage Lobotomy'; 'Psycho Therapy'; 'Do You Remember Rock 'n' Roll Radio?'; 'I Believe in Miracles'; 'Gimme Gimme Shock Treatment'; 'Rock 'n' Roll High School'; 'I Wanna Be Sedated'; 'Beat on the Brat'; 'Chinese Rocks'; 'Bonzo Goes to Bitburg'; 'Go Mental'; 'Sheena Is a Punk Rocker'; 'Rockaway Beach'; 'Pet Sematary'; 'Don't Bust My Chops'; 'She's the One'; 'Mama's Boy'; 'Animal Boy'; 'Wart Hog'; 'Surfin' Bird'; 'Cretin Hop'; 'I Don't Wanna Walk Around with You'; 'Today Your Love, Tomorrow the World'; 'Pinhead'; 'I Wanna Live'; 'Somebody Put Something in My Drink'; 'Do You Wanna Dance?'; 'Palisade Park'; 'We're a Happy Family'.

THE CHINESE WALL
New York, July 20, 1982
(Europe: Rarities & Fews TKCD 1054) 'Do You Remember Rock 'n' Roll Radio?/Do You Wanna Dance?'; 'Blitzkrieg Bop'; 'This Business Is Killing Me'; 'All's Quiet on the Eastern Front'; 'Gimme Gimme Shock Treatment'; 'Rock 'n' Roll High School'; 'I Wanna Be Sedated'; 'Beat on the Brat'; 'The KKK Took My Baby Away'; 'Commando'; 'Come on Now'; 'Suzy Is a Headbanger'; 'Let's Dance'; 'Needles and Pins'; 'I'm Affected'; 'Chinese Rocks'; 'Rockaway Beach'; 'Teenage Lobotomy'; 'Surfin' Bird'.

COUNTY JAIL
The Club, Cambridge, MA, May 12, 1976
(Italy: Aulica A 130) 'Blitzkrieg Bop'; 'I Remember You'; 'Gimme Gimme Shock Treatment'; 'I Wanna Be Your Boyfriend'; '53rd and 3rd'; 'Havana Affair'; 'California Sun'; 'Judy Is a Punk'; 'I Don't Wanna Walk Around with You'; 'Today Your Love, Tomorrow the World'; 'Beat on the Brat'; 'Now I Wanna Sniff Some Glue'; 'Swallow My Pride'; 'Glad to See You Go'; 'Chainsaw'; 'Listen to My Heart'; 'Babysitter'; 'Oh, Oh, I Love Her So'; 'Commando'; 'Let's Dance'.

ESCAPE FROM ZAGREB
November 24, 1990
(Long Knife Records) 'The Good, the Bad, and the Ugly'; 'Durango 95'; 'Teenage Lobotomy'; 'Psycho Therapy'; 'Blitzkrieg Bop'; 'Do You Remember Rock 'n' Roll Radio?'; 'I Believe in Miracles'; 'I Wanna Be Sedated'; 'Rock 'n' Roll High School'; 'Beat on the Brat'; 'I Wanna Live'; 'Bonzo Goes to Bitburg'; 'Commando'; 'Sheena Is a Punk Rocker'; 'Rockaway Beach'; 'Pet Sematary'; '53rd and 3rd'; 'Now I Wanna Sniff Some Glue'; 'Mama's Boy'; 'Animal Boy'; 'Wart Hog'; 'Surfin' Bird'; 'Cretin Hop'; 'I Don't Wanna Walk

Around with You'; 'Today Your Love, Tomorrow the World'; 'Pinhead'; Chinese Rocks'; 'Somebody Put Something in My Drink'; 'We're a Happy Family'; 'Do You Wanna Dance?'; 'California Sun'; 'Judy Is a Punk'.

EUROPE 1992
1992 European Tour
Same recording as Live In Rome
(Italy: Rarities & Few RFCD 1224) 'Durango 95'; 'Teenage Lobotomy'; 'Psycho Therapy'; 'Blitzkrieg Bop'; 'Do You Remember Rock 'n' Roll Radio?'; 'I Believe in Miracles'; 'Gimme Gimme Shock Treatment'; 'Rock 'n' Roll High School'; 'I Wanna Be Sedated'; 'Beat on the Brat'; 'I Wanna Live'; 'Bonzo Goes to Bitburg'; 'Commando'; 'Sheena Is a Punk Rocker'; 'Rockaway Beach'; 'Pet Sematary'; 'I Wanna Be Well'; 'Glad to See You Go'; 'Mama's Boy'; 'Animal Boy'; 'Wart Hog'; 'Surfin' Bird'; 'Cretin Hop'; 'I Don't Wanna Walk Around with You'; 'Today Your Love, Tomorrow the World'; 'Pinhead'; 'Chinese Rocks'; 'Somebody Put Something in My Drink'; 'We're a Happy Family'; 'Punishment Fits the Crime'; 'California Sun'; 'Judy Is a Punk'.

EUROPEAN TOUR SUMMER '89 (released 1990)
European Tour, May 1989
Same recording as Blitzkrieg In Athens
(Europe: RS RECORDS RSCD 13) 'Durango 95'; 'Blitzkrieg Bop'; 'Teenage Lobotomy'; 'Psycho Therapy'; 'Do You Remember Rock 'n' Roll Radio?'; 'I Believe in Miracles'; 'Gimme Gimme Shock Treatment'; 'Rock 'n' Roll High School'; 'I Wanna Be Sedated'; 'Beat on the Brat'; 'Chinese Rocks'; 'Bonzo Goes to Bitburg'; 'Go Mental'; 'Sheena Is a Punk Rocker'; 'Rockaway Beach'; 'Pet Sematary'; 'Don't Bust My Chops'; 'She's the One'; 'Mama's Boy'; 'Animal Boy'; 'Wart Hog'; 'Surfin' Bird'; 'Cretin Hop'; 'I Don't Wanna Walk Around with You'; 'Today Your Love, Tomorrow the World'; 'Pinhead'; 'I Wanna Live'; 'Somebody Put Something in My Drink'; 'Do You Wanna Dance?'; 'Palisade Park'; 'We're a Happy Family'.

GABBA GABBA HEY "FUCK THE GRIND"
Palladium, New York City, December 31, 1978
(Autica A.119) 'Teenage Lobotomy'; 'Psycho Therapy'; 'Blitzkrieg Bop'; 'Do You Remember Rock 'n' Roll Radio?'; 'Bop 'Till You Drop'; 'Gimme Gimme Shock Treatment'; 'Rock 'n' Roll High School'; 'I Wanna Be Sedated'; 'I Don't Want You'; 'Chinese Rocks'; 'Weasel Face'; 'Commando'; 'Sheena Is a Punk Rocker'; 'Rockaway Beach'; 'Garden of Serenity'; 'I Just Wanna Have Something to Do'; 'Too Tough to Die'; 'Animal Boy'; 'Wart Hog'; 'Surfin' Bird'; 'Cretin Hop'; 'I Don't Wanna Walk Around with You'; 'Today Your Love, Tomorrow the World'; 'Pinhead'; 'I Wanna Live'; 'Somebody Put Something in My Drink'; 'Bonzo Goes to Bitburg'; 'Do You Wanna Dance'; 'Listen to My Heart'; 'We're Happy Family'; Interview with Joey Ramone.

HAPPY NEW YEAR 1979 (released 2001)
Palladium, New York City, December 31, 1979
'Blitzkrieg Bop'; 'Teenage Lobotomy'; 'Rockaway Beach'; 'I Don't Want You'; 'Go Mental'; 'Gimme Gimme Shock Treament'; 'I Wanna Be Sedated'; 'I Just Wanna Have Something to Do'; 'She's the One'; 'This Ain't Havana'; 'I'm Against It'; 'Sheena Is a Punk Rocker'; 'Havana Affair'; 'Commando'; 'Needles and Pins'; 'I Wanna Be Your Boyfriend'; 'Surfin' Bird'; 'Cretin Hop'; 'All the Way'; 'Judy Is a Punk'; 'California Sun'; 'I Don't Wanna Walk Around with You'; 'Loudmouth'; 'Pinhead'; 'Do You Wanna Dance?'; 'Suzy Is a Headbanger'; 'Let's Dance'; 'Chinese Rocks'; 'Beat on the Brat'; 'We're a Happy Family'; 'Bad Brain'; 'I Wanted Everything'.

HEY, HO . . . IT WAS TWENTY YEARS AGO
(E.E.C: Mastersound MS 700) The Club, Cambridge, MA, May 12, 1976
Blitzkrieg Bop'; 'I Remember You'; 'Gimme Gimme Shock Treatment'; 'I Wanna Be Your Boyfriend'; '53rd and 3rd'; 'Havana Affair'; 'California Sun'; 'Judy Is a Punk'; 'I Don't

Wanna Walk Around with You'; 'Today Your Love, Tomorrow the World'; 'Beat on the Brat'; 'Now I Wanna Sniff Some Glue'; 'Swallow My Pride'; 'Glad to See You Go'; 'Chainsaw'; 'Listen to My Heart'; 'Babysitter'; 'Oh, Oh, I Love Her So'; 'Commando'; 'Let's Dance'. Roxy Theatre, Los Angeles, CA, August 12, 1976: 'Loudmouth'; 'Beat on the Brat'; 'Blitzkrieg Bop'; 'I Remember You'; 'Glad to See You Go'; 'Chainsaw'; '53rd and 3rd'; 'I Wanna Be Your Boyfriend'; 'Havana Affair'; 'Listen to My Heart'; 'California Sun'; 'Judy Is a Punk'; 'I Don't Wanna Walk Around with You'; 'Now I Wanna Sniff Some Glue'; 'Let's Dance'. Sundragon Studio, NYC, November 1976: 'Carbona Not Glue'.

UP IN THE ZONE
Radio Show for broadcast the weekend of August 28/29, 1999
'Durango 95'; 'Teenage Lobotomy'; 'Psycho Therapy'; 'Blitzkrieg Bop'; 'Do You Remember Rock 'n' Roll Radio?'; 'Rock 'n' Roll High School'; 'I Wanna Be Sedated'; 'Censorshit'; 'Sheena Is a Punk Rocker'; 'Rockaway Beach'; 'Pet Sematary'; 'I Wanna Be Well'; 'Somebody Put Something in My Drink'; 'Poison Heart'; 'Strength to Endure'.

RAMONES—LEATHERS FROM NEW YORK 1997
(Sonic Book SB 08) CD case-sized book by Vanni Neri and Giorgio Campani (biography in English and Italian, photos, and extensive discography): 'Carbona Not Glue'; 'Blitzkrieg Bop' [live]; 'Chop Suey'; 'The Wonderful Widow of Eighteen Springs'.

LET'S DANCE
(Luxembourg: Flashback Flash 06.91.0149) The Club, Cambridge, MA, May 12, 1976: 'Blitzkrieg Bop'; 'I Remember You'; 'Gimme Gimme Shock Treatment'; 'I Wanna Be Your Boyfriend'; '53rd and 3rd'; 'Havana Affair'; 'California Sun'; 'Judy Is a Punk'; 'I Don't Wanna Walk Around with You'; 'Today Your Love, Tomorrow the World'; 'Beat on the Brat'; 'Now I Wanna Sniff Some Glue'; 'Swallow My Pride'; 'Glad to See You Go'; 'Chainsaw'; 'Listen to My Heart'; 'Babysitter'; 'Oh, Oh, I Love Her So'; 'Commando'; 'Let's Dance'. Acres, Utica, New York, November 14, 1977: 'Here Today, Gone Tomorrow'; 'I Can't Give You Anything'; 'Let's Dance'.

LIVE IN ROME (released 1995)
1992 European Tour
The same recording as Europe 1992.
(Italy: On Stage Records CD/ON 2367) 'Durango 95'; 'Teenage Lobotomy'; 'Psycho Therapy'; 'Blitzkrieg Bop'; 'Do You Remember Rock 'n' Roll Radio?'; 'I Believe in Miracles'; 'Gimme Gimme Shock Treatment'; 'Rock 'n' Roll High School'; 'I Wanna Be Sedated'; 'Beat on the Brat'; 'I Wanna Live'; 'Bonzo Goes to Bitburg'; 'Commando'; 'Sheena Is a Punk Rocker'; 'Rockaway Beach'; 'Pet Sematary'; 'I Wanna Be Well'; 'Glad to See You Go'; 'Mama's Boy'; 'Animal Boy'; 'Wart Hog'; 'Surfin' Bird'; 'Cretin Hop'; 'I Don't Wanna Walk Around with You'; 'Today Your Love, Tomorrow the World'; 'Pinhead'; 'Chinese Rocks'; 'Somebody Put Something in My Drink'; 'We're a Happy Family'; 'Punishment Fits the Crime'; 'California Sun'; 'Judy Is a Punk'.

LIVE IN USA
(Germany: Imtrat Music IMM 2CD 42.90048) 'Do You Remember Rock 'n' Roll Radio?'; 'Do You Wanna Dance'; 'Blitzkrieg Bop'; 'This Business Is Killing Me'; 'All's Quiet on the Eastern Front'; 'Gimme Gimme Shock Treatment'; 'Rock 'n' Roll High School'; 'I Wanna Be Sedated'; 'Beat on the Brat'; 'The KKK Took My Baby Away'; 'Commando'; 'Come on Now'; 'Suzy Is a Headbanger'; 'Let's Dance'; 'I'm Affected'; 'Chinese Rocks'; 'Teenage Lobotomy'; 'Surfin' Bird'; 'I Wanna Be Your Boyfriend'; '53rd and 3rd'; 'Havana Affair'; 'California Sun'; 'Judy Is a Punk'; 'I Don't Wanna Walk Around with You'; 'Today Your Love, Tomorrow the World'; 'Now I Wanna Sniff Some Glue'; 'Swallow My Pride'; 'Glad to See You Go'; 'Chainsaw'; 'Listen to My Heart'; 'Babysitter'; 'Oh, Oh, I Love Her So'; 'Here Today, Gone Tomorrow'; 'I Can't Give You Anything'; 'Needles and Pins'; 'Rockaway Beach'.

LEGEND OF A ROCK STAR

BIRTHDAY BASH 1977 (released 1994)
Whiskey a Go-Go, Los Angeles CA, November 24, 1977
(Italy: Red Line Records RFCD 1317) 'Loudmouth'; 'Beat on the Brat'; 'Blitzkrieg Bop'; 'I Remember You'; 'Glad to See You Go'; 'Gimme Gimme Shock Treatment'; 'You're Gonna Kill That Girl'; '53rd and 3rd'; 'Sheena Is a Punk Rocker'; 'Rockaway Beach'; 'Commando'; 'Here Today, Gone Tomorrow'; 'Surfin' Bird'; 'Cretin Hop'; 'Listen to My Heart'; 'California Sun'; 'I Don't Walk Around with You'; 'Pinhead'; 'Suzy Is a Headbanger'; 'Chainsaw'; 'Today Your Love, Tomorrow the World'; 'Now I Wanna Be a Good Boy'; 'Let's Dance'.

MARCH OF THE PINHEADS
The Vogue Theatre, Indianapolis IN, 1978
(Italy: Hawk 064) 'Drum Intro'; 'Blitzkrieg Bop'; 'Teenage Lobotomy'; 'Rockaway Beach'; 'I Don't Want You'; 'Go Mental'; 'Gimme Gimme Shock Treatment'; 'Rock 'n' Roll High School'; 'I Wanna Be Sedated'; 'I Just Want to Have Something to Do'; 'Bad Brain'; 'I'm Against It'; 'Sheena Is a Punk Rocker'; 'Havana Affair'; 'Commando'; 'Needles and Pins'; 'I'm Affected'; 'Surfin' Bird'; 'Cretin Hop'; 'All the Way'; 'California Sun'; 'I Don't Walk Around with You'; 'Today Your Love, Tomorrow the World'; 'Pinhead'; 'Do You Wanna Dance?'; 'Suzy Is a Headbanger'; 'Let's Dance'; 'Chinese Rocks'; 'Beat on the Brat'; 'We're a Happy Family'.

MORE UNRELEASED TRACKS
(RAM-12616) 'Happy Birthday Mr. Burns' (from *Simpsons* episode); '1969' (from "We Will Fall: The Iggy Pop Tribute"); 'I'm Seeing U.F.O's' (from Dee Dee Ramone "I'm Seeing U.F.O.'s" Single); 'Boomerang' (from the Japanese version of Marky Ramone & The Intruders CD)'; 'Blank Generation' (from the Japanese version of Marky Ramone & The Intruders CD); 'Chop Suey' (from "Get Crazy" original motion picture soundtrack); 'The Wonderful Windows of Eighteen Spring' (from John Cage Tribute); 'I Wanna Be Sedated' (from the Various Artists "In Their Own Words Vol.1" recorded at the Bottom Line, N.Y.C. November 7, 1991); 'Gilligan' (performed by Furious George with Joey Ramone, from "Gets a Record" CD); 'Merry Christmas' (Extended Version—B Side of "I Wanna Live" U.K. 12" Single); 'Nothing Can Change the Shape of Things to Come' (performed by the Seclusion & Joey Ramone on bkg vocals, from Single & LP "Isolation For Creation"); 'Medley' (from the MTV Awards 1996); 'Sonic Reducer' (Joey Singing with Pearl Jam recorded live on 1985); 'I Won't Let It Happen' (recorded live); 'Bring It on Home to Me' (recorded live); 'Glad All Over' (recorded live—Joey Ramone on vocals); 'Sleeping Trouble' (demo); 'Baby Say You Beg' (demo); '7-11' (demo); 'I Wasn't Looking For Love' (demo & outtakes From Pleasant Dreams); 'You're Not Fooling Me' (demo); 'Working It Over' (demo); 'Chasing the Night' (demo & outtakes from Too Tough To Die); 'Humankind (demo & outtakes from Too Tough To Die).

ON THE ROAD TO RUIN
(Da Bruddha RAM 001) Studio Demo 1975: 'I Don't Wanna Go Down to the Basement'; '53rd and 3rd'; 'I Wanna Be Your Boyfriend'; 'Judy Is a Punk'; 'Loudmouth'. Recorded Live in Philadelphia April 9, 1977: 'Beat on the Brat'. Palladium, N.Y.C. January 7, 1978": 'Havana Affair'; 'Commando'. Recorded Live in New York October 7, 1982: 'Surf City'; 'Here Today Gone Tomorrow'; 'I Can't Give You Anything'; 'Let's Dance'. Old Grey Whistle Test 1978 U.K. TV Show: 'Don't Come Close'; 'She's the One'. Don Kirschner Rock Concert August 9, 1977: 'Listen to My Heart'; 'California Sun'; 'Judy Is a Punk'; 'I Don't Wanna Walk Around with You'; 'Sheena Is a Punk Rocker'; 'Loudmouth'; 'Beat on the Brat'; 'Blitzkrieg Bop'; 'Glad to See You Go'; 'Gimme Gimme Shock Treatment'; 'Rockaway Beach'; 'Commando'. Tomorrow Show January 9, 1981: Introduction & 'I Wanna Be Sedated '; 'The KKK Took My Baby Away'. Paradisio, Amsterdam, September 15, 1978: 'Needles and Pins'; 'Surfin' Bird'; 'Cretin Hop'; 'Listen to My Heart'; 'California Sun'; 'I Don't Wanna Walk Around with You'. Tomorrow Show, January 9, 1981: Introduction & 'We Want the Airwaives'.

PSYCHO THERAPY

Hammersmith Odeon, London, June 5, 1986
'Teenage Lobotomy'; 'Psycho Therapy'; 'Blitzkrieg Bop'; 'Do You Remember Rock 'n' Roll Radio?'; 'Freak of Nature'; 'Gimme Gimme Shock Treatment'; 'Rock 'n' Roll High School'; 'I Wanna Be Sedated'; 'KKK Took My Baby Away'; 'Crummy Stuff'; 'Loudmouth'; 'Love Kills'; 'Sheena Is a Punk Rocker'; 'Glad to See You Go'; 'I Don't Care'; 'Too Tough to Die'; 'Animal Boy'; 'Wart Hog'; 'Surfin' Bird' (White/Frazier/Harris/Wilson); 'Cretin Hop'; 'I Don't Wanna Walk Around with You'; 'Today Your Love, Tomorrow the World'; 'Pinhead'; 'Chinese Rocks'; 'Somebody Put Something in My Drink'; 'Rockaway Beach'; 'Do You Wanna Dance?' (Freeman); 'California Sun'; 'We're a Happy Family'; 'I Just Want to Have Something to Do'; 'Judy Is a Punk'; 'Beat on the Brat'; 'Go Mental'.

WART HOG

Sporthalle, Boblingen, Germany, November 30, 1978
'I Wanna Live'; 'Bonzo Goes to Bitburg'; 'Weasel Face'; 'Sheena Is a Punk Rocker'; 'Rockaway Beach'; 'Pet Sematary'; 'Don't Bust My Chops'; 'She's the One'; 'Mama's Boy'; 'Animal Boy'; 'Wart Hog'; 'Surfin' Bird'; 'Cretin Hop'; 'I Don't Wanna Walk Around with You'; 'Today Your Love, Tomorrow the World'; 'Pinhead'; 'Chinese Rocks'; 'Somebody Put Something in My Drink'; 'Let's Dance'; 'Do You Wanna Dance?'; 'Havana Affair'; 'We're a Happy Family'; 'I Just Wanna Have Something to Do'; 'Indian Giver'; 'California Sun'.

AMERICA KILL

Stadhalle, Offenbach, Germany, November 22, 1998
'The Good, the Bad, the Ugly'; 'Durango 95'; 'Teenage Lobotomy'; 'Psycho Therapy'; 'Blitzkrieg Bop'; 'Do You Remember Rock 'n' Roll Radio?'; 'I Believe in Miracles'; 'Gimme Gimme Shock Treatment'; 'Rock 'n' Roll High School'; 'I Wanna Be Sedated'; 'Beat on the Brat'; 'I Wanna Live'; 'Bonzo Goes to Bitburg'; 'Weasel Face'; 'Sheena Is a Punk Rocker'; 'Pet Sematary'; 'Don't Bust My Chops'; 'She's the One'; 'Mama's Boy'; 'Animal Boy'; 'Wart Hog'; 'Surfin' Bird'; 'Cretin Hop'; 'I Don't Wanna Walk Around with You'; 'Today Your Love, Tomorrow the World'; 'Pinhead'; 'Chinese Rocks'; 'Somebody Put Something in My Drink'; 'California Sun'; 'Do You Wanna Dance?'.

RAISING HELL

(DIYE 9) Paradiso, Amsterdam, February 11, 1980 'Go Mental'; 'Gimme Gimme Shock Treatment'; 'Rock 'n' Roll High School'; 'I Wanna Be Sedated'; 'Do You Remember Rock 'n' Roll Radio?'; 'Judy Is a Punk'; 'California Sun'; 'I Don't Walk Around with You'; 'Today Your Love, Tomorrow the World'; 'Pinhead'. Roxy, Los Angeles, CA, August 12, 1976: 'Loudmouth'; 'Beat on the Brat'; 'Blitzkrieg Bop'; 'I Remember You'; 'Glad to See You Go'; 'Chainsaw'; '53rd and 3rd'; 'I Wanna Be Your Boyfriend'; 'Havana Affair'; 'Listen to My Heart'; 'California Sun'; 'Judy Is a Punk'; 'I Don't Wanna Walk Around with You'; 'Now I Wanna Sniff Some Glue'; 'Let's Dance'. The 914 Session (1975): 'I Don't Wanna Go Down to the Basement'; '53rd and 3rd'; 'I Wanna Be Your Boyfriend'; 'Judy Is a Punk'; 'Loudmouth'.

RAMONES 2000

CD ROM
Russia
This CD contains the entire set of Ramones studios albums.
(Sound in MP3 Format 160 Kbps - 44 KHZ), Lyrics and Pictures
Ramones (1976) 14 tracks; Leave Home (1977) 14 tracks with "Sheena Is a Punk Rocker"; Rocket to Russia (1977) 14 tracks; Road to Ruin (1978) 12 tracks; End of the Century (1980) 12 tracks; Pleasant Dreams (1981) 12 tracks; Subterranean Jungle (1983) 12 tracks; Too Tough to Die (1984) 13 tracks; Animal Boy (1986) 12 tracks; Halfway to Sanity (1987) 12 tracks; Brain Drain (1989) 12 tracks; Mondo Bizarro (1992) 13 tracks; Acid Eaters (1994) 12 tracks; Adios Amigos (1995) 14 tracks with "Spiderman" Song.

LEGEND OF A ROCK STAR

RAMONES 2000
CD ROM
Russia
Sound in MP3 format "160 kbps - 44 KHZ", Lyrics & Pictures
It's Alive (1979) 28 tracks; *Ramones Mania* (1988) 30 tracks; *All the Stuff & More* Vol.1 (1990) 33 tracks; *All the Stuff & More* Vol.2 (1991) 30 tracks; *Loco Live* (European Version) (1991) 33 tracks; *Loco Live* (U.S. Version) (1991) 32 tracks; *Greatest Hits Live* (1996) 18 tracks; *We're Outta Here* (1997) 32 tracks.

THE RAVAGE OF SLUMBERLAND
Various Shows
(Mogul Nightmare Records MNR 001) 'Durango 95'; 'Teenage Lobotomy'; 'Psycho Therapy'; 'Blitzkrieg Bop'; 'Do You Remember Rock 'n' Roll Radio?'; 'I Believe in Miracles'; 'Gimme Gimme Shock Treatment'; 'Rock 'n' Roll High School'; 'I Wanna Be Sedated'; 'The KKK Took My Baby Away'; 'I Wanna Live'; 'Bonzo Goes to Bitburg'; 'Commando'; 'Sheena Is a Punk Rocker'; 'Rockaway Beach'; 'Pet Sematary'; '53rd and 3rd'; 'Glad to See You Go'; 'Mama's Boy'; 'Animal Boy'; 'Wart Hog'; 'Surfin' Bird'; 'Cretin Hop'; 'I Don't Wanna Walk Around with You'; 'Today Your Love , Tomorrow the World'; 'Pinhead'; 'Chinese Rocks'; 'Somebody Put Something in My Drink'; 'We're a Happy Family'.

SOLID GOLD—EASY ACTION 1993
Stadhalle Offenbach December 2, 1992
(Europe: 1-2-3-4 Records BONZO 32) 'Durango 95'; 'Teenage Lobotomy'; 'Psycho Therapy'; 'Blitzkrieg Bop'; 'Do You Remember Rock 'n' Roll Radio?'; 'I Believe in Miracles'; 'Gimme Gimme Shock Treatment'; 'Rock 'n' Roll High School'; 'I Wanna Be Sedated'; 'Censorshit'; 'I Wanna Live'; 'Bonzo Goes to Bitburg'; 'Tomorrow She Goes Away'; 'Sheena Is a Punk Rocker'; 'Rockaway Beach'; 'Pet Sematary'; 'I Wanna Be Well'; 'Glad to See You Go'; 'Take It As It Comes'; 'Somebody Put Something in My Drink'; 'Commando'; 'Wart Hog'; 'Cretin Hop'; 'Judy Is a Punk'; 'Today Your Love, Tomorrow the World'; 'Pinhead'; 'Poison Heart'; 'Chinese Rocks'; 'We're a Happy Family'; 'Strength to Endure'; 'Beat on the Brat'; 'California Sun'.

THANK YOU ROCK 'N' ROLL—ADIOS RAMONES
River Plate Stadium, Bueno Aires, Argentina, March 16, 1996
(Dynastyx DIYE 62) 'The Good, the Bad and the Ugly'; 'Durango 95'; 'Psycho Therapy'; 'Blitzkrieg Bop'; 'Do You Remember Rock 'n' Roll Radio?'; 'I Believe in Miracles'; 'Gimme Gimme Shock Treatment'; 'Rock 'n' Roll High School'; 'I Wanna Be Sedated'; 'Spider Man'; 'The KKK Took My Baby Away'; 'I Don't Want to Grow Up'; 'I Just Want to Have Something to Do'; 'Sheena Is a Punk Rocker'; 'Rockaway Beach'; 'Pet Sematary'; 'Strength to Endure'; 'Do You Wanna Dance?'; 'Somebody Put Something in My Drink'; 'Wart Hog'; 'Cretin Hop'. Studio Material: 'R.A.M.O.N.E.S.'; 'Today Your Love, Tomorrow the World'; 'Pinhead'; 'The Crusher'; 'Poison Heart'; 'We're a Happy Family'; '53rd and 3rd'; 'Beat on the Brat'; 'Chinese Rocks'; 'Have You Ever Seen the Rain?'; 'R.A.M.O.N.E.S.; 'Spider Man'; 'Blitzkrieg Bop'; 'Can't Say Anything Nice'.

HALFWAY TO RUSSIA
Provinssirock, June 4, 1988
'Durango 95'; 'Teenage Lobotomy'; 'Psycho Therapy'; 'Blitzkrieg Bop'; 'Do You Remember Rock 'n' Roll Radio?'; 'Bop'Til You Drop'; 'Gimme Gimme Shock Treatment'; 'Rock 'n' Roll High School'; 'I Wanna Be Sedated'; 'I Don't Want You'; 'Chinese Rocks'; 'Weasel Face'; 'Commando'; 'Sheena Is a Punk Rocker'; 'Rockaway Beach'; 'Garden of Serenity'; 'I Just Want to Have Something to Do'; 'Too Tough to Die'; 'Animal Boy'; 'Wart Hog'; 'Surfin' Bird'; 'Cretin Hop'; 'I Don't Wanna Walk Around with You'; 'Today Your Love, Tomorrow the World'; 'Pinhead'; 'I Wanna Live'; 'Somebody Put Something in My Drink'; 'Bonzo Goes to Bitburg'; 'Do you Wanna Dance?'; 'Listen to My Heart'; 'We're a Happy Family'; Interview with Joey Ramone.

TRASH SURFIN' 1996
All tracks from Ramones live albums *Loco Live* and *Greatest Hits Live*
(Germany: Grifon Records GR 88006) 'Teenage Lobotomy'; 'I Wanna Be Sedated'; 'Pet Sematary'; 'Somebody Put Something in My Drink'; 'The KKK Took My Baby Away'; 'Sheena Is a Punk Rocker'; 'Do You Remember Rock 'n' Roll Radio?'; 'Pinhead'; 'Judy Is a Punk'; 'Surfin' Bird'; 'Beat on the Brat'; 'Rockaway Beach'; 'Rock 'n' Roll High School'; 'I Believe in Miracles'; 'Chinese Rocks'; 'Today Your Love, Tomorrow the World'; 'I Don't Wanna Walk Around with You'; 'Wart Hog'; 'Cretin Hop'.

UNRELEASED TRACKS
(RAM-12615) 'R.A.M.O.N.E.S.'; 'Spiderman'; 'Carbona Not Glue'; 'Can't Say Anything Nice'; 'See My Way'; 'On the Beach'; 'Don't Be So Strange'; 'Blitzkrieg Bop'; 'Smash You'; 'Street Fighting Man'; 'Life Goes On'; 'Go Home Ann'; 'Rockaway Beach'; 'I Got You Babe'; 'Surfin' Safari'; 'What About Me'; 'Chatterbox'; 'The Crusher'; 'I'd Love to Save the World'; 'Keeping Time'; 'Know What I Got Here'; 'Quick to Cut'; 'Ride'; 'I Don't Wanna Go Down to the Basement'; '53rd and 3rd'; 'I Wanna Be Your Boyfiend'; 'Judy Is a Punk'; 'Loudmouth'.

WEASELFACE 1992
(Luxembourg: Jewels of Live JOL 9204)
Whiskey a Go-Go in Los Angeles, CA, November 24th, 1977
'Rockaway Beach'; 'Commando'; 'Here Today Gone Tomorrow'; 'Surfin' Bird'; 'Cretin Hop'; 'Listen to My Heart'; 'California Sun'; 'I Don't Wanna Walk Around with You'; 'Pinhead'; 'Suzy Is a Headbanger'; 'Chainsaw'; 'Today Your Love, Tomorrow the World'; 'Psycho Therapy'; 'Blitzkrieg Bop'; 'Do You Remember Rock 'n' Roll Radio?'; 'Bop' Til You Drop'; 'Chinese Rocks'; 'Weasel Face'; 'Garden of Serenity'; 'Pinhead'; 'I Wanna Live'; 'Somebody Put Something in My Drink'; 'Bonzo Goes to Bitburg'. Recorded September 19, 1975 at 914 Studios, Blauvelt, New York: 'I Don't Wanna Go Down to the Basement'; 'Loudmouth'.

RAMONES—YOU DON'T COME CLOSE (2000)
Enhanced Audio and Video CD
(U.K.: Burning Aurlines PILOT 79) 'Rockaway Beach'; 'Teenage Lobotomy'; 'Blitzkrieg Bop'; 'Don't Come Close'; 'I Don't Care'; 'She's the One'; 'Sheena Is a Punk Rocker'; 'Cretin Hop'; 'Listen to My Heart'; 'California Sun'; 'Don't Wanna Walk Around with You'; 'Pinhead'.

Ramones appear on:

MUSIC FOR OUR MOTHER OCEAN (July, 1996), Universal/Interscope,
'California Sun'.

GET CRAZY (1983)
Morocco 6065, 'Chop Suey'.
ROCK 'N' ROLL HIGH SCHOOL (1983), Warner Brothers, 'Rock 'n' Roll High School'; 'I Want You Around'; 'Come on Let's Go'; medey of 'Blitzkrieg Bop', 'Teenage Lobotomy', 'California Sun', 'Pinhead', and 'She's the One'; 'Rock 'n' Roll High School'.

LEGEND OF A ROCK STAR

Ramones Songs Appear on:

THE SONG RAMONES THE SAME

Dee Dee Ramone Solo
As Dee Dee Ramone:

7" singles:
'I'm Seein UFOs'/'Bad Horoscope' (1997), U.K.: Blackout Records 5008-7.

'Born to Lose'/'Hop Around' (2002), Finland: Woimasointu Records 005

12" single:
'Do the Bikini Dance'/'Twist and Shout' (2002), Germany: Wanker Records 002.

Studio albums:

ZONKED October, 1997
(Other Peoples Music 2118) 'I'm Zonked, Los Hombres'; 'Fix Yourself Up'; 'I Am Seeing UFOs'; 'Get Off of the Scene'; 'Never Never Again'; 'Bad Horoscope'; 'It's So Bizarre'; 'Get Out of My Room'; 'Someone Who Don't Fit in'; 'Victim of Society'; 'My Chico'; 'Disguises'; 'Why Is Everybody Always Against Germany'.

AIN'T IT FUN 1997
(Europe: Blackout 5008ECD) 'I'm Zonked, Los Hombres'; 'Fix Yourself Up'; 'I Am Seeing UFOs'; 'Get Off of the Scene'; 'Never Never Again'; 'Bad Horoscope'; 'It's So Bizarre'; 'Get Out of My Room'; 'Someone Who Don't Fit in'; 'Victim of Society'; 'My Chico'; 'Disguises'; 'Why Is Everybody Always Against Germany'; 'Please Kill Me'

HOP AROUND (Canadian Version) January, 2000
(Other Peoples Music 1234) 'I Don't Wanna Die in the Basement'; 'Mental Patient'; 'Now I Wanna Be Sedated'; 'Rock 'n' Roll Vacation'; 'Get Out of This House'; '38th and 8th'; 'Nothin''; 'Hop Around'; 'What about Me'; 'I Saw a Skull Instead of My Face'; 'I Wanna You'; 'Master Plan'; 'Born to Lose'; 'Hurtin' Kind'; 'I'm Horrible '.

HOP AROUND (European Version) 2000
(Corazong 2000 006) 'I Don't Wanna Die in the Basement'; 'Mental Patient'; 'Now I Wanna Be Sedated'; 'Rock 'n' Roll Vacation'; 'Get Out of This House'; '38th and 8th'; 'Nothin''; 'Hop Around'; 'What About Me'; 'I Saw a Skull Instead of My Face'; 'I Wanna You'; 'Master Plan'; "Chinese Rocks"; 'Hurtin' Kind'; 'I'm Horrible'.

Compilation:

GREATEST & LATEST September 2000
(EMI 65601) 'Blitzkrieg Bop'; 'Timebomb'; 'Sheena Is a Punk Rocker'; 'Shaking All Over'; 'I Wanna Be Sedated'; 'Cretin Hop'; 'Teenage Lobotomy'; 'Gimme Gimme Shock Treatment'; 'Motorbikin''; 'Come on Now'; 'Cathy's Clown'; 'Pinhead'; 'Rockaway Beach'; 'Fix Yourself Up'; 'Sidewalk Surfin''; 'Beat on the Brat'.

dee dee ramone

As Dee Dee King:

12"single:
'Funky Man'/'Dub' (1987), Rock Hotel Records 7159.

Standing in the Spotlight July, 1988
(Red Eye 25884) 'Mashed Potato Time'; 'Much 2 Drink'; 'Baby Doll'; 'Poor Little Rich Girl'; 'Commotion in the Ocean'; 'German Kid'; 'Brooklyn Babe'; 'Emergency'; 'The Crusher'; 'I Want What I Want When I Want It'.

Unreleased:

'The Great Adventurer'; 'The Goon'; 'Max the Cat'.

As Dee Dee Ramone & The Chinese Dragons:

7" Single:
'What About Me'/'Chatterbox' (1993), American Gothic Records 306.

As Dee Dee Ramone I.C.L.C.:

12" Maxi Single:
'Chinese Bitch'; 'I Don't Wanna Get involved with You'/'That's What Everybody Else Does'; 'We're a Creepy Family' (1994), U.K.: Rough Trade Records 157.1756.0 17

I HATE FREAKS LIKE YOU 1994
(U.K.: Rough Trade Records 157.1757) 'I'm Making Monster for My Friends'; 'Don't Look in My Window'; 'Chinese Bitch'; 'It's Not for Me to Know'; 'Runaway'; 'All's Quiet on the Eastern Front'; 'I Hate It'; 'Life Is Like a Little Smart Alleck'; 'I Hate Creeps Like You'; 'Trust Me'; 'Curse on Me'; 'I'm Seeing Strawberries Again'; 'Lass Mich in Rube'.

As The Ramainz:

LIVE IN N.Y.C. June, 1999
(G.B. Music 1004) 'Rockaway Beach'; 'Commando'; 'I Don't Care'; 'Teenage Lobotomy'; 'Beat on the Brat'; 'Chinese Rocks'; 'Rock 'n' Roll Vacation in L.A.'; 'Listen to My Heart'; 'I Don't Wanna Walk Around with You'; 'I Wanna Be Sedated'; 'Cretin Hop'; 'Hop Around'; 'Sheena Is a Punk Rocker'; 'I Just Wanna Have Something to Do'; 'Gimme Gimme Shock Treament'; 'Wart Hog'; 'Chain Saw'; 'Judy Is a Punk'; 'Loudmouth'; 'Blitzkrieg Bop'; '53rd and 3rd'.

Dee Dee's Appearances Elsewhere:

"Bad Little Go-Go Girl" (March 2000). Recorded exclusively for musicblitz.com.

Dee Dee Ramone Appears on These Compilation Albums:

Smells Like Bleach: A Punk Tribute to Nirvana (January 2001), Cleopatra 0934-2. 'Negative Creep'
A Punk Tribute to Metallica (January 2001), Cleopatra 0992-2, 'Jump in the Fire',
Beyond Cyberpunk (March 2001), Europe: Music Blitz 22 202532.
New Prohibition: A Musical History of Hemp (May 2001), Orchard 800824.
Ramones Maniacs (2002), Trend is Dead!

LEGEND OF A ROCK STAR

Dee Dee Ramone appears on these albums and singles:

Joan Jett, *Bad Reputation* (1981, reissue 1998) Blackheart JJ 707-2.
G.G. Allin, *Hated* (1992), Performance 7.
Nina Hagen, *Freud Euch* (1995), Germany: RCA/BMG 32064.
Stiv Bators, *Last Race* (1996), France: Bondage 7562819.
Nina Hagen, *Beehappy* (1996), Europe: BMG 74321-36936-2.
Furious George, *Furious George Goes Ape* (September 1996), Lookout 163.
Youth Gone Mad, *Rotten;* '(7" single, 1997), France: Panx 044.
Jump Little Children, *Magazine* (September, 1998), Germany: Breaking Records 7567-83134-2; Atlantic 83134.
G.G. Allin, *Res-erected* (October, 1999), Roir 8258.
Youth Gone Mad, *Oompa Loompa* (2000), France: Panx 057.
The Dead Boys, *We Have Come For Your Children* (June, 1978) Sire 6054; 2001 CD: WEA international 26054.
Youth Gone Mad, *Touching Cloth* (2000), Germany: Empty Records 446,
Youth Gone Mad, *Cry Baby* (7" single, 2002), Germany: Empty Records 490.

Dee Dee Ramone's songs appear on:

A.N.I.M.A.L., *Poder Latino* (June, 1998), WEA international 22762.
Green Day, *Shenanigans* (July, 2002), Warner Brothers 48208.
Nina Hagen, *Abgehaun*, RCA/BMG 35823.
The Huntingtons, *File Under Ramones* (April, 1999), Tooth & Nail 1138.
Impaler, *Undead Things* (1996), Vlad 3323.
Jon Cougar Concentration Camp, *Too Tough To Die* (June, 1998), Liberation 37810.
Jim Rome, *Welcome to The Jungle* (September, 1998), Outpost 30009.
Skid Row, *B-sides Ourselves* (September, 1992), Atlantic 82431.
Ronnie Spector, *Siren* (1980), Polish 808.
Stop, *Never* (December, 1995), Smut Pedlurz 10.

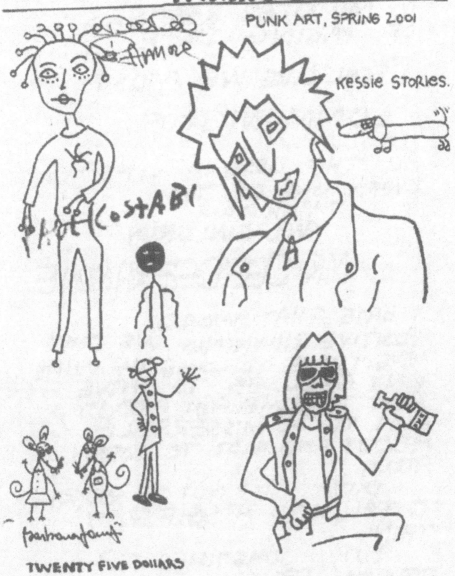

TO MY DEAR READERS
OF TAKING DOPE

I FEEL LIKE WE MUST

COMMUNICATE

ALL THE BEST IN LIFE TO
EVERY ONE OF YOU
          THANK YOU
               AND SINCERLY

MR DEEDEE RAMONE

I HATE THAT WORD
POSITIVE THINKING. WE DONT
EVEN HAVE TO COME UP WITH
ANY EXCUSES TO HAVE
ALOT TO COMPLAIN ABOUT,
ALOT TO BE MISSERABLE,
ABOUT AND ALOT TO WORRY
ABOUT.
     BUT !!!. ITS NOT TO SMART
TO FALL INTO A SELF PITY
THING.
     BUT,,, SOMETIMES ITS
OKAY TO "CRY.

IF YOU DO YOUR CRYING IN
PRIVATE SO NO ONE CAN SEE
YOU, THEN IT'S OKAY.

WHEN i FOUND OUT A COUPLE
OF YEARS AGO THAT MY DAD
HAD DIED i DID THE SAME THING
i DID WHEN i FOUND OUT
THAT JOEY RAMONE HAD
DIED.
 i TOOK ALOT OF WALKS
ALONE IN THE WOODS AND
LET MY SELF CRY. i WAS UPSET
BECAUSE i WOULD NEVER GET
TO SEE THESE GUYS EVER AGAIN
AND THAT THE ONLY WAY i
COULD EVER RESOLVE THE
PROBLEMS i HAD, ████, WITH
THEM WAS TO PRAY FOR THEM
TO FORGIVE ME AND FOR MY
SELF TO FORGIVE THEM
 BUT i CANT SEEM TO GET
OVER IT THAT IT'S OVER, IT'S
PAINFUL.   i DIDNT KNOW THAT
i WOULD CARE WHEN ████████
MY DAD DIED BUT i DID. i ALSO
TOOK IT AS HARD AS EVERY ONE
ELSE DID WHEN JOEY DIED.

SOME PEOPLE I MET AT A BOOK
SIGNING TOLD ME THAT
WHEN JOEY DIED. THEY FELT
THAT THERE YOUTH DIED
ALSO.

I KNOW HOW THEY
FEEL. THE RAMONES KEPT
US ALL YOUNG.

I CANT PREDICT
MY FUTURE BUT I REALY
CANT SEE MYSELF TOURING
ARROUND PLAYING RAMONES
SONGS NOW. I'AM SORRY.
MY HEART JUST WONT BE
READY FOR THAT FOR A
WHILE OR MAYBE EVEN
EVER AGAIN.

MAYBE THAT'S THE
ONLY WAY I CAN SHOW
RESPECT OR RESOLVE SOME
DIGNITY

I REALY APPRECIATE HOW
POPULAR THE RAMONES STILL
ARE AND HOW MUCH PEOPLE
STILL LOVE THE RAMONES
MUSIC.   JOEY, AND MY SELF
AND THE REST OF THE RAMONES
WILL ALLWAYS BE FONDLY
REMEMBERED IN ROCK AND
ROLL FOR BEING A REAL
COOL, WONDERFUL BAND.
NOTHING LIKE US COULD
EVER HAPPEN AGAIN BUT
ITS NICE TO HAVE BEEN
THREW IT ALL AND HAVE
THE MEMORIES OF THE
WHOLE SCENE LIKE I DO.
    BUT WHEN I SAW
THE TWIN TOWERS BLOW
UP IN NEW YORK ON T.V.
I FREAKED AND I
CRIED. I AM SAD SAD
SAD FOR NEW YORK.

I NEVER THOUGHT THAT
WOULD HAPPEN.
    I FEEL LIKE NEW YORK
IS GONE LIKE I KNEW IT
NOW ALONG TIME AGO
BUT NOW FOREVER FINALY.
AND I WONT BE THERE
ANY MORE EVER AGAIN.
    I DIDNT HAVE ANY WOODS
TO WALK ARROUND AND CRY
ALONE IN ABOUT TEN YEARS
AGO WHEN JOHNNY THUNDERS
AND STIV AND JERRY NOLEN
ALL DIED ON ME ONE AFTER
THE OTHER.
    NEW YORK WAS DIFFERENT
THEN. IT WAS MORE LONELY
I COULD WALK ARROUND AT
5 OR 6 IN THE MORNING THEN
BEING MISSERABLE AND PRETTY
MUCH BE INVISIABLE.
    BACK THEN JUST ABOUT
EVERY ALLY, HALL WAY
STREET BLOCK OR NEIGHBOR
HOOD HELD SOME LIFE OR
DEATH OR PAINFUL MEMORY
OF MY PAST AND FRIENDS

THAT DIDNT MAKE IT
THREW HELL AND BACK
WITH ME

TO THE BEST OF MY
ABILITY I TRY TO SEE
THE GOOD INSTEAD OF
THE BAD

POSITIVE THINKING MEANS
THAT WHEN YOU GET
UP IN THE MORNING TO
START YOUR DAY YOU
BEGIN BY LETTING GOD
KNOW THAT YOU ARE VERY
HAPPY THAT HE HAS GIVEN
YOU THE PRIVILAGE OF LIFE
SOMETHING WILL MAKE
YOU SMILE, EVEN IF YOU
CANT LET ANY BODY SEE
YOU SMILE AND HAVE TO
SMILE SOMEWHERE IN PRIVATE.

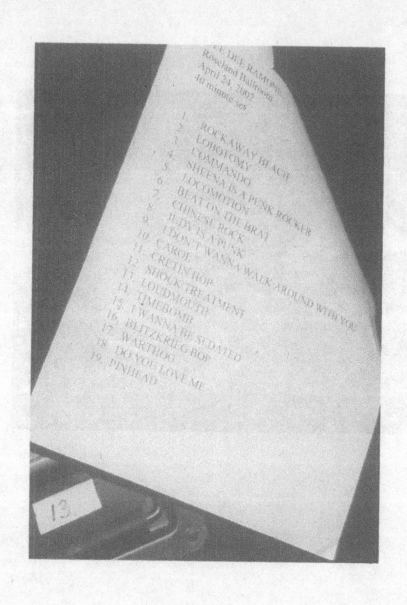

Photo Credits

77 Joey, Barbara, Marky, Dee Dee, and Walter Lure, ex-Heartbreakers. © 2002 John Nikolai. Courtesy of the photographer.

83 © 2002 Michel Solis. Courtesy the photographer and Paul Kostabi.

85 With Jayne County Djing at Coney Island High, 1997. © 2002 John Nikolai. Courtesy of the photographer.

89 © 2002 John Nikolai. Courtesy of the photographer.

94 © 2002 Andy Poncherello. Courtesy of the photographer.

101 With Richard Hell at Max's Kansas City, 1976. © 2002 Roberta Bayley. Courtesy of the photographer.

107 All photos © 2002 Paul Kostabi except bottom photo, © 2002 Michel Solis. Courtesy the photographer and Paul Kostabi..

108 © 2002 deedeeramone.net. Courtesy Paul Kostabi, except third photo from top, Dee Dee and Paul Kostabi in front of one of their collaborations, © 2002 Heidi Follin. Courtesy of the photographer. Bottom photo: Paul Grimes, Paul Kostabi, Dee Dee, Walter Lure.

110 On Second Avenue, 1976. © 2002 Roberta Bayley. Courtesy of the photographer.

116 © 2002 Keith Green. All rights reserved. Courtesy of the photographer.

119 New Jersey, 1980. © 2002 David Godlis. Courtesy of the photographer.

136 © 2002 David Godlis. Courtesy of the photographer.

148 Johnny, Joey, and Dee Dee at CBGB's, 1976. © 2002 David Godlis. Courtesy of the photographer.

158 Clockwise from top left: Marky, Tommy, Arturo Vega, Legs McNeil—still punks. All photos by Keith Green. © 2002 Keith Green. All rights reserved. Courtesy of the photographer.

161 Dee Dee's 44th Birthday at the Lakeside Lounge, NYC, September 18, 1996. It was the first time Joey and Dee Dee had shared a stage in years. © 2002 John Nikolai. Courtesy of the photographer.

165 CBGB's on the Bowery, summer, 1977. © 2002 David Godlis. Courtesy of the photographer.

169 Clockwise from top: A.Dee Dee, Marky, Paul Kostabi perform at Book

IN LOVING MEMORY

Dee Dee Ramone

September 18, 1951 - June 5, 2002

O.K...
I've gotta go now.

HOLLYWOOD
FUNERAL HOME
FD#1651

HOLLYWOOD FOREVER
6000 SANTA MONICA BLVD.
HOLLYWOOD, CA 90038
1(877)844-3837